D1594113

CLASSICAL THEORIES OF MONEY, OUTPUT AND INFLATION

Classical Theories of Money, Output and Inflation

A Study in Historical Economics

Roy Green
Senior Lecturer in Economics
University of Newcastle, New South Wales
Australia

St. Martin's Press

First published in Great Britain 1992 by
THE MACMILLAN PRESS LTD
Houndmills, Basingstoke, Hampshire RG21 2XS
and London
Companies and representatives
throughout the world

This book is published in Macmillan's *Studies in Political Economy* series
General Editor: John Eatwell

A catalogue record for this book is available from the British Library.

ISBN 0–333–56562–2

Printed in Great Britain by
Ipswich Book Company Ltd
Ipswich, Suffolk

First published in the United States of America 1992 by
Scholarly and Reference Division,
ST. MARTIN'S PRESS, INC.,
175 Fifth Avenue,
New York, N.Y. 10010

ISBN 0–312–08556–7

Library of Congress Cataloging-in-Publication Data
Green, Roy, 1951–
Classical theories of money, output and inflation: a study in historical economics / Roy Green.
p. cm.
Includes index.
ISBN 0–312–08556–7
1. Money. 2. Inflation (Finance) 3. Credit. I. Title.
HG220.A2G68 1992
332.4—dc20 92–20308
CIP

To Deidre, Otto and Claude

Contents

Preface

Controversy is not new to the field of monetary economics. It is well known that the contemporary monetarist challenge to the 'Keynesian' post-war consensus had its origins in the quantity theory of money formulated by the eighteenth- and nineteenth-century classical school. It is not so well known, however, that the classical school also supplied the most trenchant critics of quantity theory, both as a doctrine and policy. Yet these critics, like their modern counterparts, ultimately failed to make their case. The question is why.

This book examines the historical antecedents of monetarism and its critics in significant phases of monetary controversy over a period of two centuries. We find, paradoxically, that the key to understanding the debates of this period lies less in the theory of money and prices than in the approach adopted to the analysis of output in a market economy. From this perspective, the problem facing the critics of classical quantity theory is thrown into sharp relief. It is that, due to the universal acceptance of Say's law, they lacked a theory of output comparable with their theory of value and distribution. As a consequence, however sound their policy prescriptions, their theoretical analysis was fatally flawed, and seen to be so.

The implications for modern debate, I shall suggest, are profound. They affect not only the neoclassical revival of quantity theory but also its aftermath in financial deregulation and the unrestrained credit expansion of recent years. Although neoclassical economics does encompass a theory of output, it is one which logically implies a monetarist approach to the relationship between changes in the money supply and the price level. My argument here is that an alternative approach must be founded upon a synthesis of the classical analysis of value and distribution, on the one hand, and the theory of output embodied in Keynes's 'principle of effective demand' on the other. This approach has the merit both of internal consistency and practical support for a policy of credit control which is better equipped to avoid the destructive excesses of restriction and expansion associated with monetarism and the neoclassical orthodoxy.

The main body of my research for this book, which is a revised version of a Ph.D. thesis for Cambridge University, was begun as monetarism reached its high watermark in Britain and North America in the late 1970s. It was completed after an interval of some years as policy-makers recognised the inconsistency of the theory with both the experience and future requirements of economic management. The problem with the debate at this time, from the viewpoint of my research findings, was that it proceeded almost entirely along pragmatic rather than theoretical lines. There was no sense in which the critics of monetarism, despite its eventual fall from grace, could be said to have 'won'. Nor, as a result, was there any guarantee that it could not simply be resurrected at some future date when it suited the convenience of those self-same policy-makers. The research conducted for the book is therefore an attempt to demonstrate the importance of a theoretically coherent alternative to monetarism in the context of a study in 'historical economics'.

During such an extended period of research, it is only natural that I should be indebted to the guidance and constructive criticism offered by many colleagues. I owe a particular debt of gratitude to my supervisors, John Eatwell and the late M. M. Postan, both of whom exercised a strong influence on the direction of my work. I also benefited at various stages from the advice of Bob Rowthorn, Murray Milgate, Pierangelo Garegnani, Geoff Harcourt, Chris Gregory and Barry Gordon, and from the helpful comments of my examiners, Bernard Corry and Jane Humphries.

The manuscript was typed by Kay Lawrence and read by Gwyn and Miriam Prins, all of whom were my neighbours in the lovely village of Great Eversden, near Cambridge in England. However, any remaining errors are mine alone.

I would like finally to express my appreciation to Trinity College, Cambridge, which made a Research Studentship available to initiate my studies, to Clare Hall, Cambridge, which subsequently appointed me to a Research Fellowship and to my parents who supported me throughout. I hope that this book is worthy of their faith in me.

ROY GREEN

Part I

Introduction

1 Aim of the Inquiry

> Of all the constituent parts of the science of Political Economy none is perhaps so inseparably bound up with the totality of the general theory as is the theory of money.
>
> Karl Helfferich, *Das Geld* (1903)

The aim of this work is two-fold. It is intended first, to challenge the prevailing view that monetarism, or the quantity theory of money, is a necessary part of classical economic analysis, and, second, to show that the framework upon which classical (and Marxian) analysis is based suggests an alternative account of the inflationary process. This may be seen as an exercise in the history of economic thought, but the conclusions are also relevant to modern debate. In particular, the converse of the argument is that the monetarist approach to inflation *is* a logically necessary component of neoclassical analysis, and that consequently any attempt to criticise that approach in a fundamental way must involve an explicit rejection of the conceptual structure of neoclassical economics.

The common feature of classical and neoclassical quantity theory is the notion that expansion or contraction of the money supply – other things being equal – will lead to an equiproportional change in the price level. That other things remain equal is ensured by the assumption of a fixed level of output. Here the resemblance between the classical and neoclassical approaches comes to an end. Whereas in the latter approach the fixed output assumption, and hence the causal relationship between money and prices, is the result of a theoretical analysis of the determination of output, in the former it follows automatically from the adoption of Say's law of markets. Classical quantity theory is based not on a theory of output but on the *absence* of such a theory comparable with its theory of value and distribution. This important difference between the classical and neoclassical approaches may be expressed as a distinction between two kinds of 'Say's law.' One I shall call Say's identity, and the other Say's equality.[1]

The idea of a unilinear progression from classical to neoclassical quantity theory owes as much to J. M. Keynes as to the orthodoxy of his time. The conflation in the *General Theory* (1936, p. 3 fn) of the Ricardian and Marshallian systems encouraged a misconception which has persisted to the present day. Followers of Keynes have either tried to refute quantity theory from a neoclassical standpoint, which is self-contradictory (e.g.,

Tobin, 1974; Hahn, 1982); or they have identified their position with the anti-quantity theory school of classical economics, thus ignoring the important difference between Say's identity and Say's equality (Kaldor and Trevithick, 1981). Both groups have failed to appreciate that the quantity theory of money *as a theory* only took shape with the marginal revolution, and that classical quantity theory was not a theory at all, but simply a logical consequence of assuming an independently given level of output.[2] This major concession by their opponents has allowed modern monetarists such as Milton Friedman to claim an unbroken intellectual ancestry stretching back to Hume, if not Copernicus, which indeed makes the period of Keynesian ascendency look like a 'temporary eclipse of the quantity theory of money' (Friedman, 1968, p. 47).

STRUCTURE AND APPROACH

The work is divided into four parts. In the remainder of Part I (Chapter 2), I shall outline the framework of classical analysis. This is a necessary precondition for the discussion of monetary phenomena, which are treated in isolation only at the cost of their coherence with the process of production. I shall begin by introducing the basic distinction between 'natural' and 'market' price and go on to explain the separability in classical economics of the theory of the value and the theory of output. I shall then be in a position to define the nature of the problem of price inflation in the context of the equation of exchange. Since the quantity theory of money is occasionally confused with the equation of exchange, it will also be important to bear in mind Friedman's observation that '[t]he quantity theory is not . . . this tautology. It is, rather, . . . [t]he conclusion . . . that substantial changes in prices or nominal income are almost invariably the result of changes in the nominal supply of money' (ibid., p. 39). The essence of quantity theory, as we shall see, is a statement of *causality*.

In Parts II and III, the nature of this causality and its direction will be illustrated by three key phases of monetary controversy, which show that the conceptual categories we are dealing with have real counterparts in historical experience.[3] The development of theories of metallic money, fiduciary money and credit both presuppose and directly influence corresponding stages in the evolution of the financial structure. The analysis of these theories requires an approach which combines their logical and historical aspects. This approach I have called 'historical economics'. It suggests, with Engels, that the logical method 'is indeed nothing but the historical method, only stripped of the historical form and diverting chance occurrences. The point where this history begins must also be the starting point of the train of thought, and its further progress will be simply the reflection, in abstract and theoretically consistent form, of the historical course'. The reflection may be corrected at various points; but 'it is corrected in accordance with laws provided by the actual historical course, since each factor can be examined at the stage of development where it reaches its full maturity, its classical form' (Engels, 1859, p. 225).[4]

The scene is set in Chapter 2 with an account of pre-classical debate. The immediate stimulus was the 'price revolution' of the sixteenth and seventeenth centuries, which was in turn associated with the influx of gold and silver from the New World. The mercantilist orthodoxy was unable to reconcile this persistent and generalised inflationary trend with its concept of money; for, instead of augmenting wealth, the precious metals appeared simply to devalue the unit of account. An explanation was required of the empirical connection between the increased quantity of metallic money and the rise in the price level.

Two opposing hypotheses emerged from investigation and analysis. The first – associated mainly with David Hume – was a simplistic but influential quantity theory of money, which retained the mercantilist 'pure exchange' approach to price formation. In this approach, prices were determined simply by the proportion of supply to demand for individual commodities. However, quantity theory went a step further and calculated prices not just individually but in the aggregate by relating the total volume of money in a country to the total volume of circulating commodities. In other words, quantity theory was concerned not so much with *relative* prices as with the *general* price level. Nevertheless, as we shall see, it could not move beyond this superficial supply and demand framework; and its assumption of a constant level of output and velocity proved unsustainable.

The second hypothesis – developed in its essential features by Adam Smith, David Ricardo and Karl Marx – was based upon the classical 'surplus' approach to value and distribution. This approach, which I shall examine in Chapter 4, did take economic analysis beyond the supply and demand framework, shifting the object of inquiry from a concern merely with exchange ratios between commodities and money to the underlying conditions of production which ultimately determined the pattern of prices and profits. Correspondingly, the supply and demand viewpoint, which has become 'almost an axiom in political economy' was now identified as 'the source of much error in that science' (Ricardo, 1951/58, I, p. 382). It will therefore be necessary to contest an apparent trend among modern authorities to the effect that Ricardo, in his monetary analysis, 'was only following the ideas laid down by Hume' (O'Brien, 1979, p. 145; Hollander, 1979, p. 436; but cf. pp. 438–4).[5]

According to the classical hypothesis, the first historical phase of inflation could be explained by an increasingly sophisticated labour theory of value, which in turn both derived from and helped to shape the study of distribution in the 'real' economy. In what I shall call the classical 'law of monetary circulation', long-run causation ran from prices to the money supply, rather than the reverse. Where the classical authors themselves differed was in their assessment of the *short-run* effects of exogenous monetary disturbances; since output was independently given by past accumulation, only the price level or the velocity of circulation could vary. Those adhering to a short-run 'quantity theory' placed the burden of adjustment entirely upon prices, whereas their 'anti-quantity theory' opponents insisted upon a velocity adjustment, i.e., hoarding and dishoarding. Lacking a theory of output, however, these opponents proved singularly ineffective in the face of the new classical monetary orthodoxy.

The next significant inflationary episode accompanied the French Napoleonic wars at the beginning of the nineteenth century. The issue here – in the famous 'bullion controversy' – was the part played by inconvertible paper money in the divergence of the market price of bullion from its mint price, which mirrored a commensurate increase in the price level. The classical circulation law developed for a system of metallic money was now to be applied to the more advanced case of a paper currency. This had already been attempted in a long-run context by eighteenth century writers, culminating in the monetary analysis of Smith's *Wealth of Nations*. Their considerable achievement, especially in formulating the principle of limitation which became known as the 'real bills doctrine', is the subject of Chapter 5. The suspension of cash payments in 1797, however, seemed to create a new situation, calling for new explanatory concepts. Although economists accepted the classical circulation law in the long-run, they were once again divided over the short-run adjustment process consequent upon fluctuations in the money supply. This division did not present itself clearly in the bullion dispute, where a system of credit money was mistaken for a fiduciary system by Ricardo and the proponents of classical 'quantity theory'. Hence, the account in Chapter 6 focuses primarily on the classical theory of fiduciary money and its associated principle of limitation.

A theory of credit, on the other hand, could only evolve with the increasingly pronounced industrial cycle of the mid-nineteenth century, whose monetary character was expressed at a certain stage in a sudden rush for means of payment in the shape of gold or bank notes. The causes and cures of these periodic crises were the occasion for a further round of controversy, which is generally termed the 'currency–banking debate'. Again, both sides were in broad agreement on the long-run relationship between money and prices; as before, it was price behaviour in the short-run and the connection with monetary movements that produced the main division of opinion, which on this occasion was more sharply defined and understood.

With the return to cash payments in 1821, classical economists were concerned that paper money ought to conform to the operation of a metallic currency. The 'currency school' argued that this could only be secured by relating the money supply in accordance with the flow of gold and silver across the foreign exchanges. The 'banking school', by contrast, maintained that '*economic* convertibility' – the convertibility of notes into gold coin at par – was automatically guaranteed by *legal* convertibility and that the source of the problem of crises lay in the overextension of the credit structure as a whole, not just of means of circulation. Marx endorsed the Banking School position so far as it went, but investigated crises from the standpoint of real as well as 'fictitious' capital accumulation. The development of the classical theory of the credit system is traced in Chapter 7. There I shall discuss the concept of fictitious capital, the determination of the rate of interest and the rehabilitation by the Banking School of the early real bills doctrine – in the guise of the 'law of reflux' – as a mechanism of credit control.

Finally, in Part IV (Chapter 8), I shall draw together the implications of the theoretical debate for economic policy. In particular, we find that the absence of a theory of output in classical analysis blunted opposition to the quantity principle, and, as a corollary, that the inclusion of such a theory within the framework of the 'surplus' approach would result in a more formidable alternative than those based upon neoclassical value and distribution analysis. A further, more general, implication for modern debate is the crucial importance of theory itself. There are many who would accept that, in assessing the validity of monetarism, '[t]he issues raised . . . are clearly empirical rather than theoretical' (Friedman, ibid., p. 49); and yet, in each of the historical episodes we shall consider, the facts alone (so far as they could be established) were not conclusive of debate.[6] This was settled only by the logical consistency and explanatory power of competing theories.

2 The Classical Framework

> Money is but the Fat of the Body-politick, whereof too much doth as often hinder its Agility, as too little makes it sick. 'Tis true, that as Fat lubricates the motion of the Muscles, feeds in want of Victuals, fills up uneven Cavities, and beautifies the Body, so doth Money in the State quicken its Action, feeds from abroad in time of Dearth at Home; even accounts by reason of its divisibility, and beautifies the whole, altho more especially the particular persons that have it in plenty.
>
> W. Petty, 'Verbum Sapienti', in *The Political Anatomy of Ireland* (1691)

In the conventional interpretation of classical economics, the quantity theory of money is held to be an integral part of its conceptual framework. I shall seek to disprove that interpretation in what may be regarded as the negative, or essentially critical, aspect of my discussion. There is, however, an additional, positive task to be undertaken. I shall also attempt to draw together the elements of an alternative theory of price behaviour, which, it will be argued, is implicit in the classical framework. The discussion will therefore begin with a brief resume of this framework, a preliminary step made all the more necessary in view of successive attempts to recast the classical approach as a primitive variant of neoclassical analysis (e.g., Hollander, 1979).

In the first section of this chapter, I shall introduce the *method* of classical economics and the *theory* based upon that method. The fundamental contribution of the classical tradition is its characterisation of the dominant 'long-run' forces in the capitalist economy in isolation from the arbitrary 'short-run' phenomena which reflect its day-to-day operation. This has been called the 'long-period method', whose purpose is to identify and circumscribe the 'object of analysis' in economic thought (Garegnani, 1976; Eatwell, 1979; Milgate, 1982). It is a method which has since been abandoned, but only sometime after the rejection of classical theory in the marginal revolution of the late nineteenth century. The function of theory, on the other hand, is to explain the nature and magnitude of the object selected for investigation. Whereas neoclassical theory attempts to determine the value of commodities simultaneously with the level of output, it was a feature of classical economics that these key variables were treated separately.

The significance of an independent determination of value and output will become apparent in the second section of the chapter when I introduce the 'equation of exchange'. This expresses a definite, arithmetical relationship between money and its velocity of circulation on the one hand and the level of prices and output on the other. Although the equation is no more than a formal identity, the direction of causation between its variables may be established theoretically. Moreover, the behaviour of the variables also has a historical dimension. The evolution of monetary categories, in particular, tended both to generate and to define the immediate problem requiring theoretical resolution, and this consequent resolution, whatever its degree of validity, in turn gave rise to the practical policies which were then to influence the next stage in the development of the financial structure. The interconnection between the historical and theoretical aspects of classical analysis thus serves as a foundation for the whole discussion. It is an approach which is here encapsulated in the term, 'historical economics'.

THEORY AND METHOD

The key to the method of classical economics is the crucial distinction between the 'natural price' of commodities in a system of capitalist production and their 'market price'. Indeed, it may be argued that this distinction is the key to economic science as such. Every science has as its aim the discovery of 'laws' governing the matter or process selected for investigation. The usual procedure is first to abstract from superfluous aspects of the problem in order to permit the formulation of general theoretical propositions, and then, if possible, to take into account these aspects for the purpose of testing their consistency with the theory and extending it from the explanation of simple to more complex phenomena. This was the procedure adopted by the classical economists whose common attribute – whatever their other differences – was a commitment to theorise permanent tendencies in isolation from random and temporary occurrences.[1]

A pioneer of the classical method was Ferdinando Galiani, who, in his important study of prices and profits, *Della Moneta* (1751), set forth two guiding principles. The first was, 'that initial variations in anything are not to be taken into account but rather permanent and steady states, and in this, order and equality are always found; as when waves are made in a vessel of water, after the confused and irregular movement the water returns to its original level.' The second principle was, 'that it cannot be an accident in nature which brings things to an ultimate limit, but a certain moral gravity which is in everything will never allow them to maintain a straight linear progression, twisting them in a perpetual but finite circle' (cited by Cesarano, 1976, p. 382). These principles have not been bettered as a description of the classical approach.

The classical school deduced from the growth of the social division of labour and the emergence of generalised commodity production in the seventeenth and eighteenth centuries that price formation – and thus economic activity as a whole – are regulated by definite laws. The first comprehensive analysis of these laws was provided by Adam Smith in the *Wealth of Nations*. He showed that the process of competition in a market economy tended to establish average or 'natural' rates of wages, profits and rent. When the price of a commodity was just sufficient to pay for the land, labour and 'stock' used in its production at their natural rates, the commodity sold at its *natural price* (Smith, 1776, p. 43). This was the 'central price', to which the prices of all commodities were 'continually gravitating'.[2]

Smith thus isolated the concept of natural price – whose magnitude was determined by systematic forces – from the arbitrary fluctuations of market prices.[3] A deviation of market from natural price simply indicated an excessive or deficient 'effectual demand' in relation to the available quantity of a particular commodity. This deviation, however, was self-correcting, for the supply response 'naturally suits itself to the effectual demand' (ibid.). That is not to say that natural prices are *explained* by the interaction of supply and demand: once they balance, the problem is not solved but only formulated in a more transparent way.

The mechanism by which the pattern of natural prices is determined was further elaborated, as we shall see, by Ricardo and Marx. They too showed that the formation of natural prices, or 'prices of production', is associated with a *uniform rate of profit* on capital in all lines of production. With the breakdown of feudal restrictions and the development of the credit system, the movement of capital in search of the highest return on investment tended to equalise the rate of profit throughout the economy. In Ricardo's view, this constant tendency towards uniformity served merely to offset and eliminate the disparity between market and natural prices. For Marx, however, it served a more significant purpose which overcame some of the unsolved difficulties in Ricardo's presentation. Equalisation of the rate of profit redistributed surplus value among capitals with different organic compositions such that prices of production departed systematically from the values of commodities. Prices of production could only be a direct monetary expression of values when the organic composition of capital was equal in all sectors of the economy.

I shall examine these developments in the theory of value and distribution in more detail later. For the moment, it is sufficient to note that, despite their theoretical differences, the abstract method employed by Smith, Ricardo and Marx was a powerful unifying strand of classical thought. In his chapter' On Natural Price and Market Price' in the *Principles*, for example, Ricardo explicitly adopted Smith's reasoning. While acknowledging the temporary sources of influence on commodity prices, he insisted that, 'we will leave them entirely out of our consideration, whilst we are treating of the laws which regulate natural prices, natural wages and natural profits, effects totally independent of these accidental causes (1951/58, I, pp. 91–2).[4]

Marx began from a similar premise in *Capital*, whose analysis was addressed to the 'laws of motion' of capitalist society. In the first volume, where values and prices of production were assumed to be equal, he deliberately excluded factors superfluous to the investigation. Chief among these factors were the oscillations in the market prices of commodities. If these prices differed from values, he argued, 'we must first of all, reduce the former to the latter, in other words, *treat the difference as accidental in order that the phenomena may be observed in their purity*, and our observations not interfered with by disturbing circumstances that have nothing to do with the process in question'. Marx went on to point out that, 'this reduction is no mere scientific process. The continual oscillations in prices, their rising and falling, compensate each other, and reduce themselves to an average price, which is their hidden regulator. . . . (1867/94, I, p. 163 fn., emphasis added).[5] This 'average price', of course, is not to be interpreted merely in the sense of a statistical average over a given time scale. The essential character of the 'normal' or long-run position of the economic system as a 'centre of repose and continuance' is quite consistent with short-run deviations which, in a formulation Smith may have exaggerated for rhetorical effect, 'continue for whole centuries' (1776, p. 47).

Hence, the greater analytical complexity of Marx's presentation need not persuade us to set it apart from the classical framework. On the contrary. Not only does its theoretical content represent a logical progression of classical ideas, but it clearly shares their methodological starting-point. This becomes even more apparent in the third volume of *Capital*, where prices of production are analysed separately from values in conjunction with a uniform profit rate. Again, Marx abstracted from supply and demand to be 'able to study phenomena in their fundamental relations, [that is] in the form corresponding to their conception' (1867/94, III, p. 189).

In sum, the distinguishing feature of the classical method was that it focused theoretical inquiry upon the persistent, long-run forces governing circulation and production in a market economy. We shall find that the criticism which Marx directed against his classical precursors stemmed not from the method they adopted so much as their failure or reluctance to exploit it to the full.[6] In assessing the validity of this criticism, however, we shall also have occasion to observe that Marx's own contribution was not immune from it.

Separability

Having introduced the method of classical analysis, we can now turn to its theoretical dimension. Since this will occupy a considerable proportion of the chapters which follow, little needs to be anticipated here except the underlying 'separability' of the theories of value and output (Garegnani, 1978/79; Eatwell, 1979). The theory of the value, that is to say the discovery and elucidation of the laws regulating the exchange of commodities, is the core of classical economics. By contrast with the neoclassical approach, this theory was developed *separately* from a theory for the determination of output – or the social product. In order to determine relative prices and the rate of profit, classical theory treated two sets of magnitudes as given, or independently variable, along with the technical conditions of production. One was the real wage, which was determined by the amount of labour socially necessary to reproduce the labourer. The other was output, which was held to depend upon the level of capital accumulation.

The notion of a given real wage governed by conventional as well as physiological factors was, as we shall see, comprehensively discussed in classical writing. It was introduced by the Physiocrats into a 'circular flow' model of production to prove the existence of a surplus measurable in physical and monetary terms. Generalisation of the Physiocratic notions of surplus by Smith, Ricardo and Marx from agriculture to all lines of production brought a corresponding development in value theory: the reduction of exchange ratios between heterogeneous goods to ratios between homogeneous abstract labour. The transformation of these value ratios into price ratios associated with a uniform rate of profit on capital then became a central task for political economy.

The theory of output, on the other hand, was not adequately dealt with in the classical approach. The reason may be found in the universal assumption of Say's law of markets, which holds that 'saving is spending', i.e., that saving and investment are identical (see Milgate, 1982, pp. 46–57). As indicated earlier, I call this assumption Say's identity, to distinguish it from the version of Say's law adopted by neoclassical economics. Say's identity was used by Ricardo to prove that 'demand is only limited by production' (Ricardo, 1951/58, I. p. 290), and similarly by Marx to show, first, that expanded reproduction implied no 'realisation' problem and, second, that 'permanent crises' did not exist (Marx, 1867/94, III, pt. III).[7] Having thus assumed full capacity utilisation (though not full employment of labour), the problem of determining the 'normal' level of output did not arise: output simply expressed the stage of accumulation.

Marx's quarrel with Ricardo on the issue of Say's law related solely to the possibility and characteristics of deviations from this position, and not the determination of output.[8] Ricardo's denial of the possibility of a 'general glut' was refuted by Marx, who argued that the introduction of money separates the act of purchase from the sale of commodities. A crisis of overproduction – the polarisation of commodities and money – reflected the *temporary* overaccumulation of capital in relation to surplus value. The inability to sell commodities except at market prices far below their prices of production inevitably reduced output and capacity utilisation, but there was no mechanism in the analysis to identify the level of output towards which the system would tend. It has been said of Ricardo that, 'Say's law was not the result of an analysis of the investment-saving process but rather the result of the *lack* of any such analysis' (Garegnani, 1978/79, p. 280). His critics either accepted the identity of saving and investment and then vainly tried to escape its logic (Malthus), or distinguished the two aggregates, but only to present an account of temporary or cyclical crises (Marx).

Neoclassical economics, on the other hand, does have an analysis of the investment–saving process. It takes as data consumer preferences, technology and endowments, and asserts a functional relationship between prices and quantities in all commodity markets – including those for factors of production. 'Equilibrium' prices are established simultaneously with output on the basis of a distribution analysis which not only determines wages by the operation of demand and supply in the labour market but also interest (rate of profit) by demand and supply in the capital market, i.e., the equalisation of investment and saving (see Milgate, 1982, pp. 57–8; and Eatwell, 1983). I refer to this version of Say's law as Say's equality. Unless otherwise specified, I shall be using the term Say's law in this work to mean Say's identity.

EQUATION OF EXCHANGE

The brief account in the previous section of the method and theory of classical economics was by way of background to the competing interpretations of the well-known 'equation of exchange', to which I now turn my attention. This account will also be supplemented by a broad sketch of the unfolding historical context in which successive generations of economists made their mark. Schumpeter has pointed out that, 'the state of any science at any given time implies its past history and cannot be satisfactorily conveyed without making this implicit history explicit' (1954, p. 4). This is a view whose application, I hope to demonstrate, enhances rather than detracts from the status and significance of 'theory' as such. In the field of economics, perhaps more than in any other, 'an adequate understanding of our modern institutions presupposes a satisfactory knowledge of the historical development of these institutions' (Niebyl, 1946, pp. 2–3).

The equation of exchange forms a common point of reference for all approaches to the problem of inflation since the relationships it expresses simply constitute a truism and do not in themselves imply causality:

$$MV = PT$$

where M denotes the money supply, V the velocity of circulation, P an index of prices and T the number of commodity transactions. This is the way in which the equation was usually formulated by classical economists, as we shall see in Chapter 4.

The equation may also be written:

$$MV = PY$$

where Y denotes total output, the index P is correspondingly adjusted and V no longer reflects the circulation of a stock of commodities but the rate of expenditure of a flow of income (corresponding to the flow of output). I shall adopt this alternative formation of the equation of exchange. The only difference of substance is the replacement of the sum of commodity transactions with a measure of net output over a given period, hence excluding non-produced assets (such as land) from the exchange process. The advantages of the alternative formulation is its congruence with the economic categories we have already identified, and its closer conformity with modern usage.[9]

We are now in a position to ask what is the nature of the relationship between the money supply and the price level. This was the central question posed in the three historical phases which I am about to investigate. It was not the existence of an empirical correlation that was in dispute, but rather the *direction of causation.* To find an answer therefore required a theoretical approach as well as knowledge of the facts. The basic structure of the solution in all three situations is already clear from the discussion so far. For the classical school, when economic activity is regulated by permanent forces, the magnitude of P in the equation of exchange is determined on the basis of the law of value, Y is fixed due to the Say's law assumption and V is externally given. Thus P is the independent variable in the equation and M the dependent variable. Any movement in P as a result of changes in the production costs of commodities (or money) has a commensurate effect on M.

This determination of aggregate monetary requirements in the 'real' sector of the economy I shall call the 'classical law of monetary circulation'. Causation ran from prices to money in classical economics and not the reverse as we find in neoclassical monetarism. The type of money employed in the circulation process has no bearing on this conclusion, since V is determinate at all numerical values of M. The important point is that this conceptual framework excluded market fluctuations from the analysis.

The short-run

Had the scope of classical economics extended no further than the study of the permanent economic forces, it would have been impossible to attribute to it a quantity theory of money. But the limitations of this approach in explaining concrete developments and formulating relevant policies convinced most classical writers to take into account the role of temporary factors. In particular, the effects of exogenous changes in the money supply needed to be explained. Now the problem became complicated by the definition of money and the nature of financial organisation. If Say's law kept Y constant, only two possibilities remained open: a price adjustment, i.e., a change in P, or a quantity adjustment, i.e. a change in V (by hoarding or dishoarding). This was the essence of the division among the classical economists.[10]

The dominant Ricardian school held not only that Say's law implied a fixed value for Y but also that V remained externally given by institutional factors. Just as every unit of saving automatically became investment, so every commodity bought had to be sold *without any variation in monetary velocity*. The role of money as a store of value and means of payment was subordinated to its role as a medium of circulation, interposing itself as a mere instrument in a system of direct barter. In the words of James Mill, 'of two men who perform an exchange, the one does not come with only a supply, the other with only a demand; each of them comes with both a demand and a supply. . . . The supply which he brings is the instrument of his demand; and his demand and supply are, of course, exactly equal to one another' (1844, p. 120). Since the operation of a hoarding mechanism was thus excluded from the analysis, the stability of V was assured (see Schumpeter, 1954, p. 620). In that context, the quantity 'theory' of money was no theory at all, but simply the logical outcome of assuming Say's law.[11]

The opponents of quantity theory, on the other hand, were prepared to sacrifice 'consistency' in an attempt to interpret the real events with which they were confronted. Their often pioneering expositions generally placed the weight of adjustment on V, although the extent was seen as contingent upon the composition of M, that is to say, whether the money supply was metallic, fiduciary or credit. These economists questioned the general identification of supply and demand (in the product market) but not of saving and investment (in the capital market). They recognised that in the process of buying and selling, 'the effect of the employment of money . . . is, that it enables this one act of interchange to be divided into two separate acts or operations' (J. S. Mill, 1874, p. 70). Moreover, they understood that the seller 'does not therefore necessarily add to the *immediate* demand for one commodity when he adds to the supply of another' (ibid.).

The role of money as a store of value – irrespective of whether 'money' was a produced commodity or paper substitute – gave rise to the possibility of hoarding and hence to changes in the rate of monetary circulation. Yet the Ricardian school regarded any such relaxation of the fixed V assumption as no more than a sleight of hand. After all, the possibility of hoarding arose even in a barter system, though in the form of goods rather than money. In the end, it became clear that the stability or otherwise of V in the equation of exchange was not the solid rock on which to construct an 'anti-Ricardian' alternative. What was missing was any coherent attempt to overthrow Say's law and to develop an analysis of the saving–investment process itself, i.e., a theory of output. Had this been undertaken, the challenge to the incorporation of quantity theory into classical economics would have stood a better chance of success.

To summarise the argument so far, all classical economists held that the amount of money necessary for normal circulation was determined in the 'real' sector of the economy by the theory of value and that the level of output was independently given by Say's law. Hence causation in the equation of exchange ran from the supply side *PY* to the demand side *MV*, and more specifically from *P* to *M*. However, when the economy departed from its normal position due to an exogenous change in the money supply, there was a division of opinion about the consequences. In the following chapters, I shall examine that division in three historical phases of relatively high price inflation and rapid social change. In each phase, theoretical controversy was associated with new developments in the predominant form of money. The growing complexity of the conceptual categories therefore mirrored the evolution of the real economic categories, and represented an attempt not merely to comprehend them but also to influence the pace and form of their progress.

This interdependence of the logical and historical aspects of the classical framework is fundamental to my discussion of the behaviour of the variables in the equation of exchange. Its analysis, as I have indicated, is the task and objective of historical economics, the method I shall employ in this work. It is in the nature of such an approach that a principle of 'periodisation' must be devised, both to impose a sense of order on the historical process and to illuminate the connection with the development of theory at successive stages of this process.

Historical periodisation

It will be appropriate here, before I embark upon the substance of the investigation, to make some reference to the principle of historical 'periodisation' I have adopted and to the orders of magnitude which give it concrete application. This principle has been advanced by Stark as follows:

> What we need, then, is a principle of periodization which is taken from economics proper, but comprehends it as a progressive development. Now, if economics is considered as the science of exchange economy, its progressive development must consist in a growing knowledge of the laws which constitute the inner order of the system of economic intercourse known by that name. . . . The principle of periodization which we seek must express at once the absolute knowledge, and the much more important relativity of its tenets; it must take into account, not only our growing comprehension of the capitalist order, but also its great historical variations which the science describing it could not but share. (Stark, 1944, p. 65)[12]

The three distinct periods of monetary debate covered in the discussion each corresponded with fundamental developments in the UK financial structure. These periods of debate I shall denote as follows:

the 'price revolution', this period corresponded with a system based on metallic money;
the 'bullion controversy', this period corresponded with a system of paper money decoupled from its metallic base; and
the 'currency–banking debate', this period corresponded with the rise of a mature credit system.

Although inflationary pressures acted as the chief stimulus to debate in all three instances, the focus of analysis shifted successively from one form of money to another. While metallic money, as the simplest economic category, held the key to understanding more advanced and complex phenomena, decisive theoretical steps had still to be taken before an explanation of those phenomena became possible (see Green, 1987b). Similarly, real progress in financial organisation had to occur before phenomena such as credit could become categories of major significance for the capitalist economy.[13] It was in this sense that theory 'shared' in the historical periodisation and established the preconditions for historical economics:

> Money may exist, and did exist historically, before capital existed, before banks existed, before wage labour existed, etc. Thus in this respect it may be said that the simpler category can express the dominant relations of a less developed whole, or else those subordinate relations of a more developed whole which already had a historic existence before this whole developed in the direction expressed by a more concrete category. To that extent the path of abstract thought, rising from the simple to the combined, would correspond to the real historical process. (Marx, 1973, p. 102)

Let us now proceed to the orders of magnitude involved in the three inflationary episodes. In each case, the inflation may be characterised for the purposes of our discussion as 'a cumulative process persisting into the long-term and riding over short-term fluctuations in prices generated by temporary disturbances on the side of either demand or output' (Deane, 1979, pp. 1–2). Most economic historians would now accept that, of all the empirical data available on the development of modern society, price indices are among the most enlightening and sophisticated. Beveridge, for example, has pointed out that, '[t]he importance to economic and social science of having a comprehensive history of prices and wages hardly needs to be emphasised. Prices and wages are the social phenomena most susceptible of objective statistical record over long periods of time' (1939, cited by Mitchell and Deane, 1962, p. 465). Yet, as Mitchell and Deane tell us (ibid.), prior to the efforts of Beveridge's own Price and Wage History Research group, there were few long series of prices in existence – the major exceptions being those by Thomas Tooke (1838/57) and Thorold Rogers (1866/1902).[14]

By 1957, however, it could be said that, 'the material now available on past wages and prices is incomparably richer than anything hitherto known or imagined' (Beveridge, 1957, cited by Mitchell and Deane, 1962, p. 465). Much of this material has recently been assembled by Deane (1979) in a survey of the key inflationary episodes in Britain since the middle ages. She uses the price indices constructed by Phelps-Brown and Hopkins (1955a, 1955b, 1957) to show that, while commodity prices rose at an average yearly rate of only 0.5 per cent between the thirteenth and twentieth centuries, this long-term trend was interrupted by several episodes in which their rate of increase accelerated sharply. More recently still, Phelps-Brown and Hopkins have published their completed work in *A Perspective of Wages and Prices* (1981). Here they provide two indices: first, of the price of a 'composite unit of consumables', and second, of the 'equivalent of wage-rate of building craftsmen', expressed in the above composite physical unit, in southern England between 1264 and 1954. The table given in the Appendix to this work reproduces the price index only, and not the 'equivalent of wage-rate'. It therefore measures the commodity value of money, not the real value of money incomes.

Price behaviour

During the first of the inflationary episodes which comprise the historical background to this study – the 'price revolution' of the sixteenth and seventeenth centuries – inflation averaged around 2 per cent for Europe as a whole, with a slightly higher rate in Spain. Although this inflation could hardly be described as spectacular by modern standards, its scope and persistence were nevertheless economically significant for the time. As Deane comments, 'the most remarkable feature of the Price Revolution was not the pace at which prices rose but the fact that a rising trend was sustained for so long and that the violent periodic upswings in staple foodstuff prices characteristic of a pre-industrial economy were rarely fully compensated by subsequent downswings in periods of plenty' (1979, p. 3). The data on price movements from the mid fifteenth century to the end of the seventeenth century may be found in the Appendix.

While no single explanation for these movements emerges unequivocally from the data alone, this has not dissuaded economic historians from suggesting a range of factors – such as population pressure, inelastic food supplies and, perhaps most consistently, the influx of American treasure.[15] However, Deane persuasively concludes that, 'the one thing that seems clear from recent researches and analyses is that neither the simple monetarist interpretation, nor the undiluted demographic interpretation suffices to explain the Price Revolution . . .' (ibid., p. 9; see also Hammarström, 1957). This was the view taken by *all* of the classical economists, who, even without the benefit of reliable statistics, were able to shift the focus of theoretical inquiry away from the sheer quantity of treasure to its cost of production.

For classical theorists, as we shall see, money was first and foremost a *produced commodity* and therefore, like other commodities, subject to the law of value. It is their analysis which is borne out by the available evidence. Vilar, for example, has recently shown that it is 'possible to relate on the one side, the periodicity of gold and silver imports into Europe, the rate of 'general' price increases (which show a fall in the value of the monetary metals), and certain financial difficulties of the Spanish state which affected the whole European economy to, on the other, *changes in the conditions of production of precious metals in America*' (1976, p. 115, emphasis added). This 'long-run' aspect of the 'price revolution' could not be comprehended by a pure exchange quantity theory of money.

The inflationary upsurge which accompanied the French Revolutionary and Napoleonic wars at the end of the eighteenth and the beginning of the nineteenth centuries was both more rapid and more erratic than anything previously experienced in Britain. (France itself was only just beginning to recover from the trauma of John Law's financial experiment.) Indeed, Deane calls it 'the first major inflation in modern British history' (1979, p. 10).[16] Between 1792 and 1813 – the peak year for the 'war inflation' – the annual compound rate of growth of prices (domestic and imported) averaged nearly 3.2 per cent. This trend and what seemed at the time to be apocalyptic fluctuations around it are also illustrated in the Appendix. The decisive institutional change in this period came in 1797 – after an unprecedented expansion of the war debt – with the suspension of cash payments by the Bank of England. In other words, bank notes were no longer redeemable in gold coin or bullion.

The emergence of 'short-run' considerations lay at the heart of the subsequent 'bullion controversy' which sharply divided classical economists. The absence of legal convertibility required the development of an effective principle of limitation to maintain 'economic convertibility'. Those who proffered direct monetary control as just such a principle were convinced that the Bank of England had introduced a fiduciary system into the nation's economy, that is to say an inconvertible paper currency issued at will by the state. They sounded the alarm when a premium appeared on gold and singled out the overissue of bank notes as the primary cause. The apparent correlation between the rise in the price level and the growth of the money supply (notes and coin) was cited in evidence; though, more often than not, broadly defined elements of the money supply – especially securities held by the Bank – tended to move in the opposite direction. In addition, the domestic picture was complicated both by factors associated with the war, such as the continental blockade and the military's insatiable appetite for funds, and by recurrent harvest failures. Here again, any explanation of price movements called for sound theoretical analysis – the facts did not speak for themselves. It was during this period, however, that quantity theory became established as a new monetary orthodoxy, even though, as Deane observes, 'subsequent events did not seem to confirm the monetarist argument' (ibid., p. 18).

By the middle of the nineteenth century, inflation was no longer the result simply of random economic disasters and the need to finance war expenditure, but had become an endemic feature of the industrial cycle then taking shape in Britain and Europe (see Landes, 1969, ch. 2). The more regular pattern of price movements may be gleaned from the Appendix. In this final episode of our investigation, while the legal convertibility of bank notes had been restored, fluctuations in the price level were far from eliminated; for example, in 1846–7, prices increased by about 10 per cent, only to drop sharply in the subsequent deflation. Once again, since there was on observable correlation with monetary expansion and contraction, the principle of limitation devised for a fiduciary system was applied to a system dominated by credit; this had the effect of adding unnecessarily large swings in the interest rate to the prevailing financial instability. An alternative explanation of price behaviour was required to sustain alternative policies, but the quantity theory of money was not to be displaced until well into the following century.

These, then, are the three historical phases of price inflation which inform the development of monetary analysis. We are now in a position to evaluate this analysis in greater detail. The sequence of the argument has been anticipated. In short, it progresses from the supply and demand framework of mercantilism and early quantity theory to the establishment of a long-run monetary circulation law on the basis of classical value theory. It then examines the differing approaches of classical economists to the short-run in systems of commodity money, fiduciary money and credit. Finally, it assesses the classical approaches in relation to neoclassical monetarism and the extent to which they were limited in their application to policy by the absence of a theory of output.

Part II

Metallic Currency

3 Mercantilism and the Quantity Theory of Money

> Whence it comes to pass that the doctrine of money is so extremely difficult and involved? This I ascribe chiefly to the introduction of a money-jargon, employed by people who have had the management of mints, or who have been practical merchants, without knowing anything of the theory of their business.
>
> Sir James Steuart, *Principles of Political Oeconomy* (1767)

The theoretical analysis of inflation has its origin in the attempts to explain the so-called 'price revolution' of the sixteenth and seventeenth centuries. This is the term used to describe the secular rise in commodity prices which occurred throughout Europe, punctuated by sharper, localised fluctuations around a general trend. Then as now, many of the operative short-run factors were widely recognised. Harvest failure, war, disease and currency manipulation all exercised a disproportionately severe influence upon price behaviour in a continent whose predominant economic activity remained agriculture – notwithstanding the rapid dissolution of the feudal social structure and the growing diversification and interdependence of national markets. Such disturbances by themselves, however, could not account for the persistence and generality of the price inflation, which continued at an average rate of around 2 per cent a year for well over a century.

The question was how to 'theorise' or at least make sense of this sustained rise in the price level. Two fundamentally different hypotheses were offered, each more or less in conflict with the mercantilist orthodoxy. The first was a 'long-run' quantity theory of money, which, as we shall see, made the price level depend upon an *exchange relationship* between the money supply and a determinate volume of marketed output. The observable correlation between the influx of precious metals from the New World and the movement in commodity prices – first in Spain and then in the rest of Europe – was transformed into a one-way causal connection (see especially Viner, 1937, ch. 1). The most influential exponent of quantity theory in the eighteenth century was David Hume, whose economic essays may be seen as 'a reaction against the mercantilist concept of money and a *theoretical generalization from the phenomena of universal price rises* that Europe experienced during the "price revolution" ' (Rubin, 1929, p. 83).

The other hypothesis was an embryonic classical theory of value based upon *relationships of production*, which attempted to establish the level of prices independently of both output and money supply. We shall also find that, as a corollary, the classical 'law of monetary circulation' turned the quantity of money into a *dependent* variable, at least in the long-run. The association of quantity theory with classical analysis in the history of economic thought is due to the fact that both emerged almost simultaneously as parallel critiques of mercantilism. Both treated the level of output as given in the long-run, whereas the mercantilist approach assumed output to vary with changes in the amount of money in circulation.

This chapter looks at the nature of the quantity theory challenge to mercantilism. It will be argued that this challenge was insufficient on its own to dislodge orthodox thinking because it was conducted exclusively within a supply and demand or 'pure exchange' framework. The central propositions of quantity theory were left indeterminate and hence open to rebuttal by 'neo-mercantilist' writers, such as Sir James Steuart, whose 'system' relied upon the same framework. It was only with the development of classical economics that determinate propositions could be sustained about long-run price behaviour; and to the extent that quantity theory was accommodated within this approach, it was transformed into a purely short-run phenomenon. This will be the subject of Chapter 4.

ORIGIN OF QUANTITY THEORY

Mercantilism was the dominant system of economic policy and ideas in the sixteenth and seventeenth centuries. The wealth of a nation, according to the underlying principle, comprised only its money, i.e., gold and silver. The principle was formulated in two stages. The first has come to be known as 'bullionism' (see Viner, 1937, pp. 3–5).[1] This constituted the 'pre-history' of mercantilism and expressed the principle in its most superficial guise. Here wealth was objectively located in the *physical substance of money*. The second stage of mercantilism still accepted that wealth consisted solely of money but found its source in the *subjective activity of labour* which produced things exchangeable for money, rather than in the material object.[2] This version, as we shall see, served as a point of departure for the labour theory of value (see Rubin, 1929, p. 56).

Commodity prices in the mercantilist system were analysed, however, without any reference to production. They were either accounted for tautologically by the exchange ratio between a specific commodity and money, which simply expressed the relationship between supply and demand, or derived from some notion of 'just price'.[3] Since at that early stage of capitalist society, value took 'the form of the universal commodity as distinct from all particular commodities' (Marx, 1859, p. 158), the magnitude of value appeared to be established by exchange, and surplus value by exchange with other countries, i.e., by the balance of trade.[4] By contrast, the labour theory of value was to determine value and surplus value – and hence prices and the rate of profit – independently of the exchange process.

In effect, mercantilism as a concept of prices was indeterminate. It did not progress beyond an elementary supply and demand framework and hence cannot be regarded as a *theory* of price behaviour. Its overriding concern was rather to justify measures taken by the state to promote capital accumulation on a national basis. As Landes has observed:

> [M]ercantilist doctrine was shapeless, inconsistent. It was inconsistent because it reflected policy as much as guided it, and each state did with its economy what circumstances warranted, knowledge (or ignorance) suggested, and means permitted. Mercantilism was, in short, pragmatism gilded by principle. (Landes, 1969, p. 32)

When we turn to the quantity theory of money, we find that it too, like mercantilism, fell short of the criteria necessary to justify theoretical status. Here again, price formation was 'explained' by the ratio of exchange between money and commodities; in other words, it was not so much explained as merely *described* in terms of the operation of the market. The novelty of quantity theory thus lay in its *application* of 'pure exchange' analysis, rather than in any conceptual advance which might have set it apart from the traditional framework. Its main achievement, perhaps, was a shift in emphasis from the study of 'relative prices' which were determined by the proportion of money to individual commodities, to the 'general price level' established by the relationship between the total money supply and the aggregate sum of commodities in circulation at a given time.

The underlying point of difference with mercantilism was the rejection by quantity theory of the identification of money with capital. Money was simply a commodity, according to this principle, and, like other commodities, was subject to the laws of supply and demand. The one special attribute of money was its function as a medium of circulation. This underpinned the assumption of an externally given level of output and, as I shall now try to demonstrate, characterised the distinct quantity theory interpretation of the 'price revolution'.

The predominant feature of the price revolution which affected all the countries of Europe was the influx of precious metals from the newly discovered American mines. Instead of augmenting wealth – or stimulating output – in the manner suggested by mercantilist doctrine, the metals seemed only to devalue the unit of account. The quantity theory of money rapidly became accepted not only because it provided a consistent interpretation of this new phenomenon, but also because it contributed to the ideological campaign against the increasingly anachronistic economic role of the state.[5] Money was no longer regarded as capital whose accumulation in a country was to be accelerated by state controls, but rather as a commodity performing the role of circulating medium. The supply and demand analysis which mercantilist writers applied to individual commodities was now extended to the money commodity, whose value was said to depend upon its quantity (see Viner, 1937, pp. 40–5). It was logical, therefore, that an increased supply of gold and silver in a country should result in an equiproportional rise in the price level. Both output and the velocity of circulation were assumed constant by proponents of quantity theory, although, as we shall see, some permitted a short-run non-price response.

Early attempts

Just as Spain was the first country in Europe to experience the price inflation associated with the inflow of metals, so it was the source of the first coherent statements of the quantity theory of money. Pierre Vilar (1976) recounts the pioneering contributions of two theologians, Martin de Azpilcueta and Tomas de Mercado, who in the middle of the sixteenth century noticed that the price of a silver ingot changed 'for the same reason as cloth did', and constructed out of this observation an hypothesis which would ultimately help to form the theoretical structure of eighteenth-century economic liberalism. In his Manual 'for confessors and penitents', an authoritative guide to business morality published in 1556, Azpilcueta asked why a currency does not retain its value at all times in all places. In a series of eight reasons, he argued that, 'the seventh reason why money falls or rises is lack or abundance of it' (cited by Vilar, ibid., p. 163).[6]

The pure exchange analysis of mercantilism was therefore generalised to the monetary material itself, and money became 'merchandise' whose value was set simultaneously with the prices of other goods by the relative quantities available in the market-place:

> All goods grow dearer for the great need and small quantity of them; and in that money can be sold or changed in any other way, it is merchandise, as said above, and so it too becomes dearer for the great need and small quantity of it. Similarly, in the countries where there is a great want of money, everything, even men's labour, is given for less money, than where there is an abundance of it, as experience shows that in France, where there is less money in Spain, bread, wine, cloth and men's labour are worth much less, and even in Spain, when there was less money goods and labour were given for much less than after the discovery of the Indies flooded it with gold and silver. (Ibid.)

Mercado went further in discussing what he called 'the esteem of money', by which he meant its purchasing power. He even foreshadowed the decline of Spain as its goods became uncompetitive in the world market: 'Hence the disorder: for rich and poor alike load the ships, and in so doing destroy both commonweals, Spain and the Indies, in Spain making prices rise with their great demand, and the great number of merchants approaching foreigners as well as Spanish for ridiculously high prices' (ibid., p. 165).

The argument was taken up in France in 1568 by Jean Bodin in his well-known debate with de Malestroict. He concluded that the 'main and almost the sole' cause of the increased level of prices was 'the abundance of gold and silver' (1568, p. 3), though he still justified this abundance by the need to promote production and trade. The main elements of quantity theory were also developed with some profundity by Bernado Davanzati and a line of Italian economists. Only at the turn of the century were similar ideas advanced in England, though even then they were by no means universally accepted. Malynes's *Treatise of the Canker of England's Commonwealth* of 1601 is usually regarded as the first example of English quantity theory (Viner, 1937, p. 41). However, Outhwaite has shown that he is predated by an anonymous author (probably Sir Thomas Smith) who tried in 1581 to explain why, if price rises were caused by debasement of the coinage, they did not fall to their previous level with the restoration of the coinage to 'its former purity and perfection' twenty years earlier. He eventually fastened upon 'the great store and plenty of treasure, which is walking in these partes of the world, far more in these our dayes, than ever our forefathers have sene in times past. Who doth not understand of the infinite sums of gold and silver, which are gathered from the Indies and other countries, and so yearly transported unto these costes?' (cited by Outhwaite, 1969, p. 22).

This alleged causal relationship between the supply of metallic money and the price level was not seen by early writers as necessarily incompatible with mercantilism. Indeed, the juxtaposition of quantity theory and the prevailing national objective of monetary accumulation expressed not only the shared conceptual limitation of pure exchange analysis but also the practical capacity of the mercantilist system to withstand – or at least internalise – the gathering momentum towards free trade and the deregulation of economic life. All the ambiguities and hesitations of this period can be found in Thomas Mun's *England's Treasure by Foreign Trade*, written in 1630 and published posthumously in 1664. There it is argued that although a favourable balance of trade would benefit individuals, the country as a whole would suffer a deterioration in the *terms* of trade due to the effect of the expanded money supply on prices:

> For all men do consent that plenty of money in a Kingdom doth make the natife commodities dearer, which as it is to the profit of some private men in their revenues, so is it directly against the benefit of the Publique in the quantity of trade; for as plenty of mony makes wares dearer, so dear wares decline their use and consumption . . . And although this is a very hard lesson for some great landed men to learn, yet I am sure it is a true lesson for all the land to observe, lest when wee have gained some store of mony by trade, wee lose it again by not trading with our mony. (Mun, 1664, p. 17)

Mun's selective opposition to the existing network of feudal restrictions and special privileges did not proceed entirely from a detached view of the national interest. As a director of the East India Company, he was convinced that the factors making for the success of this monopoly venture had a general application to the growth of commercial capital. Hence, the exemption granted to the East India Company from the outward exchange controls which were then operating could hardly be denied to other trading enterprises. Changes in the predominant forms of property meant that the old argument for privileges could now be superseded by universal right. Since Mun still advocated state control and protectionism as a means of accelerating the growth and concentration of capital on a national basis, it was left to John Locke to develop the new conception of right.

A new philosophy

In his political philosophy, Locke counterposed constitutional monarchy to absolutism and, correspondingly, in his theory of economic development, he identified individual self-interest as the motive force which could give a unifying coherence to analysis and policy. Locke was therefore able to separate the essential characteristics of quantity theory from the mercantilist apparatus to a greater extent than his predecessors, and to promote it as a critical and even subversive doctrine. As Roll pointed out:

> Here is a philosophy suited to the new conditions of the economy. It is the embodiment of the victory over the Middle Ages. But it is more than that; it is a symptom of the decline of state power which commercial capital had created at an earlier stage of its war against feudalism. . . . [T]he new state was beginning to be seen for what it was: the creature of economic power no less than its master. (1973, pp. 91–2)[7]

While Locke's monetary writings were neither as extensive nor as important as his contribution to philosophy, his treatment of the connection between money and prices allowed a first glimpse of quantity theory in its modern form. Again, however, this was not a *theory* in the strict sense. Since Locke conducted his analysis in terms of supply and demand, he simply *assumed* that the level of output was externally fixed; and, unlike his contemporary, Sir William Petty, he could provide no theoretical explanation of price behaviour. Indeed, the fact that Locke modified the fixed output assumption in the course of his argument as a concession to mercantilism indicated the transitional and indeterminate character of his approach. Support could be derived from it by David Hume *and* Sir James Steuart, both of whom regarded Locke with equal justification as an authority for their respective viewpoints.

Most of Locke's economics is contained in a pamphlet *Consequences of the Lowering of Interest, and Raising the Value of Money*, published in 1691 but written some twenty years earlier. Its main purpose was to oppose legal regulation of the rate of interest, but it also included a polemic against devaluation of the monetary standard. This had been proposed by Lowndes, the Secretary to the Treasury, to take account of the effect of wear and tear on the coinage. As we shall see, Locke's practical criticism of Lowndes was inconsistent with the abstract model he constructed as the basis of his quantity theory. This is all the more surprising since, as Locke himself pointed out, the model was designed to 'serve rather to give us some light into the nature of money, than to teach here a new measure of traffic' (1691, p. 251). The primary role of money was identified as being an 'instrument of commerce' (medium of exchange) due to its possession of 'intrinsic value'. Money also functioned, therefore, as a measure of this value, whose determination became a key issue in the debate with Lowndes.[8]

For Locke, money was 'perfectly in the same condition with other commodities, and subject to the same laws of value' (ibid., p. 243). This meant that the value of money, like the value of commodities generally, was determined not in the sphere of production but in the sphere of exchange – by supply and demand: 'For mankind having consented to put an imaginary value upon gold and silver, . . . the intrinsic value, regarded in these metals, made the common barter, is *nothing but the quantity* which men give or receive of them' (ibid., p. 233, emphasis added). In other words, the monetary metals were initially things without value, but once in the sphere of circulation they acquired an imaginary value whose magnitude was dependent (other things being equal) upon their quantity. This formulation was a defining characteristic of 'pre-classical' quantity theory, and it constituted the first direct opposition to the mercantilist doctrine that gold and silver alone possessed real value. The function of money as a measure of value – and as the exclusive form of capital – was thus subordinated to its role as medium of exchange in which capacity it also served as a 'counter' (money of account). Since the process of exchange could bestow only an imaginary value on money, quantity theory, as Schumpeter has pointed out, 'essentially amounts to treating money not as a commodity but as a voucher for buying goods' (1954, p. 313). This representative function of money became even more explicit in Hume's discussion.

The implications of this approach for the devaluation of controversy should have been obvious. Locke could scarcely maintain along with Lowndes that the representation of a particular weight was purely conventional and imaginary. Despite his abstract quantity theory, Locke clung to the metallic content of the silver: 'And thus silver, which makes the intrinsick value of money, compared with itself, under any stamp, or different countries, cannot be related. For an ounce of silver, whether in pence, groats, or crown-pieces, stivers, or ducatoons, or in bullion, is and always eternally will be, of equal value to any other ounce of silver, under what stamp, or denomination soever . . .' (ibid., pp. 275–6).[9]

International context

It was at the level of the world economy that Locke's quantity theory came into its own, confining the application of mercantilism to the comparative positions of nation states: 'Riches do not consist in having more gold and silver, but in having more in proportion than the rest of the world, or than our neighbours. . . . Nor would they be one jot the richer, if, by the discovery of new mines, the quantity of gold and silver in the world becoming twice as much as it is, their shares of them should be doubled' (ibid., pp. 226–27). Hence *world* output was assumed to be externally given and changes in the money supply would ultimately bring about an equiproportional shift in the *world* price level – with each country submitting to its shares of the inflationary process. Locke here introduced the effect of American treasure as the chief illustration of this causal linkage: '[T]here being ten times as much silver now in the world, (the discovery of the West-Indies having made the plenty) as there was [in the reign of Henry VII], it is nine-tenths less worth now, than it was at that time; that is, it will exchange for nine-tenths less of any commodity now, which bears the same proportion to its vent, as it did 200 years since . . . ' (ibid., p. 250).

Quantity theory was therefore only an international phenomenon: '[T]he value of money in general, is the quantity of all the money in the world, in proportion to all the trade . . .' (ibid., p. 252). Having come this far, however, Locke was logically bound to concede its application to a *closed* economy as well: [S]upposing any island separate from the commerce of the rest of mankind; . . . any quantity of that money (if it were but so much, that every body might have some) would serve to drive any proportion of trade, whether more, or less' (ibid., p. 251). No longer was a determinate amount of money required for circulation – any amount would do. This formulation anticipated that of Hume eighty years later. It was when Locke once again took into account international trade that he reverted back to the mercantilist preoccupation with an export surplus in the form of bullion. The contradiction with his quantity theory was 'resolved' by a crude terms of trade argument, previously employed by Malynes but soon afterwards discarded, as we have seen, by Mun.

Seemingly unaware of the problem he was creating for his model, Locke maintained that an insufficient stock of money in a country would depress domestic activity either directly or through a corresponding reduction of export prices and increase of import prices:

> [I]n a country, that hath open commerce with the rest of the world, and uses money, made of the same materials with their neighbours, any quantity of that money will not serve to drive any quantity of trade; but there must be a certain proportion between their money and trade. The reason whereof is this, because, to keep your trade going without loss, your commodities amongst you must keep an equal, or at least, near the price of the same species of commodities in the neighbouring countries: which they cannot do, if your money be far less than in other countries: for then, either your commodities must be sold very cheap, or a great part of your trade must stand still, there not being money enough in the country to pay for them (in their shifting of hands) at that high price, which the plenty, and consequently low value of money makes them at in another country. (Ibid., p. 252)

Hume was to deal with this problem in an ingenious way; he separated the transitional effects of a variation in the money supply from its ultimate consequences. Hence, any output response could be seen as a purely short-run phenomenon which would be eliminated automatically on an international scale by a specie-flow mechanism, not counterposed to the original principle. By holding both views simultaneously, Locke demonstrated the inevitable compatibility of mercantilism and the quantity theory of money within a supply and demand framework. Of course, they differed in their assumptions about the behaviour of output – assumptions which flowed from whether money was conceived as means of circulation or as the unique form in which capital was accumulated. Nevertheless, both propositions had to rest upon *ad hoc* assumptions since they lacked a *theory* of output and a *theory* for the determination of prices other than by reference to market forces.

The crucial point here is that within this pre-classical framework, the prices of all commodities were established simply by the amount of money consumers were prepared to pay for them – a tautological assertion.[10] In the mercantilist system, relative prices emerged from individual exchange, whereas quantity theory accorded primacy to the general price level, which might then be decomposed into the exchange ratios for individual commodities. Once the indeterminacy of output becomes apparent within this framework and the competing interpretations of price behaviour are shown to turn merely upon different levels of aggregation, it will be seen that there is less to the dispute between Hume and Steuart than at first meets the eye. Only with the development of classical economics by the other major figure of the Scottish Enlightenment,

Adam Smith, could any attempt be made to theorise the determinate relationship between money and prices.

HUME'S ESSAY

The quantity theory of money received its definitive exposition in David Hume's economic essays of 1752. Their purpose was to refute mercantilism once and for all against the empirical background of the sixteenth and seventeenth century price inflation. If success is measured by the practical outcome, then it was assured in this case for the mercantilist system had already begun to disintegrate under the growing pressure of industrialisation. This was the period characterised by Christopher Hill as a 'new epoch' in the development of capitalism (1969, p. 241; also Landes, 1969, ch. 2): the mass production of iron, and its substitution for wood in machines, set the stage for the Industrial Revolution, and indeed for the rise of classical political economy.

There is much to be said for Schumpeter's claim, that the formidable reputation acquired by Hume's seminal essay 'Of Money' was 'due to the force and felicity with which it formulated the results of previous work rather than to any novelties' (1954, p. 291). The timing and presentation of the essay certainly far outweighed its originality. Viner observed in his detailed study of the evolution of quantity theory that 'its most important constituent elements had been stated long before Hume' (1937, p. 74; also p. 84); and Marx had earlier reached the same conclusion (1867/94, I, p. 124 fn.).[11] Indeed, in response to the counter-claims of Hume's latter-day disciples, Marx went to some length to show that Hume was 'anything but an original investigator': 'The influence of his economic essays on the educated circles of his day was due, not merely to his brilliant exposition, but also and principally to the fact that the essays were a progressive and optimistic glorification of industry and trade, which were then flourishing – in other words of the capitalist society which at that time was rapidly developing in England, and which was bound to provide the Essays with a "success"' (1894, p. 264).

While all conceptual breakthroughs in the history of economic thought are in some sense a synthesis of pre-existing ideas, it would be no exaggeration to say that that was the limit of Hume's achievement. He simply combined the abstract model of quantity theory developed by Locke, Jacob Vanderlint, Montesquieu and others with a 'transmission mechanism' to mask any potential inconsistency between price and output responses to changes in the money supply. His attempt to distinguish between temporary and long-run effects gave his approach a superficial similarity to the method of classical economics, but it was still trapped in the theoretical void of supply and demand analysis.[12]

Hume's main objective was to show that, contrary to mercantilist premises, the total amount of money in the economy is a matter of indifference, 'for men and commodities are the real strength of any community' (1752, p. 175). The corollary of this argument was that the only permanent effect of an alteration in the amount of money would be a proportional and uniform change in commodity prices, at any given velocity of circulation. In order to prove this hypothesis, however, Hume also had to reconcile it with evidence of an initial output response to the inflow of American bullion. No one could deny that at least the first phase of bullion imports was accompanied by a rapid growth of material prosperity throughout Europe, creating the technological preconditions for the advance of large-scale manufacturing enterprise. Moreover, this expansion of the productive forces was followed by an equally significant downturn – now known as the 'general crisis of the seventeenth century' – which enabled landed interests, backed by government policy, to obstruct the transfer of capital into manufacturing projects, and thus to delay the industrial revolution until Hume's era of social progress and economic revitalisation (see Hobsbawm, 1954).

As Locke had also found, the quantity theory here ran up against a problem: how was the hypothesis of an equiproportional price response to be maintained in the face of these 'real' effects? To overcome the apparent contradiction,[13] Hume's first step was to discard not only the mercantilist confusion of money with capital but also the associated 'dual value' of money. The quantity of money (all other things being equal) simply established its value as a *medium of circulation* – i.e., its purchasing power – and hence the general price level. The value of money as *capital* – i.e., the (capitalised) rate of interest – depended exclusively upon the 'real forces' of the system, which alone determined output. The level of output was given independently by the 'arts and industry' in each country.

The change in the concept of money together with the independent determination of output were the central features of the pure exchange quantity theory:

> Money is not, properly speaking, one of the subjects of commerce; but only the instrument which men have agreed upon to facilitate the exchange of one commodity for another. . . . If we consider any one Kingdom by itself, it is evident, that the greater or less plenty of money

> is of no consequence; since the prices of commodities are always proportioned to the plenty of money. . . . [M]oney is nothing but the representation of labour and commodities, and serves only as a method of rating or estimating them. Where coin is in greater plenty; as a greater quantity of it is required to represent the same quantity of goods; it can have no effect, either good or bad, taking a nation within itself; any more than would make an alteration on a merchant's books, if, instead of the Arabian method of notation, which requires few characters, he should make use of the Roman, which requires a great many. (Ibid., pp. 167, 169)

Locke's hesitations were thus put to one side. Money was seen here as having *no* intrinsic value. It was simply a means of circulation, performing nothing more than an accounting role. All the precious metals in a country *represented* commodities in the process of exchange, hence reducing these metals to mere tokens, things without value.[14] Hume illustrated his proposition with a comparison between two systems of notation. For this to prove anything, however, would it not have to be demonstrated that in a *given* system, the numerical value is governed by the quantity of characters employed as opposed to the quantity of characters depending upon their numerical value (see Marx, 1859, p. 162)? Hume made no attempt to do so.

Although gold and silver had no value and hence were not real commodities when they entered the sphere of circulation, once in the circulation they were spontaneously transformed into commodities through their acquisition of a 'fictitious value' (Hume, 1752, p. 170). This value was determined, like Locke's 'imaginary value', by the ratio of their own volume to the volume of other commodities.[15] It led to the peculiar result that every commodity being a fraction of the total mass of commodities was directly exchangeable for a commensurate fraction of the existing stockpile of coin.[16] Instead of calculating the general price level as an index of relative prices, i.e., as a measure of individual commodity values expressed in terms of the monetary standard, Hume's failure to analyse value separately from output forced him to reverse the procedure and derive relative prices from a price level established by supply and demand. These relative prices were determined by reciprocal quantities of use values converted into money by means of barter, thus superimposing upon exchange a criterion which could not be reduced to any common measure, or, in other words, an aspect of commodities which could not be denominated or quantified in units of equal quality.

When Dugald Stewart, in his account of Adam Smith's life and writings, remarked that Hume's ideas, 'though always plausible and ingenious . . . involve some fundamental mistakes', it is apparent from the context that he was alluding to this deduction of exchange values of commodities from a comparison of their physical quantities, i.e., their distinct character as use values. The misconception to which it gave rise over the nature and dynamic movement of commodities and money, 'affords striking proof, that in considering a subject so extensive and so complicated, the most penetrating sagacity, if directed only to particular questions, is apt to be led astray by first appearances' (Smith, 1812, V, pp. 501–2).

Specie-flow doctrine

The specie-flow doctrine did no more than *extend the scope* of quantity theory to the international context. Mercantilism had identified surplus value with the surplus money derived from a favourable balance of trade. Hume, disregarding the problem of surplus value in the same way that he avoided the concept of value itself, again contended that the amount of money was irrelevant, and furthermore, that the international distribution of circulating media was subject to automatic regulation. He supposed four-fifths of all the money in a country to be 'annihilated' in one night:

> Must not the price of all labour and commodities sink in proportion . . . ? What nation could then dispute with us in any foreign market, or pretend to navigate or to sell manufactures at the same price, which to us would afford sufficient profit? In how little time, therefore, must this bring back the money which we had lost, and raise us to the level of all the neighbouring nations? Where, after we have arrived, we immediately lose the advantage of the cheapness of labour and commodities; and the further flowing in of money is stopped by our fulness and repletion. (Hume, 1752, pp. 185–6)

The converse situation brought about the opposite effect: money flowed out 'till we fall to a level with foreigners, and lose that great superiority of riches, which laid us under such disadvantages' (ibid.).[17] Hume nevertheless recognised the possibility of a lag between an exogenous change in the money supply and the ultimate price response. This lag allowed him to introduce a 'transmission mechanism', which came to be seen as the main innovation of his essay. Yet, as we shall discover shortly, the elements of even this analytical device had been presented earlier (and in greater detail) by Richard Cantillon. Moreover, the two reasons he gave for the lag were inconsistent with his own theory.

First, monetary expansion could result in a higher propensity to hoard, i.e., a fall in the velocity of circulation. In this case, the general price level, and value of money, was determined not by the absolute amount present in a country but by the sum actually *in circulation* at any given level of marketed output. In the long run, however, *all* the available specie must be absorbed as coin into the circulation process:

> It is also evident, that the prices do not so much depend on the absolute quantity of commodities and that of money which are in a nation, as on that of the commodities which come or may come to market, and of the money which circulates. If the coin be locked up in chests, it is the same thing with regard to prices, as if it were annihilated; if the commodities be hoarded in magazines and granaries, a like effect follows. As the money and commodities, in these cases, never meet, they cannot affect each other. . . . [T]he whole [of prices] at last reaches a just proportion with the new quantity of specie which is in the Kingdom. (Ibid., pp. 170, 172–3)

The second reason for a lag lay in the output response to a monetary stimulus. Hume was well aware that, 'since the discovery of the mines in America, industry has increased in all nations of Europe, except in the possessors of those mines; and this may justly be ascribed, amongst other reasons, to the increase of gold and silver' (ibid., pp. 169–70). He explained the paradox in this way: '[T]hough the high price of commodities be a necessary consequence of the increase of gold and silver, yet it follows not immediately upon that increase; but some time is required before the money circulates through the whole state, and makes its effect be felt on all ranks of people' (ibid., p. 170). It was in the interval or intermediate situation, between the influx of money and the upward gravitation of prices to their new equilibrium position, that the expanded supply of bullion gave a boost to economic activity and employment (see Price, 1909, ch. 3). The additional sum was initially a source of windfall profits for exporters, who received it in payment for goods. These profits were then reinvested in the business, specifically in enlarging the workforce at the current wage rate. If the demand for labour outstripped supply, the employer might concede higher wages, but only on condition of a comparable growth in productivity. Before that happened, however, the increase in consumption expenditure would have ramified throughout the economy (in agriculture, services, etc.) until, finally, the whole spectrum of prices was readjusted in conformity with the mechanical equalisation of commodities and money originally envisaged by Hume's principle. 'It is easy,' he concluded, 'to trace the money in its progress through the whole commonwealth; where we shall find, that it must first quicken the diligence of every individual, before it increases the price of labour (ibid.; also p. 209).[18]

The possibility of changes in velocity and output as a result of monetary fluctuations exposes the theoretical vacuity of Hume's approach. Why should the short run effects not become permanent? James Oswald made exactly this point, foreshadowing the critique by Steuart; he argued that the quantity theory of money 'is so far from being universally true, that in any country which has a free communication with its neighbours, it is, I think, evidently false. . . . The increased quantity of money would not necessarily increase the price of all labour and commodities; because the increased quantity, not being confined to the home labour and commodities, might, and certainly would, be sent to purchase both from foreign countries, which importation, unless obstructed by arbitrary and absurd laws, would keep down the price of commodities to the level of foreign countries' (Oswald to Hume, 10 October 1749, in Hume, 1955, pp. 191–2; see Law, 1705, pp. 74–5). Hume's reply was '[H]ere, then, is the flowing out of the money already begun'; and, in a telling admission, 'I agree with you, that the increase of money, if not too sudden, naturally increases people and industry, and by that means *may retain itself*' (Hume to Oswald, 1 November 1750, ibid., pp. 197–8, emphasis added).[19]

Despite the appearance of an analytical structure, pure exchange quantity theory was shown to be indeterminate; Hume was unable to escape Locke's confusion of money with capital after all. Having conceded that the immediate effect of monetary expansion on the level of economic activity could enter into the determination of his 'long-run' equilibrium, he was only one step away from a justification of protection and coercive measures by the state to promote capital accumulation on a national basis. Indeed, as we shall see in a later chapter, while he condemned hoarding as 'destructive' (1752, p. 192), he nevertheless advocated the creation of a public bank which would have the task of retaining its total deposits – a 100 per cent reserve ratio – and thus of holding down prices and restricting the development of a credit system (ibid., pp. 169–92). Presumably such a policy would be designed to maximise export price competiveness and encourage import substitution. This inclination to keep a mercantilist finger on the pulse of the world market led Hume to join with a target of his criticism, Thomas Mun, in proclaiming merchants 'one of the most useful races of men' (ibid., p. 179), a stage passed by Petty long before.

Transmission mechanism

Hume is sometimes compared with his little known predecessor, Richard Cantillon, whose *Essai sur la nature du commerce en général* was completed in manuscript form by 1734, but only published (in French) two decades later. Jevons, for example, described Cantillon's work as 'the Cradle of Political Economy'; and, on the subject of money and prices, he was particularly impressed with its 'scientific precision' as against the 'vague literary elegance' of Hume's more popular exposition (Jevons, 1881, pp. 342, 353).[20] It is true, as we shall see, that Cantillon's portrayal of the 'transmission mechanism' in pre-classical quantity theory was superior to that of Hume. Yet it must also be recognised that his analysis, despite formal gestures towards the new ground broken by Petty, invariably fell back upon the supply and demand approach employed by Locke; thus, from the viewpoint of this investigation, it did little more than anticipate the *ad hoc* quantity theory for which Hume achieved recognition.

In examining the sources and implications of monetary growth, Cantillon wanted to establish the following hypothesis: 'All this money, whether lent or spent, will enter into circulation and will not fail to raise the price of products and merchandise in all the channels of circulation which it enters. Increased money will bring about increased expenditure and this will cause an increase of Market prices . . .' (1755, p. 161). He began with the discovery of new gold or silver mines: '[E]verybody agrees that the abundance of money or its increase in exchange, raises the price of everything. The quantity of money brought from America to Europe for the last two centuries justifies this truth by experience' (ibid.). This he saw simply as an application of Locke's 'fundamental maxim', to the effect that, 'the quantity of produce and merchandise in proportion to the quantity of money serves as the regulator of Market price' (ibid.).[21] However, for Cantillon, Locke had not looked at the issue in sufficient depth: '[H]e has clearly seen that the abundance of money makes everything dear, but he has not considered how it does so. *The great difficulty of this question consists in knowing in what way and in what proportion the increase of money raises prices* (ibid., emphasis added). Long before Hume, therefore, he elucidated a 'transmission mechanism', though with one significant difference. Whereas the point of departure for Hume's presentation was the windfall profits accruing to exporters who received bullion in payment for goods and services, for Cantillon it was the increased consumption and investment expenditure of the mining sector.[22]

Cantillon went on to show how this mechanism operated in the case of a trade surplus with the rest of the world, as well as an enlarged supply of precious metals, introducing his own international specie-flow doctrine. Again, however, it was dependent entirely upon the working of market forces, whose outcome was indeterminate:

> If an annual and continuous balance has brought about in a State a considerable increase of money it will not fail to increase consumption, to raise the price of everything and even to diminish the number of inhabitants unless additional produce is drawn from abroad proportionable to the increased consumption. Moreover it is usual in States which have acquired a considerable abundance of money to draw many things from neighbouring countries where money is rare and consequently everything is cheap: but as money must be sent for this the balance of trade will become smaller. The cheapness of land and labour in the foreign countries where money is rare will naturally cause the erection of Manufactories and works similar to those of the State, but which will not at first be so perfect nor so highly valued. (Ibid., p. 169)[23]

Once Cantillon had conceded the possibility of variations in both output and velocity, he was unable to offer a theoretically precise statement of the effect of monetary expansion: 'I conceive that when a large surplus of money is brought into a State the new money gives a new turn to consumption and even a new speed to circulation. But it is not possible to say exactly to what extent' (ibid., p. 181). Like Hume, therefore, Cantillon hedged quantity theory with qualifications so fundamental that little was left for critics to dispute. A difference of opinion about anything other than empirical issues within the supply and demand framework proved ultimately to be futile.

A 'NEO-MERCANTILIST' CRITIQUE

The most extensive – if not the most successful – repudiation of the quantity theory of money in the eighteenth century was undertaken by Sir James Steuart, a 'neo-mercantilist'. His *Inquiry into the Principles of Political Oeconomy* (1767), though inevitably overshadowed by Smith's *Wealth of Nations* a decade later, was called by Marx the first 'general system' of economics in Britain (1859, p. 57).[24] Its poor reception clearly had more to do with the 'temper of the times' than with strictly scientific criteria; for while Steuart may well have been 'the last of the mercantilists' (Haney, 1949, p. 138), his analytical contribution went beyond a narrow commitment to state regulation, let alone the special pleading which characterised the writings of many of his predecessors.

A further problem for Steuart was a self-confessed 'prolixity', arising from his method of historical economics. 'Historical economics' is a term I have used to denote the investigation of specific categories in the process of social evolution. In the hand of classical writers, it was, at least potentially, a powerful tool; but, on its own, the historical method could not provide a basis for abstract reasoning and, in Steuart's case, implied a pragmatic standpoint: 'If one considers the variety which is found in different countries, in the distribution of property, subordination of classes (etc.) . . . one may conclude, that the political economy in each must necessarily be different . . .' (1767, I, p. 17).[25]

It was from this standpoint that Steuart confronted the quantity theory of Hume and Montesquieu: 'I am forced to range this ingenious exposition of a most interesting subject among those general and superficial maxims which never fail to lead to error (ibid., II, p. 344). We shall see that Steuart was unable to overturn this 'maxim' for his pragmatism confined him to their pure exchange approach. Yet much of his analysis was superior. Instead of dividing money and commodities into separate heaps whose equalisation determined individual exchange ratios, Steuart made some attempt to deduce the essential features of money, and the laws regulating its movement, from the phases and requirements of commodity exchange (see Skinner, 1967). He contended that a definite amount of money was necessary to circulate as the equivalent of a given level of 'alienations', or commodity transactions:

> These uses of money may be comprehended under two general heads. The first, *payment* of what one owes; the second, *buying* what one has occasion for: the one and the other may be called by the general term of *ready-money demands*. . . . Now the state of trade, of manufactures, of modes of living, and of the customary expence of the inhabitants, when taken altogether, regulate and determine what we may call the mass of ready-money demands, that is, of alienation. To operate this multiplicity of payments, a certain proportion of money is necessary. This proportion again may increase or diminish according to circumstances; although the quantity of alienation should continue the same. . . . From this we may conclude, that the circulation of a country can only absorb a determinate quantity of money. (Ibid., II, pp. 496–8)

This analysis accorded with the classical view that prices are established independently of the amount of money which happened to be in a country, but it was based upon supply and demand. Steuart's concept of money drew upon the 'consent hypothesis' advanced earlier by Locke: 'By money, I understand any commodity . . . which acquires such an estimation from his opinion of it, as to become the universal measure of what is called value, and an adequate equivalent for any thing alienable' (ibid., I, pp. 44). It was not just the nature of the monetary material that was conventionally established, however, but also its *value*. In the case of gold and silver, for example, 'the substance of which the coin is made, is a commodity, which rises and sinks in its value with respect to other commodities, according to the wants, competitions and caprices of mankind' (ibid., II, pp. 419–20). It followed that any change in the weight of the coin implied a commensurate alteration in its value.

Steuart took the part of Lowndes in the debate with Locke on devaluation (see pp. 31–2). Moreover, he regarded the susceptibility of the precious metals to fluctuations in their value as a defect which could only be eliminated by the adoption of an 'invariable' standard. This was proposed as a device which would be immune not merely to changes in the weight of metal (due, say, to wear and tear), but also to changes in the value of a *given* weight. In effect, although the laws of supply and demand were seen as paramount, they could be suspended in their application to money by administrative fiat. This was the predicament in which Steuart found himself with a pure exchange approach to money and prices.[26]

In the absence of such an 'invariable' standard, the value of money, and hence the prices of all commodities, were established by the ebb and flow of the market; though Steuart made a noteworthy attempt to differentiate his interpretation from quantity theory: '[I]t is the complicated operations of demand and competition, which determines the standard price of everything. . . . Let the specie of a country, therefore, be augmented or diminished, in ever so great a proportion, commodities will still rise and fall according to the principles of demand and competition; and these will constantly depend upon the inclinations of those who have *property* or any kind of *equivalent* whatsoever to give; but never upon the quantity of *coin* they are possessed of' (ibid., pp. 344–5). In other words, aggregate demand need not conform with the total money supply, as Locke (in the specific context of a closed economy) and Hume had assumed.

The significant factor was not the sum of money available in a country at any point but 'the money circulating, multiplied by the number of transitions from hand to hand' (ibid., p. 715). Calculation of this magnitude was 'impossible', because velocity could not be treated as stable:

'[T]he solution of the question does not depend on the quantity of coin alone, but also upon the disposition of those who are the possessors of it; and as these dispositions are constantly changing, the question thereby becomes insoluble' (ibid., I, p. 325). Thus any exogenous changes in the quantity of money would not necessarily affect prices at all, but could be absorbed by fluctuations in velocity:

> If the coin of a country, therefore, falls below the *proportion* of the produce of industry *offered to sale*, industry itself will come to a stop; or inventions, such as symbolical money [Steuart means credit: RG], will be fallen upon to provide an equivalent for it. But if the specie be found above the proportion of the industry, it will have no effect in raising prices, nor will it enter into circulation: it will be hoarded up in treasures . . . [W]hatever be the quantity of money in any nation, in correspondence with the rest of the world, there never can remain *in circulation*, but a quantity nearly proportional to the consumption of the rich, and to the labour and industry of the poor inhabitants . . . [C]onsequently, the proportion is not determined by the *quantity* of money actually in the country. (Ibid., II, p. 350.)

Indeterminacy

While Steuart appeared to reach a different conclusion, it can be seen that his train of thought was not dissimilar from that of Hume, his arch-opponent. Both expained prices by the relationship between money and commodities in the circulation process; indeed, Steuart explicitly conceded that Hume's formulation 'is *almost* my proposition in other words: for the money to be employed in the purchase of any commodity, is just the measure of the demand' (ibid., II, p. 349). The price revolution of the sixteenth and seventeenth centuries was therefore caused not by monetary expansion, but by an upsurge in *demand*: 'People complain that prices are risen; of this there is no doubt with regard to many articles . . . It is not because there is now a larger mass of money in the kingdom, . . . but the direct principle which has influenced them, and which will always regulate their rise and fall, is the increase of demand (ibid., I, p. 66). Likewise, 'the treasures of the frugal Greeks . . . had not the smallest influence upon prices', for, except in times of war, demand was restricted by 'the ancient simplicity of their manners' (ibid., II, p. 374), i.e., the primitive character of their market economy. By contrast, a price inflation followed the subjugation of Greece by the Romans, who introduced these treasures into circulation; but this inflation was confined to luxury goods, and 'proceeded from the impossibility of augmenting the supply in proportion to the demand; not from the abundance of the money, which had no effect in raising the price of necessaries' (ibid., II, p. 376; see Marx, 1859, pp. 161–2).

The apparent conflict between Hume and Steuart thus turned upon empirical rather than theoretical issues. Whereas Hume was attracted to sweeping generalisation, Steuart derived four possible causes of high prices in any one country relative to another from a detailed investigation of the facts in each individual case. The causes he found were: (i) a high profit rate associated with a shift to luxury consumption; (ii) a shortage of means of subsistence due to the disproportionate growth of the manufacturing and agricultural sectors; (iii) the 'natural advantages' of competing nations, such as climate; and (iv) their 'superior dexterity' in industry, trade and finance (ibid., I, pp. 246–60). That the substance of the dispute was merely empirical was shown not just in their treatment of velocity but also of output, which will be discussed shortly.

Steuart's behavioural assumptions gave rise to a causal sequence which was the reverse of Hume's – until their respective assumptions were relaxed in as arbitrary a manner as they were selected in the first place. He maintained that, 'the riches of a country have no determinate influence upon prices; although I allow, they may accidentally affect them'; but he added in a later edition: 'what I mean is, that they may influence them; but they cannot regulate them' (ibid., II, p. 348). Whereas in classical economics, the distinction between 'influence' and 'regulate' was given a fundamental methodological status, supply and demand analysis made it simply one of time and circumstances. Hence it is not surprising to find that the practical proposals of Hume and Steuart also converged to some degree. Unlike Adam Smith, who was to conclude from the self-regulation of the money supply that external regulation by the government was unnecessary, Steuart believed that the authorities 'ought at all times to maintain a just proportion between the produce of industry, and the quantity of circulating equivalent, in the hands of his subjects, for the purchase of it' (ibid., I, p. 323). It will be recalled that Hume favoured the setting up of a public bank for precisely the same purpose.

Having indicated the role of velocity in modifying the abstract model of quantity theory, Steuart also revived the mercantilist notion that monetary movements could have an impact of the level of output. He began with the example of an open economy where any increase in prices which was supposed to result from growth in the money supply could be offset by import penetration. He asked whether it was not plain, 'that if this country have a communication with other nations, there must, in carrying on trade, be a proportion between the prices of many kinds of merchandize, and that the sudden augmentation or diminution of the specie at home, supposing it could *of itself* operate the effects of raising or sinking prices, would be restrained in its operation by foreign competition' (ibid., II, p. 345). We have seen that this was the argument used by James Oswald against Hume, whose reply conceded a fatal weakness in the international specie-flow mechanism.

Steuart took Hume's concession to its logical conclusion and allowed exogenous monetary expansion *permanently* to affect output – after a transitional price response – in a closed economy: 'Increase the money, nothing can be concluded as to prices, because it is not certain that people will increase their expenses in proportion to their wealth; and although they should, the moment their additional demand has the effect of producing a sufficient supply, prices will return to the old standard' (ibid., II, p. 355). The example Steuart gave was based upon the 'price revolution' and envisaged a ten-fold increase in the amount of specie in Europe. Since 'no man can tell to what extent demand may carry industry', the relative implications for prices and output would depend simply upon the 'circumstances'. Hence it was not difficult for Steuart to claim that, 'This solution is entirely consistent both with Mr Hume's principle and mine; because nothing is so easy in an hypothesis, as to establish proportions between things, which in themselves are beyond all the powers of computation' (ibid., II, p. 356).

Conversely a sudden restriction of the available money might throw industry into a slump from which it could not automatically recover. Steuart disputed the notion that, 'there is no such thing as a balance of trade, that money over all the world is like a fluid, which must ever be upon a level, and that so soon as in any nation this level is destroyed by any accident, while the nation preserves the number of its inhabitants, and its industry, the wealth must return to a level as before' (ibid., II, pp. 357–8). A country which lost four-fifths of its stock of money, as depicted in Hume's hypothetical example, would no longer have the productive capacity to restore output to what it was previously: 'If . . . the event alone of annihilating the specie, and reducing prices in proportion (which I shall allow to be consequence of it) will have the effect of annihilating both industry and the industrious, it cannot afterwards be insisted on, that the revolution can have the effect of drawing back a proportional part of the general wealth of Europe: because the preservation of the industrious is considered as the requisite for this purpose' (ibid., II, pp. 258–9).

We have seen that Hume was reluctant to admit any output response to monetary growth or contraction, but was forced to do so in the face of

Oswald's criticism. Only Steuart, however, was prepared to advocate trade protection as a means of retaining wealth. It was, he maintained, 'the interest of a rich nation, to cut off the communications of hurtful trade, by such impediments as restrictions, duties, and prohibitions, upon importation; in order that, as by dykes, its wealth may be kept *above* the level of the surrounding element' (ibid., II, p. 364). This practical conclusion stemmed as much from the Cameralist influence of continental Europe,[27] as from the rapidly subsiding mercantilist tradition. It was shortly to be overtaken by the classical 'free trade' ideas of Adam Smith – ideas which were more soundly based than those of either Hume or Steuart and which were capable of explaining the real cause of the sixteenth and seventeenth century price inflation.[28] This will be the subject of the next chapter.

Young's reconciliation

Just before the publication of Smith's major work, Arthur Young in his *Political Arithmetic* (1774) made a last attempt to reconcile the views of Hume and Steuart – in favour of a quantity theory interpretation of the 'price revolution'. He wanted to show that, 'Demand and competition appear to be *effects*; money the *cause*. . . . If this is not true, how are we to account for the prices of a thousand things before the discovery of America, compared with the present prices of the same commodities . . . ?' (Young, 1774, pp. 115, 117). Young's account simply confirmed that *anything* could be proved or disproved in the context of supply and demand analysis. His primary objective was to defend Hume and Montesquieu against the suggestion that they understood price fluctuations as nothing more than a uniform and proportional reflection of changes in the money supply:

> Nobody could suppose they were so short-sighted as to form such ideas: . . . [I]f any commodity in general and regular demand, is brought to market at a particular season in much greater plenty than at any other season, who can doubt but the price will be low? All such variations are perfectly consistent with the idea that the price of commodities will depend on the quantity of specie; because this idea is not relative to certain days, weeks, months, or markets, but to general periods in which money has increased or decreased. (Ibid., p. 113)

In other words, while exogenous monetary growth may not initially be matched by demand, it was inevitable in the long-run since the propensity to hoard was fixed:

> In such a comparison, and neither the French writer [Montesquieu] nor Mr Hume could have any other in view, the idea of demand and competition is absolutely lost in that of specie, because they are in fact the same thing. Sir James will keep close to the circumstance, that the quantity of money has nothing to do in the case, if a man will not spend what he possesses: but this appears to me to be taken for granted: relative to a market day, or other point of competition, I admit of it; but I think it should be rejected in application to a *period*. (Ibid., p. 114; also, p. 117)

Nevertheless, Young acknowledged a possible *output* response to monetary movements, but only as 'a partial exception' which he accused Steuart of having 'wrought into a complete hypothesis: I admit that to an unknown degree, an increase of wealth increasing the demand for certain manufactures, will increase the quantity brought to market, and prices stand as they were . . .' (ibid., p. 118). Young was convinced that such an exception was 'not of importance enough to overturn Hume's idea' (ibid., p. 119). This was eloquent testimony to the inconclusive nature of pre-classical debate and to the degree to which it rested upon assertion and counter-assertion.

In conclusion, it should be clear that the failure of Hume and Steuart to discover the basic cause of the 'price revolution' had less to do with any lack of reliable statistics than with the conceptual limitation of their approach. The correlation between the inflow of precious metals and shifts in the general price level led to a deduction of causality on the part of quantity theory, which was vainly denied by its critics. In fact, these shifts were due not to monetary expansion but to the *lowered production costs* of gold and silver at the American mines. It was this change in the conditions of production – along with demographic factors in Europe – which underlay the altered exchange relationship between money and commodities and hence the sustained and widespread price inflation.[29]

Numerous historians have since collected the evidence. Vilar, for example, concluded that, 'In the long run the basic element in any variation in the ratio of gold and commodities as a whole, can only be a change in the ratio of their comparative costs of production. We have seen countless demonstrations of how the production costs of precious metals affect long-term price movements. This was seen with gold and silver in the 16th century . . .' (1976, p. 343). This trend should have been apparent to Hume from the closure of the European mines during this period. Even the most casual observation would have suggested that they had become uncompetitive due to the falling cost of production abroad (see, for example, Nef, 1941). Hume's inability in this case to 'reconcile reason to experience' in accordance with his philosophical empiricism had its roots in the absence of a theory of value on the one hand and a theory of output on the other. He could not understand, therefore, that both the increased amount of money in circulation *and* the rise in commodity prices expressed a revolution in the measure of value of the precious metals as a result of dramatically enhanced productivity in the mining sector. As Vilar again put it, 'the movement of prices expressed in metal depends on the value of the metal, that is on the variations in the productivity of the mines, provided this is seen in the long-term perspective and at the level of the world market. Unfortunately, there are many theoreticians who forget this simple truth' (ibid.).[30]

The classical economists, by contrast, were more successful in interpreting these events. As we shall see, they analysed money not as a valueless token or as the sole repository of wealth, but rather as a *produced commodity*. Smith was the first to recognise that, 'the discovery of abundant mines of America reduced, in the 16th century, the value of gold and silver in Europe to about a third of what it had been before. . . . [I]t *cost less labour* to bring those metals from the mine to the market' (1776, p. 24, emphasis added). This approach was developed by Ricardo and Marx, who despite their important differences, proceeded from a common starting point – the 'surplus' approach to value and distribution. They also understood that for an analysis of the relationship between money and the price level to be instructive, it would have to assume that the value of money was given (Marx, 1859, p. 160).

Although the classical economists were no more successful than their predecessors in formulating a theory of *output* comparable with their theory of value, they were able to construct a framework within which such a theory was both feasible and necessary. In the context of the 'price revolution', whose main characteristic was a *change in the value of the money commodity*, the lack of a theory of output was not a serious impediment to analysis. Here the problem was presented in a relatively straightforward fashion. Since the spectacular monetary fluctuations of the period were merely a reflection of more fundamental forces at work, it became the central task of classical political economy to theorise these forces and thus to move beyond the pure exchange approach of mercantilism and quantity theory.

4 Classical Theory of the Metallic System

> Before my readers can understand the proof I mean to offer, they must understand the theory of currency and of price.
>
> Ricardo to Mill, December 30, 1815

It will be apparent from the discussion so far that mercantilism and the quantity theory of money shared a common approach which ultimately counted for more than the factors dividing them. This is the approach I have characterised as 'pure exchange' analysis. The difference between the two founding interpretations of price behaviour lay in their respective attitudes to the stability of output in the equation of exchange – attitudes which stemmed from their distinct conceptions of money. Whereas mercantilist writers identified money with capital, and consequently made the level of output a function of the stock of money available to a country, proponents of quantity theory treated output as fixed, or independently variable, magnitude, since money for them was limited to the role of a medium of circulation.

Yet in both cases the pattern of prices was viewed simply as the outcome of the operation of demand and supply. The fact that classical economists *also* adopted a fixed output assumption in their rebuttal of mercantilism has led to their being seen as standard-bearers of this quantity theory tradition – albeit in a more sophisticated form – and, indeed, forerunners of modern monetarism. It is the argument of this chapter, however, that the classical analysis of the relationship between money and prices is fundamentally different from the quantity theory I have considered up to now. In this analysis, prices as well as output are determined independently of changes in the money supply, with modifications to this principle only in the short-run. Since the classical writers uncover for the first time the relationships of production underlying the equation of exchange, they are able to establish theoretically the long-run magnitudes on the 'supply side' (*PY*), to which the 'demand side' (*MV*) must conform.

The classical theory of money and prices evolved in conjunction with, and as a solution to, the problem of distribution in a capitalist economy. This analysis has generally become known as the 'surplus' approach, and, as I have already indicated, it was based upon a method which attempted to isolate the permanent forces in the economy from temporary or random deviations. Since its structure and development have been set out elsewhere at some length (Garegnani, 1984), an account of its key elements will suffice for our purposes – allowing us to focus attention upon the monetary aspects.

I shall begin with the analysis of distribution in physical terms and derive the corresponding function of money as *medium of circulation*. This gives rise to what will be called the 'classical law of monetary circulation'. I shall then trace the development of a price theory consistent with, yet separable from, the problem, of distribution. This is associated with a further role of money as *measure of value* and it permits a further specification of the circulation law. Finally, I shall be in a position to outline the classical analysis of inflation both in the long-run and in the short-run, where the price effect of monetary fluctuations is a matter for debate *within* the pre-established theoretical framework of the 'surplus' approach. These fluctuations assume particular importance in the theory of crises, where the role of money as a *means of payment* reflects the separation of purchase and sale in commodity circulation – and promotes the development of a credit system.

It is the 'short-run' inflationary process which provides a first glimpse of the 'bullion controversy', a crucial stage in the evolution of Britain's financial structure. Although the main discussion concerned a paper currency, its participants acknowledged the significance of commodity money as a basis for theory and policy. The attempts to formulate a 'principle of limitation' for the currency were generally derived from the operation of a metallic system as they perceived it. For both sides of the bullion controversy, 'economic convertibility', or the equivalence of paper and gold, was the chief desideratum of policy, at least in the absence of legal convertibility; and it testified to the overriding importance of classical value and distribution theory as an anchor for nineteenth-century monetary analysis.

MONEY AND THE 'REAL' ECONOMY

Classical political economy took as its starting-point the analysis of distribution, since this was seen as 'the most precise expression in which factors of production manifest themselves in a given society' (Marx, 1859, p. 201). It was the existence of a 'social surplus' over and above what was needed for the reproduction of the workforce and the current stock of materials and equipment that led the classical school to go beyond the tautological supply and demand approach and to confront the problem of 'value' in a theoretical manner. The first to recognise that price formation was subject to definite laws was William Petty – the 'founder of political economy' – who in the late seventeenth century sought what he called 'a real and not imaginary way of computing the prices of commodities' (1963, I, p. 89).[1]

Yet the classical theory of prices emerged only as a result of advance – and occasional retrogression – in the study of distribution, whose 'separability' remained a defining characteristic. As Ricardo himself pointed out, 'the great questions of Rent, Wages, and Profits must be explained by the proportions in which the whole produce is divided between landlords, capitalists, and labourers, and which are *not essentially connected with the doctrine of value*' (Letter to McCulloch, 13 June 1820, in Ricardo, 1951/58, VIII, p. 194, emphasis added). In a similar vein, following the publication of *Capital*, Marx insisted that, 'even if there were no chapter on "value" in my book, the analysis of the real relations which I give would contain the proof and demonstration of the real value relations . . .' (Letter to Kugelmann, 11 July 1868, in Marx and Engels, 1975, p. 106). Hence we begin with the problem of distribution in the 'real' economy and the associated function of money as a medium of circulation and standard of price, or numeraire.[2]

Like the quantity theory of money, the 'surplus' approach developed originally as a response to mercantilism, though we shall see that there the resemblance came to an end. The mercantilists had conceived of wealth as money arising from exchange; individuals could increase their wealth only by the sale of commodities above their value. Surplus value thus appeared simply in the form of 'profit upon alienation'. For the nation as a whole, there could be no net increase in wealth, only a 'vibration of the balance of wealth between the parties' (Steuart, 1767, I, p. 179) as individual gains and losses in domestic circulation ultimately cancelled out.[3] Consequently, the social surplus was attributed to international trade, that is to say money corresponding to a favourable trade balance.[4] With the emergence of wage labour in England and France, however, classical economists began to shift the focus of inquiry from circulation to the process of production. They showed that surplus value was generated even when commodities exchanged at their values by abstracting from value altogether and analysis production in purely physical terms, i.e., in terms of use values.

Given the predominance of agriculture at the time Petty and his immediate successors were writing, it was natural for them to recognise surplus value in its primary form as rent. Their objective was, in Petty's words, 'to explain the mysterious nature of [rents], with reference as well to money' (1899, I, p. 42). They assumed for this purpose a given social product consisting almost wholly of corn and a given set of technical conditions of production. A proportion of the social product was necessarily allocated as means of subsistence for the workers, and was thus a multiple of the real wage which was itself determined separately from output. This conception of the real wage 'as something fixed, given as magnitude', Marx called 'the foundation of modern political economy' (1963/71, I, p. 45).[5] What remained of the total corn output constituted the surplus – appearing to Petty and the Physiocrats in the form of rent – thus permitting the relationship between distributive shares to be seen not as an outcome of exchange but as a relationship of production. It was only when Adam Smith showed that this surplus arose not just from agricultural production but from production in general that profits were also identified as a key component.

The theory of distribution was addressed primarily to the determination of the *absolute size* of a surplus consisting at first only of rent and then of profits as well; later, as we shall see, it would also take account of the complications introduced by the rate of profit. The data of the theory, or its independently variable magnitudes, are clear:

(i) the annual output;
(ii) the real wage, or output necessary to maintain the average labourer; and,
(iii) the social productivity of labour.

The surplus may thus be calculated by subtracting from that total output the share which goes to the labour force, or, as Ricardo called it, the share for 'necessary consumption' (1951/58, VI, p. 108). Since both output and the wage are determined prior to the division of output into its respective income shares, it becomes our next task to examine how that determination takes place, at least insofar as it is connected with the interpretation of money and prices.

Output and circulation

The first variable to be considered is the level of output itself (Y), whose independent determination is fundamental to the classical analysis of inflation. This will give us one of the two magnitude on the 'supply side' of the equation of exchange, leaving only the price index (P) to be established as the next step in the analysis. With technical progress (and hence social productivity) assumed to be given, output in the 'surplus' approach was held simply to correspond to the stage reached by the accumulation of capital. It is important to bear in mind that no attempt was made at this time to develop a *theory* of output comparable with the classical theory of value, that is to say an account of the mechanism which would bring saving and investment into equality. The reason was straightforward. The adoption of Say's law by the classical economists meant that saving and investment were treated as *identical* and that consequently no mechanism was required to equate them. Any deviation which might be postulated could only be temporary. In other words, the whole question of a theory of output was left 'open' until the development in the next century of a 'principle of effective demand' (Garegnani, 1978/79).

The assumption of full utilisation of capacity in the long-run (though not necessarily full employment of labour) was thus a distinguishing feature of the classical framework. It was displayed with particular clarity in the corn sector of the economy, or 'corn model' as I shall call it, where the production of corn was assumed to create an equivalent demand. Moreover, since the problem of measuring value did not arise in a sector where output and the wage consisted primarily of the same commodity, it was easy to see that '[p]roductions are always bought by productions', and that if money were introduced as a universal commodity to express their common substance, it could serve only as 'the medium by which the exchange is effected' (Ricardo, 1951/58, I, pp. 291–2). This conception was an essential aspect of the 'circular flow' model of Quesnay's *Tableau Economique* of 1758, which was directed not merely against traditional mercantilism but also against its disastrous application by John Law to a system of paper currency (see below, esp. Chapter 5). Whereas the mercantilists regarded money as sole embodiment of value, Quesnay and the Physiocrats abstracted from value and showed that social reproduction could proceed without a special monetary material. Once money played a part in this abstract economy, it was limited to a medium of circulation and unit of account, or standard of price.

Like gold and silver, corn was a more or less homogeneous commodity possessing the qualities of uniformity and divisibility; hence, equal quantities could be represented by fixed weights of metal. When these weights acquired a legal denomination such as 'pound' or 'franc', which turned the metal into money of account, physical flows could be estimated immediately in price terms. In the corn model, therefore, the Physiocratic assumption of constant prices meant simply that they were a function of any given quantity of output multiplied by the socially accepted denomination of the monetary standard. The significant point at this stage of our discussion is that the money supply was thus directly dependent upon the amount of corn to be circulated; or, to put it another way, the monetary flows in this economy were the exact counterpart of the physical flows. This was the aspect of Quesnay's *Tableau Economique* to which Marx drew attention as follows: 'The first point to note in this Tableau, and the point which must have impressed his contemporaries, is the way in which the money circulation is shown as determined purely by the circulation and reproduction of commodities, in fact by the circulation process of capital' (1963/71, I, p. 308).

This separation of 'real' and monetary phenomena, whereby the commodity set aside to perform the role of means of circulation is seen as a mere 'veil' superimposed upon the real forces of capitalist production, has become known as the 'classical dichotomy'. Although it was most clearly visualised in the abstract example of the corn economy, it was also applied to the more general case where both capital and product were made up of heterogeneous commodities and hence money was required to take on the additional function of a measure of value. I shall consider this general case in due course. For the moment, it is sufficient to recognise in the analysis of the corn ratio model the origin and essential foundation of what I shall denote the classical 'law of monetary circulation'. This is a law which, even when properly described, is sometimes presented as or confused with the quantity theory of money.[6] In fact, the direction of causation it suggests is precisely the reverse. According to this law, the quantity of money in circulation is *dependent upon* the level of output and prices – not the other way around – though an independent determination of the price level can be postponed so long as the assumption of a corn ratio is retained.

There is, however, an additional factor in the equation of exchange which must be noted before we go beyond a preliminary statement of this fundamental law. The amount of money required as the counterpart of a given output will also depend upon its *velocity* of circulation. The influence of this factor may be measured by the number and size of commodity transactions served by a pre-determined unit of currency in a set time, by the frequency with which such transactions take place or by the propensity of economic agents to hoard, that is to say in more recent terminology, to hold 'cash balances'.

Petty's formulation of the law of monetary circulation, which (as always) prefigured the classical standpoint, had general validity in both the corn model and in a world of heterogeneous commodities. He contended that, 'the proportion of money requisite to our Trade, is to be . . . taken from the frequency of commutations, and from the bigness of the payments' (1899, I, p. 36). Ingenious attempts were made to calculate this proportion though it turned out to be a more problematic concept than initially supposed. Indeed, we have already seen that Locke abandoned his attempt in favour of a more congenial quantity theory of money. Petty himself was content in his *Treatise of Taxes and Contributions* (1662) with an unsupported assertion that £6 million sufficed for English circulation. There he concluded that, 'of all the wealth of this Nation, viz. Lands, Housing, Shipping, Commodities, Furniture, Plate and Money, . . . scarce one part in a hundred is Coin' (ibid., p. 34).[7]

Cantillon came to a similar result and, like Petty, anticipated in his investigation the Physiocratic scheme of Quesnay. The two basic categories of income were presented as the 'three rents' of the farmer: the first was the 'true rent' paid to the landlord, the second was for the subsistence of the farmer and his workforce, and the third was the farmer's profit which was also spent on consumption (Cantillon, 1755, p. 121). These rents were 'the principal sources or so to speak the mainspring of circulation in the State' (ibid., p. 123). The amount of money needed for circulation was therefore 'not incomprehensible', although since 'this amount may be greater or less in a State according to the mode of living and the rapidity of payments . . . it is very difficult to lay down anything definite as regards this quantity in general' (ibid., pp. 129–31). Cantillon readily admitted that his computation of monetary requirements was 'only conjectural', and, indeed, after examining the variety of institutional arrangements which govern velocity, he concluded that, 'it seems impossible to lay down anything precise or exact as to the proportion of money sufficient for the circulation' (ibid., p. 147). We have seen that this was the view of Steuart; and it was also to be accepted by classical economists, who maintained with Cantillon that in practice such a proportion was 'impossible to determine' (Smith, 1776, p. 224).

Ricardo made no attempt to calculate velocity, and Marx observed that it was contingent upon 'the general nature of the mode of production, the size of the population, the relation of town and countryside, the development of the means of transport, the more or less advanced division of labour, credit, etc., in short on circumstances which lie *outside* the framework of simple money circulation and are merely mirrored in it' (1859, p. 105). Whether or not the effect of these circumstances on velocity was susceptible to accurate measurement, a further question of greater practical relevance confronted classical analysis. This question concerned the validity of assuming a *stable* velocity in the analysis of the relationship between money and prices. It was also a question which was to prove more controversial, as we shall see when we deal with it in the final section of this chapter.

Wages share

So far we have shown that the total output in the surplus approach is an independent variable which simply reflects the level of past accumulation. The corn sector hypothesis allowed the classical school to establish a law of monetary circulation without any need for a separate determination of prices. This was treated as a purely formal expression of fixed proportions of a homogeneous commodity, corn, in terms of a selected 'numeraire' or money of account. We can now turn our attention from output to the distributive shares of which it is composed. This was a necessary logical and historical step in approaching the problem of price, which is the subject of the next section.

It has already been indicated that the real wage was a datum for classical economics, alongside output and productivity. The share of output set aside for 'necessary consumption' could therefore be calculated by multiplying the wage rate by the working population. This share was at first thought to consist of no more than what was required for the subsistence of agricultural labourers. In a pioneering account, Petty made an attempt to define the minimum physiological needs of an average labourer working at maximum capacity (1899, I, p. 87 ff.).[8] The proposition that the wage was determined independently from output – and hence prior to the remaining shares – was to become the essence of the surplus approach, though Petty's successors eventually went beyond his definition of minimum subsistence.

The subsistence definition was followed by Smith and the Physiocrats, however, whose formulation was summarised by Turgot: 'The mere Workman, who has only his arms and his industry, has nothing except in so far as he succeeds in selling his toil to others . . . In every kind of work it cannot fail to happen, and as a matter of fact it does happen, that the wages of the workman are limited to what is necessary to procure him his subsistence' (1770, p. 8).[9] Smith went further than the Physiocrats, however, in showing that under conditions of prosperity, the balance of advantage in wage disputes might shift to the side of labour as employers 'voluntarily break through the natural combination of masters not to raise wages' (1776, p. 53; also p. 27). Ricardo agreed that prosperity allowed the market rate of wages to rise above their natural rate: 'Notwithstanding the tendency of wages to conform to their natural rate, their market rate may, in an improving society, for an indefinite period, be constantly above it' (1951/58, I, pp. 94–5). But, for him, it was the Malthusian population mechanism which ultimately set in train forces to correct the deviation – a regression, as Marx noted, to supply and demand analysis (1963/71, II, p. 400). Ricardo's main advance over his predecessors in the context of the surplus approach was to include in the natural rate of wages not only the bare minimum of subsistence, but also 'those comforts which custom renders absolute necessaries' (1951/58, I, p. 94).[10]

Marx viewed as one of Ricardo's 'great merits' that 'he examined relative or proportionate wages, and established them as a definite category', that is, as a relative share of the total product. For, 'up to this time, wages had always been regarded as something simple and consequently the worker was considered an animal. But here he is considered in his social relationships. The position of the classes to one another depends more on relative wages than on the absolute amount of wages' (Marx, 1963/71, II, p. 419). He went on to show in *Capital* how an 'historical and moral element' entered into the determination of the wage rate (1867/94, I, p. 168), and, furthermore, how a law of population specific to capitalism – namely, the 'industrial reserve army' of the unemployed – governed the movements of the actual wage in the accumulation process.[11]

Social surplus

With the independent determination both of total output and of the share for necessary consumption, the social surplus could be seen clearly as a residuum, and hence as the dependent variable in the classical approach. Initially, the surplus was identified with rent, that is to say with the share of output claimed by the landowners. The problem of measuring the ratio of surplus to necessary consumption was relatively simple in a corn model. Again, Petty was the first to consider the problem, even if only from the standpoint of the individual producer (1899, I, p. 143).[12] His analysis was broadened by the Physiocrats into the scheme of social reproduction portrayed in Quesnay's *Tableau Economique* (see Vaggi, 1983), which was ultimately to serve as the inspiration for the second volume of Marx's *Capital.* The collapse of John Law's financial experiment in France not only hastened the break-up of the feudal estates and the emergence of wage-labour, but it also confirmed to the Physiocrats that land was the real foundation of wealth.[13] Their account of capitalist production was accordingly based upon agriculture. Its essential elements were presented by Turgot in his remarkable *Réflexions sur la formation et la distribution des richesses* (1770), whose 'theoretical skeleton' Schumpeter described as 'distinctly superior to [that of] the *Wealth of Nations*' (1954, p. 248).

Turgot maintained that agricultural labour alone produced a surplus over and above the material requirements of the workforce: '[W]e have here neither a primacy of honour or dignity; it is one of necessity' (1770, p. 7). Total output was resolved clearly into the wages of a 'classe productrice' and a 'produit net' accruing to a 'classe disponible' of landed capitalists.[14] The products of other sectors were regarded merely as a transformation of agricultural products. The 'produit net' thus constituted 'the only fund for the wages which all the other members of the society receive in exchange for their labour. The latter, in making use of the price of this exchange to buy in their turn the products of the Husbandman, only return to him exactly what they have received from him. We have here a very essential difference between these two kinds of labours . . .' (ibid., pp. 7–8).[15] Moreover, for Turgot, as for the Physiocrats before him, the recompense of labour was not the only limit upon the size of the 'produit net'. They also took account of 'avances' for tools and raw materials (ibid., pp. 51–2), but this was not distinguished as capital from the categories of revenue. In principle, therefore, the 'produit net' could be measured without striking any major conceptual difficulties associated with the problem of value.

To the extent that Sir James Steuart was to take over the Physiocratic scheme, we have seen that he subordinated it to his demand and supply analysis. By contrast, Adam Smith in the *Wealth of Nations* recognised the purpose of the scheme and gave economic names to its material categories. 'Avances', for example, were presented as fixed and circulating capital; and the 'produit net' claimed by the landowner became rent. Smith's original contribution came in his study of the division of labour. This allowed him to broaden the notion of surplus to encompass *profits*. It was, he argued, not just the particular type of labour in agriculture that could be designated as 'productive', but labour in general, or *social labour*.

Smith began with a hypothetical society prior to the development of landed property and capital accumulation. In such a society, output would belong to the producer: 'In that original state of things, which precedes both the appropriation of land and the accumulation of stock, the whole produce of labour belongs to the labourer. He has neither landlord nor master to share with him' (Smith, 1776, p. 49). Once land and capital became the property of distinct social classes, their incomes represented a deduction from total output (ibid., p. 50); this was the essence of Smith's well-known 'deduction' theory of profit. Since the real wage was determined separately in his analysis from output and the shares into which it was resolved, both profits and rent could now be identified as constituent parts of the surplus, or 'neat produce'. It was only because Smith was concerned here with the absolute size of profits rather than with the rate of profit on capital that the problem of value could again be postponed. Indeed, insofar as he did confront it, he lapsed into circular reasoning, which, as we shall see, prevented any attempt at a general solution until Ricardo's *Principles*.

By the time Ricardo made his contribution to the analysis of value and distribution, profits were clearly demarcated as a component of the social surplus; but the rate of profits was thought to be established by the forces of demand and supply. As Malthus put it in a letter to Ricardo in 1814, 'all will in my opinion depend upon the state of capital compared with the demand for it' (Ricardo, 1951/58, VI, p. 111). Ricardo, by contrast, reintroduced consistency into the surplus approach by deriving the general rate of profit from the conditions of production: 'The rate of profits and of interest must depend on the proportion of production to the consumption necessary to such production' (ibid., VI, p. 108). Once rent was eliminated from the calculation and capital advanced in a yearly production cycle was treated as consisting entirely of wages, the rate of profit was given by the ratio between the surplus and annual wages, or 'necessary consumption':

$$\text{Rate of profit} = \frac{\text{output} - \text{necessary consumption}}{\text{necessary consumption}}$$

Ricardo formulated this result as a 'material ratio' in his *Essay on Profits* (1815), where, for purposes of exposition, he adopted the Physiocratic assumption of a 'self-reproducing' corn sector. This assumption allowed him to demonstrate the validity of his contention that, 'it is the profits of the farmer that regulate the profits of all other trades' (ibid., VI, p. 104); and, by providing a standard independent of the rate of profit in which the aggregates in the above equation could be expressed, it also allowed him temporarily to set aside the problem of value, and hence also of money as a measure of value.[16]

Once the surplus was seen to arise from sectors other than agriculture, however, its commodity composition and that of the wage could no longer be treated as uniform. In other words, corn ceased to be an adequate unit or standard in which to measure these quantities. While this was still not completely evident in Smith's analysis, where only the surplus had to be measured, it became so in Ricardo's *Essay* as soon as commodities other than corn were admitted as part of capital. Under these conditions, the rate of profit could not accurately be determined by a ratio between physical aggregates; a *theory of value* was required to reduce heterogeneous commodities to a common standard. This was acknowledged by Ricardo in a letter to Malthus as a discrepancy between money and corn calculations: 'You before contended that in consequence of increasing wealth and the cultivation of poorer land, the whole *corn* cost of production on the land would bear a *less* proportion to the whole *corn* produce – but now you say that the *money* value of the whole produce. Between these two propositions there is a very material difference . . .' (Letter to Malthus, March 27, 1815, in 1951/58, VI, p. 204).

In a letter to Mill soon after, Ricardo finally conceded that in the further development of his theory of profits, 'I know I shall soon be stopped by the word price' (ibid., p. 348 also VII, p. 20). Sraffa has called this the 'turning point' in the transition from the *Essay* to the *Principles* (ibid., I, p. xxxiv). It is also the point at which money could no longer be regarded simply as a means of circulation but had also to be analysed as itself a produced commodity and hence as the universal measure of value. We may conclude that, while the corn model was an essential precondition for the development of the role of money as a means of circulation, it excluded the function of measure of value by postponing the need for a theory of prices. It is this problem, and its relationship to monetary circulation, that I now wish to consider.

MONEY AND PRICE FORMATION

I have so far identified a classical 'law of monetary circulation', which viewed the money supply as dependent upon the level of output – subject also to the state of velocity. This law was established as an integral part of the 'surplus' approach to distribution in a corn ratio model, where prices were not yet independently determined but were given by the denomination of the monetary standard. Since the analysis was conducted in purely physical terms, money was required only as a means of circulation and standard of price. Would the circulation law still apply once the corn assumption was relaxed, and, if so, what form would it take? The answer to this question, as I shall now seek to demonstrate, turned upon the development of a theory of value to complement the theory of distribution just outlined. It became necessary for money (as a produced commodity) to perform the additional role of a measure of value, thus permitting the independent calculation of the price index (P) in the equation of exchange.

The problem of value arose in classical economics in connection with the measurement of the social surplus when output and the capital advanced for production no longer consisted of the same commodity but of different commodities, or commodities in different proportions. If the analysis was not to dissolve into apparently circular reasoning, a theory was required to determine the exchange ratios between these commodities *separately from distribution*. Only then would it become possible to calculate the general rate of profit, and hence the pattern of prices, throughout the economy. The starting point for such a theory may be found in Petty's earlier mentioned *Treatise*, where a solution to the problem of value, or at least a first approximation, was proferred in a typically forthright manner.

Petty not only located the source of material wealth in *individual* labour – a widely shared insight even at that time – but he also derived its undifferentiated *social* character from the division of labour; and thus, although he identified the value of commodities with the money for which they were exchangeable, he nevertheless succeeded in reducing their value to a common element, namely the amount of *labour* necessary for their production. This was an important breakthrough for political economy. It meant the factors underlying the formation of value could be traced, just as we have seen in the case of distribution, beyond the superficial operation of demand and supply – the hallmark of the pure exchange approach – to the conditions of production.

Having designated the surplus in the corn sector as rent, Petty was able to proceed immediately to the question of its magnitude in value as well as in physical terms: 'But a further, though collaterall question may be, how much English money this Corn or Rent is worth? I answer, so much as the money, which another single man can save, within the same time, over and above his expence, if he imployed himself wholly to produce and make it' (1899, I, p. 43). Since Petty's comparison of the values of corn and silver was based upon an estimation of labour-time, the *qualitative* aspects of the labour in each line of production were irrelevant. All that mattered was a comparison of *quantities*: 'This, I say, to be the foundation of equallizing and ballancing of values; yet in the superstructures and practices hereupon, I confess there is much variety, and intricacy . . . (ibid., p. 43).[17]

Prefiguring classical terminology, Petty called the value of commodities expressed in money their 'natural price', as distinct from their 'political price', or market price, which was established in the 'superstructure' by supply and demand. Similarly, the Physiocrats differentiated between the 'prix courant' of commodities and their 'prix fondamental' (see Vaggi, 1983). It should be noted, however, that these terms were not an expression of value as such, but rather of physical aggregates converted into a price form by a given monetary standard. For the Physiocrats, as we have seen, social reproduction could proceed with a largely homogeneous capital and output; hence, their analysis of the relationship between these physical aggregates could logically be pursued without any recourse to the corresponding value relationship. Their task was simplified, of course, by singling out agricultural labour as the source of wealth to the exclusion of every other activity embraced by the division of labour. Petty was therefore in advance of the Physiocrats in his recognition of the social aspect of the labour contained in heterogeneous commodities; and, since he discovered in this labour the substance of their value, he also understood the role of money as 'the uniform Measure and Rule for the Value of all Commodities' (ibid., I, p. 183).

The law of monetary circulation elaborated in the context of a corn model could now rest on a more general basis. Indeed, with the further development of this labour theory of value by the classical economists, the function of money as a medium of circulation could only be performed within the parameters set down by its function as a measure of value; these parameters stemmed in turn from the fact that money was ultimately a *produced commodity* like any other. Nevertheless, while the Physiocrats broke decisively with mercantilism – the overriding purpose of their abstraction from value – Petty still tended to identify the form of social labour with the monetary metal, and thus to measure the value of commodities in general by the individual labour expended in the production of this particular commodity. His great merit was to overturn the mercantilist approach to price formation, which depended merely upon the demand and supply for specific commodities, without substituting the similarly tautological quantity theory interpretation, which derived the price level from an aggregate demand and supply relationship between money and output. However, since he recoiled from the prospect of money having an 'imaginary' value superimposed by the circulation process, he attached a special significance to the production of the monetary material.[18]

Smith's framework

Smith developed a comprehensive framework in the *Wealth of Nations* for the independent determination of prices, but in the end he could not provide a solution which satisfied the condition of separability from the determination of output and its revenue shares. Steuart had earlier, and with much less success, grappled with the same problem. He had, for example, distinguished more clearly than Petty or the Physiocrats between the use value of commodities, based upon individual labour, which was 'something real in itself', from exchange value, based upon social labour, which was 'estimated according to the labour it has cost to produce it . . . [T]he labour employed in the modification represent a portion of a man's time' (Steuart, 1767, I, p. 312). Yet he failed completely to capitalise upon this promising line of inquiry, and instead, as we have seen, reverted to a more familiar demand and supply approach.[19] Moreover, while Steuart opposed quantity theory, he introduced further confusion by treating money as potentially as 'invariable standard' in which to estimate prices. It was left to Smith to reestablish the direction of political economy, and, in a pioneering account of competition and the division of labour, he presented the main elements of the classical theory of value and money. While there is little dissent today from the proposition that the *Wealth of Nations* 'must be accorded a less illustrious place in the history of [monetary analysis] than it commands in other and more general respects' (Vickers, 1975, p. 503), it did signal the final rout of mercantilist ideas and policies and it permitted the formulation of the monetary circulation law in its boldest, if not most consistent, form.

Smith traced the origin of money to increasing specialisation in the division of labour, which he mistakenly assumed to *presuppose* commodity exchange. It was therefore to overcome the technical difficulties of barter that society required a 'universal instrument of commerce', or medium of circulation. The precious metals, having been chosen for 'irresistable reasons' to perform this role (1776, p. 18), also became the standard of price: 'The denominations of those coins seem originally to have expressed the weight or quantity of metal contained in them' (ibid., p. 20). This much was evident in the corn model; indeed, Smith explicitly began his discussion of money and exchange not with production as a whole but with *surplus* production. An individual supplied the 'greater part' of his wants 'by exchanging that surplus part of the produce of his own labour, which is over and above his own consumption, for such parts of the produce of other men's labour as he has occasion for' (ibid., p. 17). Only then did Smith proceed to an explanation of the 'real measure' of exchange value, 'or wherein consists the real price of all commodities' (ibid., p. 22). Following Steuart's earlier hint, he discovered it immediately not in any particular kind of labour but in labour in general. Since this was an 'abstract notion', he readily admitted that exchange value was 'more frequently estimated by the quantity of money, than by the quantity either of labour or of any other commodity which can be had in exchange for it' (ibid., p. 24).

Yet Smith also recognised that money was itself variable. The 'price revolution' demonstrated to him unequivocally that gold and silver, like all commodities, were subject to changes in the amount of labour they cost to produce; and 'this revolution in their value, though perhaps the greatest, is by no means the only one of which history gives some account' (ibid., p. 24; also p. 26). Consequently, money could not be regarded as having an invariable value, though Smith assembled this conclusion in a way that seemed to deny its proper function as a measure of value: '[A]s a measure of quantity, such as the natural foot, fathom, or handful, which is continually varying in its own quantity, can never be an accurate measure of the quantity of other things; so a commodity which is itself continually varying in its own value, can never be an accurate measure of the value of other commodities' (ibid.). However, it is arguably the fact that gold and silver *are* variable in their value which makes them a suitable measure of value;[20] and, in their distinct role as a standard of price, they are divisible into invariable units of weight. That Smith had some appreciation of this role was shown by his retort to Steuart: 'By the money-price of goods . . . I understand always the quantity of pure gold and silver for which they are sold, without any regard to the denomination of the coin' (ibid., p. 36). Yet he persistently mixed up the various functions of money, and, having rejected its claim to being an invariable standard of value, he simply substituted labour as just such a standard. Labour alone, 'never varying in its own value, is alone the ultimate and real standard by which the value of all commodities can at all times and places be estimated and compared. It is their real price; money is their nominal price only' (ibid., pp. 24–5).

Smith's attempt to isolate the 'real price' of commodities from their 'nominal price' was an important step in developing a coherent theory of value; and it enabled him to differentiate between movements in relative prices, which registered variations in the value of individual commodities, from movements in the general price level, which would normally be due to changes in the value of the monetary material. Nevertheless, labour was by no means an invariable standard. As Ricardo pointed out, 'Adam Smith, after notably showing the insufficiency of a variable medium, such as gold and silver, for the purpose of determining the variable value of other things, has himself, by fixing on corn or labour, chosen a medium no less variable' (1951/58, I, p. 14). The problem had its source in Smith's ambiguous treatment of the way in which labour entered into the value of commodities. In the 'early and rude state of society' before capital accumulation and landed property, it seemed as though value was determined by the quantity of labour embodied in the production of commodities (1776, p. 36); but this standard was abandoned thereafter and the value of commodities determined instead by the quantity of labour they could 'purchase or command' (ibid., p. 38).[21] It was this latter formulation which Smith used to calculate the 'natural price' of commodities, a term whose methodological significance we have discussed in a previous chapter. This concept of price was in turn defined as the sum of the 'natural rates' of wages, profit and rent, 'the three original sources of all revenue as well as of all exchangeable value' (ibid., p. 40; also p. 42).

This 'adding-up' approach to the analysis of value, as Sraffa calls it (Ricardo, 1951/58, I, p. xxxv), was Steuart's legacy; its effect was to introduce a fatal circularity into Smith's argument. Since the determination of value was now dependent upon distribution, the level of output could not be ascertained before the rate of profit was known (Garegnani, 1984, p. 301). The deductive relationship between wages and profits, which was transparent in the corn model, was thus obscured in Smith's discussion; indeed, he could claim as a corollary of his argument that 'the money-price of corn regulates that of all other home-made commodities' (1776, p. 27) due to its influence upon the wage component of prices.[22] While this proposition was initially accepted by Ricardo (1951/58, VI, p. 114), he repudiated it in his *Essay on Profits*: 'If the price of corn is affected by the rise or fall of the precious metals themselves, then indeed will the price of commodities be also affected, but they vary because the value of money varies not because the value of corn is altered' (ibid., IV, p. 21). Soon afterwards, Ricardo wrote to Mill of Smith's 'original error respecting value' (ibid., VII, p. 100); and, in the *Principles*, as we shall see, when it was no longer a question of determining 'corn ratios' but values, he set his mind to correcting this error, which threatened the surplus approach with a retrogression to supply and demand analysis.

Classical circulation law

Although Smith was unable to solve the problem of value, and hence to calculate P as an independent variable in the equation of exchange, he contributed to a further development of the classical law of monetary circulation. He argued that the amount of metallic money in a country was 'not limited by anything in its local situation, such as the fertility or barrenness of its own mines', but depended primarily upon two other factors. The first was the nation's 'power of purchasing', which was subject in turn to 'the state of its industry', or 'the annual produce of its land and labour'; and the second was the productivity of the mines 'which may happen at any particular time to supply the commercial world with those metals' (1776, p. 190; also p. 262).

Assuming that the value of money and its velocity were constant, the sum required for circulation was thus determined by the value of output:

> [T]he quantity of coin in every country is regulated by the value of the commodities which are to be circulated by it. . . . The value of goods annually bought and sold in any country requires a certain quantity of money to circulate and distribute them to their proper consumers and can give employment to no more. The channel of circulation necessarily draws to itself a sum sufficient to fill it, and never admits any more. (Ibid., pp. 332–3; also p. 261)

This was the most uncompromising statement of the circulation law so far, though, as we shall see, it was susceptible to modification in the short-run.

Even in the long-run, however, Smith went on to show (following Cantillon and Steuart) that only part of the gold and silver available to the domestic economy was actually used as coin: the rest was either absorbed into luxury articles ('the plate of private families'), accumulated in reserves ('laid up in the treasury of the prince') or set aside for discharging international payments imbalances ('bullion for the purpose of foreign trade') (ibid., pp. 333, 339). In other words, the supply of money was also governed by its velocity, which was in turn dependent upon institutional factors. The circulation law encompassed both 'the *number* and value of purchases and sales' (ibid., p. 337, emphasis added). Smith reached the conclusion, therefore, that less money was needed for 'the circulation of the dealers with one another' than for 'the circulation between the dealers and the consumers', though, in doing so, he tended to equate the total revenue spent in a given period with the value of the social product (ibid., pp. 246–7).[23]

Ricardo's value theory

Ricardo's monetary theory was the logical counterpart to his analysis of value and distribution, although, as will be shown in the next section, some of its main elements had already been canvassed during the earlier 'bullion controversy'. The achievement of the *Principles* was to lead political economy out of the impasse it had reached with Smith and to accommodate monetary factors within a more consistent theoretical framework. Ricardo began with the problem of value, whose solution was a precondition for the further development of the surplus approach to distribution outlined in the *Essay on Profits*. He managed to break free from the circular reasoning of Smith by deriving the value of commodities from the amount of labour necessary to produce them, and by holding fast to this viewpoint in the face of appearances to the contrary (Ricardo, 1951/58, I, p. 13).[24]

In Ricardo's *Essay*, it will be recalled, output in the corn model was a given magnitude, determined separately from its division into revenue shares. Now, in the world of heterogeneous commodities, he argued against Smith that the *value* of output was also a given magnitude, measured not by the labour *commanded* by commodities but by the labour *embodied* in their production: '[I]f the reward of the labourer were always in proportion to what he produced, the quantity of labour bestowed on a commodity, and the quantity of labour which that commodity would purchase, would be equal, and either might accurately measure the variations of other things; but they are not equal . . .' (Ricardo, 1951/58, I, pp. 13–14). The difference between the 'reward of the labourer', or the value of the wage, and the value of his product was seen as surplus labour, or surplus value, which Ricardo analysed in the form of profit (on rented land). Since wages were treated as the sole component of capital advanced in the annual production cycle, any change in their value would affect only the rate of profit, *not* the prices of commodities. So far, according to Ricardo, economists had 'maintained that a rise in the price of labour would be uniformly followed by a rise in the price of commodities. I hope I have succeeded in showing, that there are no grounds for such an opinion . . .' (ibid., p. 46).[25]

One factor in Ricardo's refutation of Smith's 'adding up' theory was his assumption throughout that prices were expressed in terms of a money commodity whose own value was 'invariable' (ibid.). I shall examine the ambiguous meaning conferred upon invariability in monetary and value theory shortly. The point here is that the determination of the rate of profit in the agricultural sector could be generalised to the economy as a whole and calculated as a ratio between values rather than physical aggregates. Hence, in Ricardo's presentation, the general rate of profit, r, was given by:

$$r = \frac{Y - N}{N}$$

where output, Y, and necessary consumption, N, were known magnitudes.

The remaining problem for Ricardo, as Marx subsequently pointed out, was that capital could not be treated as consisting entirely of wages, or 'variable capital', but was also advanced in the form of 'constant capital' for means of production. While Ricardo recognised this fact, at least insofar as it affected the proportions of fixed and circulating capital, he could not take account of it in the development of his value theory, and, hence, as we shall see, tended to identify the rate of profit with what Marx was to call the 'rate of surplus value'.[26] It should be clear from the discussion so far that Ricardo went much further than Smith in establishing the price level as well as output as independent variables in the equation of exchange. This much is generally accepted by economists, including Ricardo's own contemporaries. But it is also recognised that he stopped short of a complete solution. This was the goal which Marx set for himself, and, as will later become apparent, he came close to achieving it.

Money and circulation

Whatever inadequacies there were in his analysis, Ricardo also succeeded to a greater extent than any of his predecessors in presenting the theory of value and money as an integrated whole. He did not dispute Smith's account of the origin of money; and he joined with him in rejecting the quantity theory characterisation of its value as 'fictitious' or 'imaginary'. Even in such early writings as his *High Price of Bullion* (1810), he contended that gold and silver, like other commodities, possessed an 'intrinsic value', whose magnitude was directly related to their cost of production (Ricardo, 1923, p. 3). Moreover, we shall see in a moment that he expanded and built upon Smith's conception of the law of monetary circulation. Where Ricardo departed from Smith was in his specification of the content of the price index in the equation of exchange. This was dependent not only upon the value of commodities in general, which we have already looked at, but also upon the value of money, the special commodity in which prices were expressed.

In his *Principles*, Ricardo stripped away the illusions created by demand and supply, and reduced the production costs of the monetary metals unequivocally to labour-time: '[T]he same general rule which regulates the value of raw produce and manufactured commodities, is applicable also to the metals; their value depending not on the rate of profits, nor on the rate of wages, nor on the rent paid for mines, but on the *total quantity of labour* necessary to obtain the metal, and to bring it to market' (1951/58, I, pp. 85–6, emphasis added; also p. 352). The value of money was therefore by no means variable, but 'subject to variation' as a consequence of any change in the productivity of the mines.

Ricardo took care to distinguish long-run variations in the 'natural price' of money (or, more accurately, in its value) from purely short-run market phenomena; thus, he argued that, 'money made of gold and silver is still liable to fluctuations in value, not only to accidental and temporary, but to permanent and natural variations, in the same manner as other commodities' (*ibid.*, p. 86). Again, the example of such long-run variations was the 'price revolution' which followed the discovery of the American mines:

> By the discovery of America and the rich mines in which it abounds, a very great effect was produced on the natural price of the precious metals. This effect is by many supposed not yet to have terminated. It is probable, however, that all the effects on the value of metals, resulting from the discovery of America, have long ceased; and if any fall has of late years taken place in their value, it is to be attributed to improvements in the mode of working the mines. (Ibid.)

It is evident, then, that in constructing his theory of value, Ricardo sharply differentiated between changes in the relative prices of commodities and those affecting the general price level, or, in his own words, 'between those variations which in the medium in which value is estimated or price expressed' (ibid., p. 48). He was therefore able to elaborate the classical monetary circulation law with a degree of precision which Smith's version ultimately lacked. Even before the *Principles*, Ricardo had clearly identified the long-run determinants of the money supply in the equation of exchange. In his *Proposals for an Economical and Secure Currency* (1816), he declared that, 'The quantity of metal, employed as money, in effecting the payments of a particular country, using metallic money . . . must depend on three things: first, on its value; – secondly, on the amount or value of the payments to be made; – and thirdly, on the degree of economy practised in effecting those payments' (1923, p. 158). This formulation resurfaced in the 'brief survey' of money in the *Principles*, where Ricardo outlined 'the general laws which regulate its quantity and value' (1951/58, I, p. 352); but, as it stood, it added little to the conclusion reached by Smith.

It was only in connection with the analysis of value, and with his search for an 'invariable measure of value', that Ricardo's representation of the circulation law acquired a deeper significance. He argued – against the prevailing Smithian view – that any rise or fall in wages would not alter the relative prices of commodities, since gold mining would be affected as much as other sectors of industry. As Sraffa has pointed out, 'it was the relative conditions of production of gold and of other commodities that determined prices, and not the remuneration of labour' (ibid., p. xxxv). The outcome would be the same in the case of a movement in the general price level when gold was mined abroad and imported:

> If then all commodities rose in price, gold could not come from abroad to purchase those dear commodities, but it would go from home to be employed with advantage in purchasing the comparatively cheaper foreign commodities. It appears, then, that the rise of wages will not raise the prices of commodities, whether the metal from which money is made be produced at home or in a foreign country. (Ibid., p. 105)[27]

Ricardo thus introduced a short-run 'specie-flow' mechanism (to which I shall return in the next section) in order to sustain his long-run analysis. Just as significantly, he assumed for the purpose of exposition that the value of the monetary metals was 'invariable', and that 'therefore all alterations in price [are] occasioned by some alteration in the value of the commodity of which I may be speaking' (ibid., p. 46; also p. 87). The problem of an 'invariable measure of value', which was to preoccupy Ricardo for much of his life, has been interpreted in the context of his monetary writings as a search for an 'index number' concept.[28] However, it is important to recognise that this interpretation does not apply to the value theory of the *Principles*.

Invariable measure

Ricardo described the 'invariability of the value of the precious metals' in a letter to Mill in 1815 as 'the sheet anchor on which all my propositions are built' (ibid., VI, p. 340). What Ricardo meant by 'invariability', however, took its colour from the successive hypotheses he was attempting to prove. In his early monetary writings, for example, the term was used simply to denote the relative stability of the value of the monetary metals, and hence their unique aptitude to serve as a measure of value:

> A measure of value should itself be invariable; but this is not the case with either gold or silver, they being subject to fluctuations as well as other commodities. Experience has indeed taught us, that though the variations in the *value* of gold and silver may be considerable, on a comparison of distant periods, yet, for short spaces of time, their value is tolerably fixed. It is this property, among other excellences, which fits them better than any other commodity for the uses of money. Either

> gold or silver may, therefore, in the point of view in which we are considering them, be called a measure of value. (*High Price of Bullion*, in Ricardo, 1923, p. 14 fn.)

At other times, the notion of invariability was applied to the role of money not as a measure of value but as a standard of price: 'A currency may be considered as perfect, of which the standard is invariable, which always conforms to that standard, and in the use of which the utmost economy is practised' (*Proposals for an Economical and Secure Currency*, ibid., pp. 157–58). In other words, although the value of gold and silver could vary, the standard of price, which represented definite units of weight, could not. Like Smith, Ricardo took the part of Locke in the debate with Lowndes over the monetary standard, and explicitly rejected Steuart's 'idea of a currency without a specific standard' (*ibid.*, p. 161). He also followed Smith, however in his failure to delineate clearly the separate functions of money. As Marx put it, 'With English writers the confusion between measure of value and standard of price . . . is indescribable. Their functions, as well as their names, are constantly interchanged' (1867/94, I, p. 101 fn.; see also Tooke, 1838/48, IV, pp. 144–6).

In the *Principles*, Ricardo's search for an 'invariable measure of value' (1951/58, I, p. 43 and *passim*), acquired an altogether different content and meaning. The initial premise that money should be treated as having a constant, or 'tolerably fixed', value for analytical purposes, and that its standard should be invariable, was now subsumed under the search for a commodity which would satisfy the conditions of Ricardo's theory of value. This was not an attempt to solve an 'index-number' problem. As Marx explained, the notion of an invariable measure of value signified primarily 'a measure of value which is itself of invariable value, and consequently, since value itself is a predicate of the commodity, a commodity of invariable value'; hence, it 'was simply a spurious name for the quest for the concept, the nature, of *value* itself . . .' (1963/71, III, pp. 133–4; see also Dobb, 1973, pp. 82–4).

This interpretation has since been fruitfully developed by Sraffa, who found that, 'the problem which mainly interested [Ricardo] was not that of finding an actual commodity which would accurately measure the value of corn or silver at different times and places; but rather that of finding the conditions which a commodity would have to satisfy in order to be invariable in value – and this came close to identifying the problem of a measure with that of the law of value' (ibid., pp. xl–xli).[29] These conditions would, in Ricardo's view, allow the argument against Smith's 'adding-up' theory to be conducted upon more secure foundations. He began by observing that, 'When commodities varied in relative value, it would be desirable to have the means of ascertaining which of them fell and which rose in real value, and this could be effected only by comparing them one after another with some invariable standard measure of value, which should itself be subject to none of the fluctuations to which other commodities are exposed' (ibid., p. 43).

By the third edition of the *Principles*, however, Ricardo conceded that, 'Of such a measure it is impossible to be possessed, because there is no commodity which is not itself exposed to the same variations as the things the value of which is to be ascertained' (ibid., pp. 43–44). While gold seemed to come close to fulfilling the necessary criteria, it would still not be an invariable measure of value, since, even if the same quantity of gold, 'it would not be produced with precisely the same combinations of fixed and circulating capital as all other things; nor with fixed capital of the same durability; nor would it require precisely the same length of time before it could be brought to market'. Thus it could only be 'a perfect measure of value for all things produced under the same circumstances as itself but for no others' (ibid., pp. 44–5).

It will be apparent that the obstacles Ricardo encountered in his quest for an invariable measure of value were of a similar nature to those left unsolved in his analysis of value generally. Although he continued to seek a 'great desideratum in political Economy' right up to his last paper on 'Absolute Value and Exchangeable Value' (ibid., IV, p. 399 and *passim*), he had to be satisfied in the end with 'as near an approximation to a standard measure of value as can be theoretically conceived': this, he argued, was gold 'produced with such proportions of the two kinds of capital as approach nearest to the average quantity employed in the production of most commodities' (ibid., I, p. 45; also p. 87). While Marx was dismissive of the 'superficial manner' in which Ricardo 'handled' this investigation (1963/71, II, p. 202), he recognised the potential significance of being able to define the characteristics of a commodity produced under average conditions.[30] Sraffa has now confirmed Marx's perceptive – and sympathetic – appreciation of Ricardo's underlying concern throughout his discussion of the invariable measure of value; it was clearly not with 'the problem of why two commodities produced by the same quantities of labour are not of the same exchangeable value', but rather with the fact that the size of the social product appeared to change when its division between classes changed. According to Sraffa, 'Even though nothing has occurred to change the magnitude of the aggregate, there may be apparent changes due solely to change in measurement, owing to the fact that measurement is in terms of value and relative values have been altered as a result of a change in the division between wages and profits'. This explained why it was imperative for Ricardo 'to find a measure of value which would be invariant to changes in the division of the product; for, if a rise or fall of wages by itself brought about a change in the magnitude of the social product, it would be hard to determine accurately the effect of profits' (ibid., pp. xlvii–xlix). Marx's own contribution to this important theme of classical economics may now be assessed in the context of his monetary theory.

Marx's approach

Although Marx's investigation of money and prices took shape outside the mainstream of economic thought, it may be regarded as the highest point in the development of classical analysis in the nineteenth century. As 'Ricardo's only great follower' (Schumpeter, 1954, p. 384), he wanted to show how commodity values were transformed into natural prices, or 'prices of production', and thus to specify more accurately the determination of the price index, P, in the equation of exchange. His criticism of Ricardo was not that he had the 'wrong' concept of value, but rather that he identified its magnitude directly with the exchange value of commodities and hence with their prices, instead of tracing the 'inner connection' between them. As Marx put it in a letter to Ludwig Kugelmann in 1868:

> Science consists precisely in demonstrating *how* the law of value asserts itself. So that if one wanted at the very beginning to 'explain' all the phenomena which seemingly contradict that law, one would have to present the science *before* science. It is precisely Ricardo's mistake that in his first chapter on value he takes *as given* a variety of categories that have not yet been explained in order to prove their conformity with the law of value. (Marx and Engels, 1975, p. 196; see also Marx, 1963/71, II, ch. 10)

This criticism also applied to Ricardo's analysis of money, whose origin and development were not treated as an essential aspect of the process of exchange but rather superimposed upon it. Classical economists from Petty onwards had been able to demonstrate that money was a commodity. For Marx, however, 'The difficulty lies not in comprehending that money is a commodity, but in discovering how, why, and by what means a commodity becomes money' (1867/94, I, p. 95). His major work, *Capital*, published between 1867 and 1894, thus began not with competition, the division of labour or even with value as such, but with the *commodity* – the 'cell-form' of capitalist production (ibid., p. 19).[31] It is instructive to follow his train of reasoning.[32]

Like Smith and Ricardo, Marx attached considerable analytical importance to the two distinctive features of commodities. As objects of utility, they were *use values*, whose sum constituted wealth whatever its social form; and, in this qualitative aspect, they were also 'material depositories' of *exchange value*, the quantitative proportion in which they exchanged with other commodities (*ibid.*, pp. 43–4). This possibility of equating heterogeneous products implied a 'common substance' contained in exchange value, and yet distinguished from it. That substance, according to Marx, was homogeneous, social labour – a 'total abstraction' both from the product, or use value, and from the particular kind of labour materialised in it (ibid., pp. 44–6). The value of a commodity was therefore determined by the labour-time socially necessary for its production, and it 'varies directly as the quantity, and inversely as the productiveness, of the labour incorporated in it' (ibid., pp. 47–8).

Although the classical school had already analysed value and its magnitude, it was unable to separate it – and hence trace the link with – exchange value, the form in which value was manifested.[33] By contrast, at the very outset of his discussion, Marx established the preconditions for a solution to the so-called 'transformation problem'. The element of the solution he wished to emphasise at this level of abstraction was the 'two-fold' nature of the labour contained in commodities – underlying the classical use value/exchange value dichotomy – which he called 'the pivot on which a clear comprehension of Political Economy turns' (ibid., p. 49). On the one hand, he observed, individuals performed various qualitatively distinct kinds of useful labour – a necessary condition for human existence – producing use values and thus constituting a division of labour; on the other, to the extent that their labour was at the same time social due to its equal, undifferentiated character, it created values.[34]

Having independently accounted for the source of value, Marx returned to the form in which it initially appeared – exchange value – in order to explain the development of money from what he called the 'elementary' value relation between two commodities. To summarise his argument (ibid., p. 54 ff.), the contrast contained in a single commodity between use value and value became apparent as soon as the value of one was expressed in the use value of another, i.e., when concrete individual labour took the form of its 'opposite', abstract social labour. It was accentuated in the 'expanded' form of value, where a series of commodities fulfilled the role of equivalent and reached its height in the 'general' form, where one commodity was excluded from the rest by social custom and figured as a universal equivalent exchangeable with all commodities. The function of universal equivalent – the direct embodiment of social labour – devolved upon gold, the material best suited to exhibit the qualities of uniformity and divisibility. Hence, the price-form was, at this level of analysis, the elementary expression of the relative value of a given commodity in gold, the money commodity. In Marx's words, 'The single commodity-form is therefore the germ of the money-form' (ibid., p. 75).[35] As a corollary, the economists who 'reason that the emergence of money is due to external difficulties which the expansion of barter encounters . . . forget that these difficulties arise from the evolution of exchange value and hence from that of social labour as universal labour' (Marx, 1859, pp. 50–1).

Functions of money

Once Marx had established the origin of money, he demarcated its various functions in the circulation process, and consequently threw further light upon its relationship to price behaviour. He insisted throughout that, 'it is not a question here of definitions, which things must be made to fit. We are dealing here with definite functions which must be expressed in definite categories' (1867/94, II, p. 230). That the act of exchange conferred upon money not its value but its 'specific value-form', was reasserted at the outset against the hypothesis of the quantity theory opponents of mercantilism, that the value of the precious metals was purely fictitious (ibid., I. p. 93). When gold entered circulation at the point of production, its value was already given by the labour realised in it:

> Money, like every other commodity, cannot express the magnitude of its own value except relatively in other commodities. This value is determined by the labour-time required for its production, and is expressed by the quantity of any other commodity that costs the same amount of labour-time. Such quantitative determination of its relative value takes place at the source of its production by means of barter. When it steps into circulation as money, its value is already given. (Ibid., p. 95)

In this capacity, therefore, as the 'socially recognised incarnation of human labour', money served as the universal *measure of value*. Insofar as it was a fixed weight of metal, it was also the *standard of price*. Marx set much store by the fact that these were 'two entirely distinct functions' (ibid., p. 100), which earlier classical authors had confused. As measure of value, money transformed the values of commodities into prices, into imaginary quantities of gold whose value was potentially variable; and, as standard of price, it measured those quantities of gold in terms of invariable units of weight. The historical separation of the money-names of these units from their actual content through debasement, etc. (a process whose implications I shall examine in the next chapter), led to the regulation of the standard by law. When value was thus represented by denominations of coin, money became 'money of account' (ibid., p. 103). Despite their inexact terminology, Marx fully supported Smith and Ricardo's dismissal of Steuart's ideal monetary standard: 'When, therefore, money serves as a measure of value, it is employed only as imaginary or ideal money. This circumstance has given rise to the wildest theories. But, although the money that performs the functions of a measure of value is only ideal money, price depends entirely upon the actual substance that is money' (ibid., p. 99; also Marx, 1859, pp. 76–86).[36]

It did not follow, of course, from the fact that price expressed a commodity's exchange ratio with money that it expressed the magnitude of that commodity's *value*. There was no overriding reason, in other words, for price to *coincide* with value. Indeed according to Marx, the possibility of 'quantitative incongruity between price and magnitude of value, or the deviation of the former from the latter, is inherent in the price-form itself. This is no defect, but, on the contrary, admirably adapts the price-form to a mode of production whose inherent laws impose themselves only as the mean of apparently lawless irregularities that compensate one another' (1867/94, I, p. 104).

Marx's correction of his classical predecessors, however, was not followed to its logical conclusion. First, he did not indicate the possibility of a 'quantitative incongruity' between the value and exchange value of the *money* commodity, whereas Ricardo, and to some extent Smith, at least recognised a potential discrepancy in the short-run between its value, on the one hand, and its market value on the other. This shortcoming in Marx's presentation will be discussed in the next section. Secondly, when he relaxed his assumption that the prices of commodities were equal to their values and introduced the formation of a general rate of profit through competition among capitals, he was unable to complete his solution to the problem of the relationship between those same values and the wholly distinct ratios in which commodities now exchanged, namely at their prices of production. I shall return to this problem below.

Whatever the correspondence or otherwise between the prices and values of commodities, the principle governing the amount of money required as a *means of circulation* was not affected. Having explained this further role of money in the sphere of circulation – a role established in the corn model and, as we shall see, the point of departure for token or fiduciary money – Marx asked himself the question, 'how much money this sphere constantly absorbs' (ibid., p. 118). In response, he reiterated the classical law of monetary circulation, 'that the quantity of the circulating medium is determined by the sum of the prices of the commodities circulating, and the average velocity of currency'. This law, he suggested, 'may also be stated as follows: given the sum of the values of commodities, and the average rapidity of their metamorphoses, the quantity of precious metal current as money depends on the value of that precious metal' (ibid., p. 124). Marx directly contrasted his formulation of the circulation law with the quantity theory of Hume and Montesquieu:

> The erroneous opinion that it is, on the contrary, prices that are determined by the quantity of the circulating medium, and that the latter depends on the quantity of the precious metals in a country; this opinion was based by those who first held it, on the absurd hypothesis that commodities are without a price, and money without a value, when they first enter into circulation, as an aliquot part of the heap of precious metals. (Ibid., pp. 124–5)[37]

The 'price revolution' of the sixteenth and seventeenth centuries was therefore ascribed by Marx to the altered value of gold and silver, rather than to their increased quantity in domestic circulation (ibid., p. 119; see also Marx, 1859, pp. 160–3). It was not sufficient, however, simply to restate this circulation law; the price level in the equation of exchange had yet to be satisfactorily ascertained.

Prices and profits

Since Marx took as the foundation of his analysis of money and prices the theory of value developed – however imperfectly – by the classical school, he was likewise faced with the problem of reconciling it with the fact that commodities did *not* exchange according to the amount of labour they embodied. This problem could only be solved, in his view, by returning to the calculation of the general rate of profit, which was, it will be recalled, the point of departure for the surplus approach. Ricardo had assumed in his calculation, following Smith, that the capital advanced for the year could be resolved into wages. Marx showed, however, that the proportion between means of production and 'labour-power' in the total capital could affect the rate of profit independently of the distribution of output between wages and profits. He called this material proportion the 'technical composition of capital', and the proportion between the value of labour-power, i.e., the sum of wages, or 'variable capital', and the value of the means of production, or 'constant capital', its 'value-composition': 'Between the two there is a strict correlation. To express this, I call the value-composition of capital, insofar as it is determined by its technical composition and mirrors the changes of the latter, the *organic composition* of capital' (ibid., p. 574; also Marx, 1867/94, III, pp. 145–6).

Hence, if commodities exchanged at their values, i.e., according to the labour contained in them, the rate of profit would be given by:

$$s/(C+V)$$

where C and V were constant and variable capital respectively (measured in terms of the labour required to produce them), and s was 'surplus value' (measured by surplus labour, or the labour expended over and above that necessary for the reproduction of wages). By contrast, Ricardo's profit equation became $r = s/V$ where V was substituted for N and s for $(Y–N)$. It was thus apparent that his equation expressed not the rate of profit but rather what Marx called the 'rate of surplus value': the confusion of these two categories in Ricardo's analysis prevented him both from distinguishing between the prices and values of commodities and, consequently, it was further argued, from devising a solution to the 'transformation problem'. In Marx's view, 'the emergence, realisation, creation of the general rate of profit necessitates the transformation of values into cost-prices that are different from these values. Ricardo on the contrary assumes the identity of values and cost-prices, because he confuses the rate of profits with the rate of surplus-value' (1963/71, II, p. 434).[38]

The fact that commodities did not exchange in proportion to the labour they embodied was acknowledged by Ricardo only as 'modifications' to the law of value; whereas, for Marx, the equalisation of the rate of profit due to competition meant that prices *necessarily* deviated from values, and the extent of that deviation would be indicated by differences in the organic composition of capital among the various branches of production. When these prices included 'average profit', they were categorised by Marx as 'prices of production' (1867/94, III, p. 157). This, he pointed out, 'is really what Adam Smith calls natural price, Ricardo calls price of production, or cost of production, and the Physiocrats call *prix necessaire*, because in the long run it is a prerequisite of supply. But none of them has revealed the difference between price of production and value . . .' (ibid., p. 198; also, Marx, 1963/71, p. 209).

Prices of production only coincided with values in the case of commodities which were produced under average conditions, or, as Marx himself put it, 'in spheres of production [where the capital invested] has a mean, or average, composition' (ibid., p. 173).[39] For these commodities, it also followed that profits were equivalent to surplus value; but, for all other commodities which exchanged for more or less than the quantity of labour contained in them, surplus value was *redistributed* 'behind the backs of the producers' from branches of production with a lower organic composition of capital than the social average to those with a higher organic composition. Marx portrayed the result as follows:

> When a capitalist sells his commodities at their price of production, therefore, he recovers money in proportion to the value of capital consumed in their production and secures profit in proportion to his advanced capital as the aliquot part in the total social capital. His cost-prices are specific. But the profit added to them is independent of his particular sphere of production, being a simple average per hundred units of invested capital. (Ibid., p. 159)

While Marx's proposed solution to the 'transformation problem' was ingenious, it was still incomplete. As he himself acknowledged, once inputs as well as outputs were transformed into prices of production, the determination of the rate of profit in value terms might no longer be accurate:

> We had originally assumed that the cost-price of a commodity equalled the *value* of the commodities consumed in its production. But for the buyer the price of production of a specific commodity is its cost-price, and may thus pass as cost-price into the prices of other commodities. Since the price of production may differ from the value of commodity, it follows that the cost-price of a commodity containing this price of

> production of another commodity may also stand above or below that portion of its total value derived from the value of the means of production consumed by it. It is necessary to remember this modified significance of the cost-price, and to bear in mind that *there is always the possibility of an error if the cost-price of a commodity in any particular sphere is identified with the value of the means of production consumed by it*. (Ibid., pp. 164–65, final emphasis added)[40]

Given that the third volume of *Capital* was left in the form of unfinished manuscripts, it is perhaps not surprising that Marx made no attempt to correct the potential 'error' which he identified. He simply went on to remark that, 'Our present analysis does not necessitate a closer examination of this point' (ibid., p. 165). Others, of course, have tried either to dismiss or to improve upon Marx's formulation. Although it is not part of our purpose to assess these contributions, we may note in passing that a fruitful approach has been taken by Garegnani (1984), who, following Sraffa (1960), has derived from Marx and the classical economists a powerful framework for the determination of the rate of profit.[41] The important point for our present discussion is that the achievements of the surplus approach in advancing the theory of price behaviour have arisen from, and been accompanied by, progress in the analysis of distribution. Furthermore, it is only in the context of this analysis that the classical view of money, and its relationship to prices, can be understood.

We have seen that the role of money as a means of circulation had its origin in the 'real economy' where both the capital outlay and the product consisted largely of the same commodity, namely corn. In contrast with quantity theory, the money supply was here treated as the dependent variable and prices as the independent variable in the equation of exchange. This primitive version of the classical law of monetary circulation – deduced from the operation of a corn ratio model – nevertheless made prices depend in turn upon the chosen denomination or standard of currency, since there was no question at this stage of measuring the values of different commodities. Hence, the amount of money required for circulation was governed directly by the given level of output, and, in addition, by its velocity. Money was indeed a 'veil', with no influence in relation to these real forces. It was only when the corn assumption was abandoned, and a theory of price formation introduced, that the role of money as a produced commodity, and hence as a measure of value, could separately be delineated. This also implied a significant modification to the content, though not the form, of the circulation law. The money supply was still dependent upon the level of output and prices depicted in the equation of exchange, but now prices as well as output were independently determined.

While the classical economists interpreted the process of price formation with varying degrees of success, the nature of their difference with the advocates of pure exchange quantity theory was clear. In the long-run, the direction of causation did not run from money to prices, but rather the reverse. When it came to short-run market fluctuations, however, a divergence of view appeared *within* the classical approach, and it is to this divergence that I can now turn. I shall then be in a position to examine its far-reaching consequences for the analysis of fiduciary money and credit.

THE INFLATIONARY PROCESS

I have now established the circumstances in which classical economists envisaged an inflation of commodity prices in the long-run. All other things being equal, a long-run inflation was seen as the outcome of changes in the conditions of production either of the monetary material itself – which would have a proportionate effect on the general price level – or of individual commodities whose weighting in a notional price index was such that they might exercise a greater than average influence.[42] Since both output and the velocity of circulation were given in the equation of exchange by the stage of accumulation and by institutional factors respectively, any associated monetary expansion was the result – not the cause – of the increased level of prices. This was the conclusion reached by all the classical authors as an integral part of the surplus approach to value and distribution.

Quantity theory was only correct in its assertion – against mercantilism – that the absolute amount of money in a country was a matter of indifference. It was flawed, however, by its inability to ascertain the relative amount necessary for the circulation process. While for quantity theory any amount could enter circulation for an indefinite time, since the prices of commodities would automatically adjust, classical economics treated the money supply as a determinate magnitude. In calculating this magnitude, a range of numerical solutions was bound to emerge as a result of the different weightings attached to velocity and of the varying degrees of development of value theory, which I have outlined in the previous section.

Notwithstanding such discrepancies, the unifying feature of the classical analysis of the relationship between money and prices under long-run 'normal' conditions was never in doubt.[43] This was the law of monetary circulation, whose discovery and development by classical economists has been a recurrent theme of preceding sections. This law stated that the quantity of money was directly dependent upon the 'supply side' of the equation of exchange, modified by the state of velocity, where both prices and the level of output were independently determined. The only context in which quantity theory appeared to acquire 'validity', or at least relevance, within the classical perspective was in the short-run, but even here it could not lay claim to the status of a theory. Let us now examine the short-run inflationary process more closely.

Having established the direction of long-run causation, classical economists were faced with the question of whether the money supply could temporarily exceed or fall short of normal circulation requirements, and, if so, which variable would adjust in the transitional period before the long-run position was restored. It was over this issue – the short-run path of adjustment – that they were divided into two opposing groups.[44] This conflict at the level of metallic currency prefigured, as we shall see, the differing lines of approach when the behaviour of fiduciary money and credit was under consideration. It had a lasting impact on British monetary policy and the evolution of the financial structure. Yet the competing ideas on which the conflict turned have not been considered in the context of classical value and distribution theory. This section makes an attempt to restore the monetary debates to their proper context and establish the significance of money as a produced commodity for the classical school.

The main group in the debates was led by Ricardo and included the Bullionists (the supporters of the 1810 Bullion Report) and later the Currency School. It was their doctrine, Keynes lamented, which 'conquered England as completely as the Holy Inquisition conquered Spain' (1933, p. 32). The other group comprised the anti-Bullionists and the Banking School and was given qualified approval by Marx. The distinguishing characteristic of the Ricardian group was their acceptance of a short-run 'quantity theory' as a logical accompaniment of Say's law. Both sides of the debate accepted that the saving–investment basis of Say's law implied a fixed level of output, but this group maintained that the exchange of products in the commodity market implied a constant velocity, as well, which would make the burden of adjustment following an exogenous change in the money supply fall exclusively upon prices. The inflationary process was therefore seen as the transitional mechanism by which monetary deviations were corrected. As Ricardo put it, 'That commodities would rise or fall in price, in proportion to the increase or diminution of money, *I assume as a fact which is incontrovertible*' (1923, p. 93 fn., emphasis added). Since Ricardo was the most consistent exponent of this view, we must be aware of the reasoning he employed to sustain it before proceeding to his adversaries.

Ricardo's quantity theory

Ricardo developed his argument in terms of the international specie-flow mechanism but in a manner distinct from that of Hume's pure exchange approach. Sayers is right only up to a point when he comments that Ricardo's 'real interest was confined to [long-run] forces, to the exclusion of short-period disturbances' (1953, p. 93); after all, his account of inflation was mainly concerned with the process by which a long-run 'equilibrium' position was restored after a temporary monetary disturbance. Sayers is closer to the mark in attributing the 'quantity theory' element of Ricardo's account to 'the attractions of Say's law' (ibid., p. 95). With output and velocity given, only prices could change as a result of monetary expansion or contraction. Even when velocity was permitted to vary in the anti-'quantity theory' propositions of Ricardo's critics, he could retort that the signal for any such adjustment had initially to manifest itself in an alteration of the general price level.

Ricardo's discussion of the short-run inflationary adjustment process thus mirrored, as we shall see below, his analysis of deflation with its celebrated denial of the possibility of a 'glut' of commodities in the market. Both depended upon the assumption of not just a fixed level of output, but also a constant velocity; and yet no alternative account could be developed without challenging the former assumption as well as the latter. In the long-run, it was plain that, 'A circulation can never be so abundant as to overflow; for by diminishing its value, in the same proportion you will increase its quantity, and by increasing its value, diminish its quantity' (1951/58, I, p. 352).[45] This is a straightforward application of the monetary circulation law. In the short-run, however, any tendency for the stock of metallic money to overflow was reflected immediately in a fall in what Cantillon called its market-value (for which Ricardo misleadingly retains the term 'value'[46]) below its 'intrinsic value' (measured by the labour content), and hence in the external rate of exchange.

Rejecting this notion of a short-run price adjustment, Marx claimed that, 'The proof consists in postulating what has to be proved, i.e., that any quantity of the precious metal serving as money, regardless of its relation to its intrinsic value, must become a medium of circulation, or coin, and thus a token of value for the commodities in circulation regardless of the total amount of their value. In other words, this proof rests in disregarding all functions performed by money except its function as a medium of circulation' (1859, p. 174). Yet Marx himself never succeeded in showing why, having accepted the saving-investment identity of Say's law, short-run market deviations could not apply to money as much as to any commodity in response to an excessive quantity in relation to long-run circulation needs. Such deviations were admitted only at a later stage in the analysis of economic crises, which, as we shall see, were 'deduced from the real movement of capitalist production, competition and credit – insofar as crisis arises out of the special aspects of capital, and not merely comprised in its existence as commodity and money' (1963/71, II, pp. 512–13). We may agree with Marx, however, that Ricardo should have presented his case within the framework of a closed economy before introducing the added complications of international trade and finance; nevertheless, it was in this international context that Ricardo's thesis became widely known – and, one might add, associated with the Humean pure exchange version of specie-flow.[47]

Ricardo began his early pamphlet *High Price of Bullion* with the assumption of a long-run equilibrium in which the monetary metals were 'divided into certain proportions among the different civilised nations of the earth, according to the state of their commerce and wealth, and therefore according to the number and frequency of the payments which they had to perform'. These metals had the same value in all countries, and hence 'no temptation' could exist for their import or export (Ricardo, 1923, p. 3). In order to trace the effects of a disturbance, Ricardo then supposed an expansion in the supply of materials in a country (due to the discovery of new mines), or, alternatively, a contraction in the aggregate value of commodities.[48] The monetary excess relative to normal circulation requirements led to a fall in the market value of the metals below their intrinsic value and to a commensurate rise in the domestic price level. This in turn created pressure for the export of the metals in exchange for commodities until their market value once more corresponded with the intrinsic value given by the production costs at the mines and national currencies were again 'equalised'.[49] In Ricardo's words, 'the temptation to export money in exchange for goods, or what is termed an unfavourable balance of trade, never arose but from a redundant currency' (ibid., p. 9; also *Reply to Bosanquet*, ibid., p. 93). This doctrine was applied by Ricardo and the nineteenth century monetary orthodoxy both to fiduciary money and to credit. As we shall see, the Bank of England was likened to a gold mine (*ibid.*, p. 5) and would have to take care to regulate paper currency in accordance with the movement of specie into and out of the country.

The classical alternative

The classical economists opposed to the Ricardian orthodoxy were less than successful in their unceasing efforts to overturn it. The reason should by now be obvious. They all shared Ricardo's acceptance of the saving–investment basis of Say's law and thus for them output was fixed. Their rejection of the short-run quantity theory simply shifted the weight of adjustment in the equation of exchange to velocity. In other words, they adopted a hoarding mechanism, or quantity response to exogenous monetary fluctuations, as against a price response. Although this proved a more realistic interpretation of economic events, it was treated by Ricardo and his followers as logically inconsistent with the Say's law assumption of full capacity utilisation. In their view, a 'glut' of money, like that of commodities, would be countered and eliminated automatically by a forced reduction in its price. The possibility of hoarding would therefore not arise.

This 'inconsistency' in the classical alternative opened it up to devastating criticism from which it never recovered. While it would be wrong to detract from the influence of economic forces in the debate – especially the changing relationship between the banks and industry – it is clear that a key factor in the continuing dominance of quantity theory was the failure of the alternative approach to mount a significant challenge to Say's law. This was in spite of the considerable analytical progress made by its adherents, which will become most evident when we discuss its application to the fiduciary and credit system.

Petty founded the alternative approach in his *Quantulumcunque concerning Money*, an uncompromising rebuttal of mercantilist doctrine. He began, as I have already noted, by denying that a country was necessarily the poorer for having less money (1899, II, p. 446). On the contrary, it might have too much money, in which case, 'we may melt down the heaviest and turn it into the splendour of plate, in vessels or utensils of gold and silver; or send it out, as a commodity, where the same is wanting or desired; or let it out at interest, where interest is high'. If, on the other hand, the money supply was inadequate, 'we must erect a bank, which well computed doth almost double the effect of our coined money' (*ibid.*). In the case both of an excess and a deficiency of metallic money, therefore, the scope for adjustment lay not in prices but in the velocity of circulation, which in turn could be influenced by changes in the financial structure.

Adam Smith's position was more ambiguous. Nevertheless, there can be little justification for Viner's description of it as 'one of the mysteries of the history of economic thought'. The alleged mystery consisted in that Smith, 'although he was intimately acquainted with Hume and with his writings', should have made 'no reference' to his self-regulating mechanism and 'should have been content with an exposition of the international distribution of specie in the already obsolete terms of the requirement by each country, without specific reference to its relative price level, of a definite amount of money to circulate trade' (1937, p. 87). In fact, as we have already seen, Smith repudiated Hume's pure exchange standpoint in favour of the classical law of monetary circulation; the value of gold and silver was not determined within the circulation process, but 'was antecedent to and independent of their being employed as coin, and was the quality which fitted them for that employment' (Smith, 1776, p. 138).[50] The ambiguity in his position was confined only to the short-run transmission mechanism, which was not presented in any systematic form but was scattered under a variety of headings in the *Wealth of Nations*.

In his chapter on money in Book I, for example, Smith introduced the concept of a 'channel of circulation' which required a determinate sum of money to fill it: 'Whatever, therefore, is poured into it beyond this sum, cannot run in it, but must overflow' (ibid., p. 22). This was clearly a hoarding response to monetary excess. Indeed, Smith added that the superfluous money was 'too valuable' to be allowed to lie idle: '[I]t will, therefore, be sent abroad in order to seek that profitable employment which it cannot find at home.' The money may be used either to purchase 'such goods as are likely to be consumed by idle people who produce nothing', or to purchase 'an additional stock of materials, tools, and provisions, in order to maintain and employ an additional number of industrious people, who reproduce, with a profit, the value of their annual consumption' (ibid.). The same result would follow a decline in the value of the social product; again, the money 'thrown out of domestic circulation' would not be allowed to lie idle. For Smith, 'The interest of whoever possesses it, requires that it should be employed. But having no employment at home, it will, in spite of all laws and prohibitions, be sent abroad and employed in purchasing consumable goods which may be of some use at home' (ibid., pp. 261–2).

It will be apparent that Smith came close here to Ricardo's characterisation of the return to equilibrium after a disturbance to the long-run relationship between the money stock and the value of output, namely through the import and export of the precious metals. This similarity was further exhibited in his conclusion that, 'the exportation of gold and silver is, in this case, not the cause, but the effect of its declension [viz. the fall in output: R. G.], and may even, for some little time, alleviate the misery of that declension' (ibid.). Nevertheless, Ricardo, who always wrote as if he was simply developing Smith's monetary analysis, pursued a different formulation of the mechanism by which the flow of specie was triggered, namely through an alteration in the domestic price level.

Francis Horner, in an influential review of Henry Thornton's *Paper Credit of Great Britain*, had earlier accused Smith of 'overlook[ing] the intermediate event' (1957, p. 35). Indeed, Thornton himself, whom I shall discuss in the next chapter, contended that:

> Dr Smith does not, in any of his observations on this subject, proceed sufficiently, as I conceive, on the practical principle of shewing how it is *through the medium of prices* . . . that the operations of importing and exporting gold are brought about. He considers our coin as going abroad simply in consequence of our circulation at home being over full . . . [T]he circulation *can never be said to be over full.* (1802, pp. 203–5, emphasis added)

It was in connection with this issue of the 'intermediate event', that is to say the mechanism of adjustment to the long-run position, that the ambiguity to which I have referred entered into Smith's presentation. This ambiguity illustrated the problems facing the classical alternative to quantity theory.

Ambiguity in Smith

In his lengthy 'Digression on Silver' in the *Wealth of Nations*, Smith began with a firm repudiation of the 'popular notion' that 'as the quantity of silver naturally increases in every country with the increase of wealth, so its value diminishes as its quantity increases' (1776, p. 150). This was clearly directed against crude versions of quantity theory (see Price, 1909, pp. 87–95). Smith instead attributed an expanded supply of monetary metals to two separate factors. The first was the 'increased wealth of the people, from the increased produce of the annual labour' (ibid.). The latter case was straightforward and has already been discussed comprehensively. Here, 'a greater quantity of coin becomes necessary in order to circulate a greater quantity of commodities; and the people, as they can afford it, as they have more commodities to give for it, will naturally purchase a greater and greater quantity of plate' (ibid., p. 151). This was simply a restatement of the classical law of monetary circulation.[51]

It was in the former situation, when more abundant mines were discovered, that Smith's account came up against a difficulty. He argued that when, as a consequence of this discovery,

> a greater quantity of the precious metals is brought to market, and the quantity of the necessaries and conveniences of life for which they must be exchanged being the same as before: equal quantities of the metal must be exchanged for smaller quantities of commodities. So far, therefore, as the increase of the quantity of the precious metals in any country arises from the increased abundance of the mines, it is necessarily connected with some diminution of their value. (Ibid., pp. 150–1)

The source of the difficulty lay in Smith's failure to indicate whether this 'diminution' in the value of the metals was due to lower production costs at the mines, or whether it was due to the fact of abundance with unchanged production costs and thus was simply an element of a short-run adjustment mechanism along the lines developed by Ricardo.

Clearly, in assessing the response to exogenous changes in the money supply, it would have been more appropriate to hold the value of money *constant*. However, Smith and his contemporaries developed their analysis against the background of the 'price revolution', when the value of the monetary metals was falling. In contrast, therefore, with the hoarding mechanism which he established at a later stage of the *Wealth of Nations*, Smith appeared to pave the way for Ricardo's short-run quantity theory. At this point, he contended not only that, 'the discovery of the abundant mines of America seems to have been the sole cause of this diminution in the value of silver in proportion to that of corn', but that, 'the increase of the supply had, it seems, so far exceeded that of the demand, that the value of that metal sunk considerably' (ibid., p. 153). While this observation was by no means a concession to the pure exchange approach of Hume, it did anticipate Ricardo's characterisation of the process by which the market value of the monetary metal was brought into conformity with their reduced value at the point of production.[52] The question remained, however, whether and in what way prices would respond if the value of money was unchanged.

In logic, the possibility of a market deviation from value should apply as much to money as to any other commodity. If, for example, the changed relationship between corn and money as a result of a bad harvest led to a price response which could be regarded 'not as a permanent, but as a transitory and occasional event' (ibid., p. 159), it would seem that the same effect ought to follow changes on the side of money. Even were a velocity adjustment postulated – on the continuing assumption of a fixed level of output – an intermediate price response might be a necessary precondition, or signal at least, for its operation. As we have seen, Smith rejected this view at one point, but now he seemed to accept it. Ruling out an interest rate response to exogenous monetary growth, he argued that, 'Any increase in the quantity of silver, while that of the commodities circulated by means of it remained the same, could have *no other effect than to diminish the value of that metal.* The nominal value of all sorts of goods would be greater, but their real value would be precisely the same as before' (ibid., p. 273, emphasis added). Although Smith did not elaborate, Ricardo was perhaps on much safer ground than otherwise might have been the case when he implicitly derived authority from the *Wealth of Nations* for his account of the short-run transmission mechanism. Any criticisms of Smith's failings or inconsistencies in monetary analysis were studiously avoided.

It must be recognised, however, that Smith subscribed to two opposing interpretations of the short-run – one based on a price response to monetary fluctuations and the other on a hoarding response. The conditions under which either or both mechanisms might operate were left obscure in his account. This was due in no small measure to the repeated confusion of changes in the *value* of the precious metals due to a rise or fall in production costs at the mines with changes in their *market value* due to fluctuations in demand and supply. The indiscriminate use of the terminology of 'value' and 'price' to cover both sets of circumstances simply heightened the confusion. Marx, the other major exponent of the 'classical alternative' did not make this mistake, arguing that, 'Any scholarly investigation of the relation between the volume of means of circulation and movements in commodity prices must assume that the value of the monetary material is given' (1859, p. 160; also 1867/94, I, p. 120). His own failing, as we shall now find, lay in a refusal to allow for any discrepancy at all between the value of money and its market value in the event of deviations from long-run 'equilibrium'.

Marx's hoarding principle

Marx conducted his investigation of money and inflation in a logical sequence which enables us to identify both the areas of advance beyond his predecessors and the shortcomings which hindered further development. His is by far the most comprehensive analysis of monetary phenomena, yet it is relatively neglected. I shall therefore devote some attention to it here. According to the plan outlined in the *Grundrisse*, the 'rough drafts' of 1857/58, he wanted first to examine the '[c]auses of the variations in the value of the precious metals and hence of metallic money' (1973, p. 237). This issue has been covered in our previous section. It was followed in Marx's sketch by the 'effects of this variation on industry and the different classes', and only then by 'quantity of circulation in relation to rise and fall of prices' with the attendant problem of 'how [money] is affected as measure by rising quantity etc.' (ibid.).

If we are to adopt Marx's own sequence, we must begin with the effects he portrayed of an alteration in the value of the monetary metals. Ultimately, as we have seen, a reduction in their value would bring about a commensurate increase in the general price level, since a 'dual evaluation of exchange values of commodities in a given country can of course occur only temporarily; gold and silver prices must be adjusted to correspond with the exchange values themselves, so that finally the exchange values of all commodities are assessed in accordance with the new value of monetary material' (1859, p. 161). Thus, in the intervening period, Marx identified an inflationary adjustment process; but, in his *Critique of Political Economy*, he postponed any 'description of this process or an examination of the ways in which the exchange value of commodities prevails within the fluctuations of market prices' (ibid.). Having deliberately abstracted both in this work and in *Capital* from the arbitrary phenomena of supply and demand,[53] he contended merely that, 'such adjustment proceeds only very gradually, extending over long periods, and does not by any means keep in step with the increase of ready money in circulation' (ibid.).[54]

In *Capital* itself, however, Marx took the analysis somewhat further. If the value of money should fall, 'this fact is first evidenced by a change in the prices of those commodities that are directly bartered for the precious metals at the sources of their production': then, Marx went on, 'one commodity infects another through their common value-relation, so that their prices, expressed in gold or silver, gradually settle down into the proportions determined by their comparative values, until finally the values of all commodities are estimated in terms of the new value of the metal that constitutes money' (1867/94, I, p. 119).[55] As commodities acquired their 'true prices' in conformity with the reduced value of the universal commodity, so the amount of money in circulation would have to increase proportionately.

Here Marx took the opportunity to criticise – more explicitly than Smith or Ricardo – the pure exchange quantity theory of Hume and his school. He called it a 'one-sided observation of the results that followed upon the discovery of fresh supplies of gold and silver', which 'led some economists in the seventeenth and particularly in the eighteenth century, to the false conclusion, that the prices of commodities had gone up in consequence of the increased quantity of gold and silver serving as means of circulation' (ibid.). Nevertheless, he did not dispute Hume's account of the actual process of adjustment, which, after all, 'does not accord with his principle' (1859, p. 161 fn.). In the chapter he contributed to Engels's *Anti-Dühring*, Marx accepted that in this 'intermediate period', monetary growth could have 'a beneficial effect on industry and trade',[56] though Hume presented it, 'in a less comprehensive way than many of his predecessors and contemporaries' (1894, p. 262). In particular, Hume was right to argue that in the 'slow process of price equalisation' the depreciation of money 'only in the last instance' increased wages – 'that is to say, it increases the profit made by merchants and industrialists at the cost of the labourer' (ibid.; see Price, 1909, p. 102).[57] Marx made no attempt to pursue this investigation and thus did not find any disparity here between the value and the market value of metallic money.[58]

In affirming the classical circulation law, Marx noted that deviations of the money supply from its 'average level' were relatively insignificant, 'especially if we take long periods into consideration', although 'excessive perturbations' could arise periodically 'from industrial and commercial crises, or, less frequently, from fluctuations in the value of money' (1867/94, I, p. 123). Once the value of money was assumed to be *given*, however, such 'perturbations' could affect only the velocity of circulation. With the level of output independently given by past accumulation, Marx, like Petty and Smith,[59] proposed a hoarding mechanism for the correction of monetary excess or deficiency in relation to long-run requirements. Indeed, this mechanism appeared to operate automatically and instantaneously: 'The hoards thus act as channels for the supply or withdrawal of circulating money, so that the amount of money circulating as coin is always just adequate to the immediate requirements of circulation' (1859, p. 136).[60]

Marx thus ruled out any short-run price response to monetary variations, at least in the context of simple circulation, though why he turned it into such an issue of principle is difficult to explain; it was still a problem to establish how the hoarding process itself was set in train, if not by transitory price changes. This problem was acknowledged in the *Grundrisse* where Marx argued that, 'if a greater quantity [of money] than required by circulation itself were artificially thrown into it *and could not run off* . . . then it would be *depreciated*; not because the quantity determines prices, but because prices determine quantity, and hence only a specific amount can remain in circulation at a specific value' (1973, p. 813, emphasis added). However, he confined this possibility of depreciation only to cases where there were 'artificial hindrances, prohibition of melting-down, or export etc.'[61] or where 'the circulating medium is merely a symbol and does not itself possess a real value corresponding to its nominal value . . .; if it is imprisoned in its existence as coin' (ibid.).

While this conclusion was certainly applicable to fiduciary money, as we shall discover in the next chapter, it would not have placed metallic money on the same footing to admit market fluctuations in its value, which, in contrast to the depreciation of 'mere symbols', would only be *temporary*. Yet Marx reaffirmed his original conclusion in the *Critique of Political Economy*, where he highlighted the 'contradiction' Ricardo was said to have erected 'between the metallic value of gold and its value as a medium of circulation' (1859, p. 173 and *passim*).

Money and crises

Marx's objective was clear, namely to refute the constant velocity assumption that lay behind Ricardo's approach not just to the short-run inflationary process but also to the deflation of prices accompanying the so-called 'general glut'. It was only in his investigation into crises that Marx was able to take both phenomena into account, though without overturning the fixed output assumption of Say's law, whose essential premise he continued to share with the classical school as a whole. At the level of simple circulation, the behaviour of hoards was his main preoccupation: 'If the total volume of circulation suddenly expands and the fluid unity of sale and purchase predominates, so that the total amount of prices to be realised grows even faster than does the velocity of circulation of money, then the hoards dwindle visibly'; on the other hand, 'whenever an abnormal stagnation of sale from purchase predominates, then the medium of circulation solidifies into money to a remarkable extent and the reservoirs of the hoarders are filled far above their average level' (1859, pp. 136–7).[62]

Just as a slow-down in velocity might reflect stagnation in the economy, so its acceleration could be a sign of the crisis to come; but '[t]he circulation itself, of course, gives no clue to the origin of this stagnation' it merely puts in evidence the phenomenon itself' (Marx, 1867/94, I, p. 122). For Marx, the fundamental cause of crises was to be sought in the process of *capital accumulation*; yet the very separation of purchase and sale in the circulation of commodities and money implied the 'possibility' of crises and, indeed, formed their precondition (see Kenway, 1980). He therefore served notice at the outset that he would oppose the 'dogma' accepted by Ricardo, 'that every sale is a purchase, and every purchase a sale, therefore the circulation of commodities necessarily implies an equilibrium of sales and purchases'. As far as Marx was concerned, 'If this means that the number of actual sales is equal to the number of purchases, it is mere tautology. But its real purport is to prove that every seller brings his buyer to market with him. Nothing of the kind' (ibid., p. 114).[63] While Marx was therefore able to refute the notion that production created its own demand, he did not at this or any succeeding stage of his analysis question the saving-investment basis of Say's law. Here, the different phases in the 'metamorphosis' of a commodity implied the mere possibility of crises, whose 'conversion . . . into a reality is the result of a long series of relations, that, from our present standpoint of simple circulation, have as yet no existence' (ibid., p. 115).[64]

The next step in comprehending the series of relations which lay behind accumulation and crises was to identify a further role of money in the circulation process. Marx, having analysed the role of money as a measure of value and medium of circulation, defined the additional function of *means of payment*. The development of money in this capacity was motivated by the separation in *time* of purchase and sale, thus extending the polarisation of commodities and money referred to earlier. Just as fiduciary money was to arise from the function of a medium of circulation, so credit had its source in the means of payment (ibid., pp. 127, 139). While this more advanced category properly belongs in later chapters, some preliminary remarks are justified here to clarify the point of difference with Ricardo on deflation, and, correspondingly, on inflation as well.

When, according to Marx, money entered commodity circulation as a means of payment, the seller's price was realised in the form of a legal claim upon money which, until payment, was converted into a reserve fund. This fund was distinguished from a hoard by the fact that it remained *within* circulation; but, of course, the possibility of crisis was thereby accentuated. To the extent that centralised institutions for the liquidation of debt (such as clearing houses) replaced individual reserves with a single balance to be paid, the means of payment could be economised. The classical law of monetary circulation was consequently modified as follows:

> If we now consider the sum total of the money current during a given period, we shall find that, given the rapidity of currency of the circulating medium and of the means of payment, it is equal to the sum of the prices to be realised, plus the sum of the payments falling due,

> minus the payments that balance each other, minus finally the number of circuits in which the same coin serves in turn as means of circulation and of payment. (Ibid., p. 138)

It was therefore unlikely that the money supply and the mass of commodities circulating in a given period would correspond; and, moreover, the debts contracted each day might be incommensurable with the payments falling due. A contradiction was thus implied between, on the one hand, money functioning only ideally as a measure of value when payments offset each other, and, on the other, insofar as outstanding debts had to be discharged, money serving not merely as a medium of exchange but as a unique store of value – 'the individual incarnation of social labour'.

This contradiction, Marx observed, 'comes to a head in those phases of industrial and commercial crises which are known as monetary crises':

> Such a crisis occurs only where the ever-lengthening chain of payments, and an artificial system of settling them, has been fully developed. Whenever there is a general and extensive disturbance of this mechanism, no matter what its cause, money becomes suddenly and immediately transformed, from its merely ideal shape of money of account, into hard cash. . . . On the eve of the crisis, the bourgeois, with the self-sufficiency that springs from intoxicating prosperity, declares money to be a vain imagination. Commodities alone are money. But now the cry is everywhere: money alone is a commodity! (Ibid., pp. 137–8)[65]

Even at the level of simple circulation, therefore, Marx was able to confront Ricardo's denial of the possibility of a 'general glut' of commodities.[66] Moreover, in contrast with Malthus, he located the cause of this glut not in 'under-consumption' by the population but in the *overproduction* of commodities, which in turn expressed the periodic overaccumulation of capital. To follow Marx's investigation of the 'reality' of deflationary crises, and of the mechanism which brought them about, we must look beyond the circulation of commodities and money and take account of the independent movement of capital" '[J]ust as the examination of money . . . has shown that it contained the possibility of crises; the examination of the general nature of capital, even without going further into the actual relations which all constitute prerequisites for the real process of production, reveals this still more clearly' (1963/71, II, p. 493).

While later economists especially those of the Banking School were prepared to admit the periodic overaccumulation of capital, if not its counterpart in the overproduction of commodities, Ricardo consistently refused to recognise either aspect of crises. It was his view that any amount of capital could be employed in a country, since demand was limited only by production.[67] Even in his earliest monetary writings, such as his response to Malthus's review of *High Price of Bullion*, Ricardo maintained that 'no country ever possessed a general glut of all commodities. It is evidently impossible' (1923, p. 48; also 1951/58, I, p. 292, and II, p. 305). There could only be an excess of *particular* commodities, including the monetary metals, which would have the same effect in every case, namely to drive down their relative price. Ricardo thus explained a short-run deflation in the same way as he accounted for inflation; it was due either to a fall in the market price of leading commodities like corn, or to a rise in the market value of gold and silver. In both cases, the specie-flow mechanism would be set into motion with an export of corn and import of specie.

However, at the time Ricardo wrote, major crises affecting the world market were as yet unknown; his denial of their possibility therefore seemed plausible, especially when more visible factors such as bad harvests and the wartime 'continental blockade' – and including those comprised under the rubric of 'sudden changes in the channels of trade' (Ricardo, 1951/58, I, ch. 19) – assumed greater prominence in the public mind. It was left to his successors to try to comprehend the cyclical prosperity and depression of the mid nineteenth century and after. These attempts will be discussed in later chapters in the context of fiduciary money and credit.

Falling rate of profit

Marx rejected Ricardo's short-run deflationary mechanism just as he had opposed his analysis of inflation. Both rested upon a constant velocity assumption which he found to be inconsistent with the behaviour of commodities and money in the circulation process. Furthermore, he argued that inflation and deflation, although reflected in circulation, could only be *explained* by reference to capital accumulation. I shall now examine the mechanism which Marx identified as the immediate cause of crises, which was analysed on the assumption that the value of money was given and that credit had not yet been introduced. This mechanism was the 'tendency of the rate of profit to decline' and the theory Marx devised to explain this tendency became the key to his analysis of inflation (Sweezy, 1970, pp. 147–55). Even Ricardo had recognised the 'natural tendency of profits . . . to fall', at least as a secular phenomenon, and had drawn attention to its potential for 'arrest[ing] all accumulation' (ibid., p. 120). Marx commented approvingly, describing the rate of profit as 'the motive power of capitalist production . . . Hence the concern of the English economists over the decline of the rate of profit. The fact that the bare possibility of this happening should worry Ricardo, shows his profound understanding of the conditions of capitalist production' (1867/94, III, p. 259).

Whereas Ricardo ascribed the falling rate of profit to the fact that 'the natural price of labour has always a tendency to rise' (1951/58, I, p. 93), Marx offered a different reason for the phenomenon. He again traced the source of Ricardo's misconception to the identification of the rate of profit with the rate of surplus value;[68] once the reproduction of constant capital was taken into account along with variable capital, the tendency for the profit rate to fall was seen to have its origin in the increase of social productivity, expressed in a rising organic composition of capital (Marx, ibid., pp. 212–13 and *passim*). Ricardo had also contended that the declining profit rate was 'happily checked at repeated intervals by the improvements in machinery, connected with the production of necessaries' (1951/58, I, p. 120). Marx showed, however, that such improvements, while reducing the value of commodities, tended both to substitute constant for variable capital in the production of those commodities and to accelerate the growth of total capital in relation to surplus value.

Thus, an increase in the rate of surplus value was by no means incompatible with the decline in the rate of profit, though it could operate as a 'counter-acting influence' to this decline if it resulted from an expansion not of 'relative' surplus value due to growing productivity but of 'absolute' surplus value, due, for example, to a lengthening of the working day. Marx therefore felt able to improve significantly upon Ricardo's discussion of this issue:

> The tendency of the rate of profit to fall is bound up with a tendency of the rate of surplus value to rise, hence with a tendency for the rate of labour exploitation to rise. Nothing is more absurd, for this reason, than to explain the fall in the rate of profit by a rise in the rate of wages, although this may be the case by way of an exception. (1867/94, III, p. 240)

At a certain point, so long as 'counteracting influences' to the falling rate of profit were not predominant, the over-accumulation of capital in relation to the existing magnitude of surplus value would appear simultaneously as an overproduction of commodities. Ricardo's justification of his refusal to contemplate such an eventuality was that consumers' 'wants' and 'needs' were inexhaustible and would be afforded simply by an 'increase of production' (1951/58, I, p. 292).[69] This argument could now be swept aside: 'What after all has overproduction to do with absolute needs?

It is only concerned with demand that is backed by ability to pay' (Marx, 1963/71, II, p. 506). In his presentation of the falling rate of profit as the mechanism of crises, however, Marx did not question the assumption he shared with Ricardo, namely an independently fixed level of output. Crises were no more than temporary deviations from 'normal' economic conditions, which were corrected by the general deflation of commodity prices and a corresponding depreciation of capital. As Marx himself pointed out;

> When Adam Smith explains the fall in the rate of profit from an over-abundance of capital, an accumulation of capital, he is speaking of a *permanent* effect and this is wrong. As against this, the transitory over-abundance of capital, overproduction and crises are something different. Permanent crises do not exist. (Ibid., p. 497 fn.)

Marx therefore treated crises as 'momentary and forcible solutions of the existing contradictions' and 'violent eruptions which for a time restore the disturbed equilibrium' (1867/94, III, p. 249).[70] In other words, the deflation of prices associated with overproduction in relation to consumers' purchasing power served to compensate for an earlier process of inflation which contributed both to the postponement of the crisis and to its depth when it could no longer be avoided. If, according to Marx, 'the market prices of the commodities . . . fall far below their cost-prices, the reproduction of capital is curtailed . . . surplus value amassed in the form of money (gold or notes) could only be transferred into capital at a loss. It therefore lies idle as a hoard in the banks or in the form of credit money. . . .' (1963/71, II, p. 494). The inflation which preceded the crisis and mirrored its deflationary aspect appeared, 'when additional capital is produced at a very rapid rate and its reconversion into productive capital increases the demand for all the elements of the latter to such an extent that actual production cannot keep pace with it; this brings about a rise in the prices of all commodities, which enter into the formation of capital' (ibid., pp. 494–5).[71]

Although Marx refused to accept the possibility of a general inflation at the level of simple circulation (provided that the value of money was held constant), he nevertheless conceded its presence in his analysis of capital accumulation. This would be puzzling were it not for Marx's overriding determination to rebut Ricardo's assumption that velocity was fixed. Just as this assumption led to a denial of the possibility of a general glut, so its repudiation by Marx prevented him from recognising the potential disparity between the value and the market value of metallic money when the latter was in excess of circulation needs, and hence the accompanying short-run price adjustment which triggered a return to the long-run position. For Marx to have admitted the possibility of such an adjustment mechanism – together with hoarding and dishoarding – as a consequence of monetary expansion would not necessarily have implied that this expansion was a fundamental cause of inflation.

Once the argument was taken beyond the circulation of commodities and money to the sphere of capitalist production, Marx himself was ready to identify a range of factors which conditioned both monetary expansion and any sustained rise in the price level which might have been connected with it. His reluctance to apply an account of the deviation of the market prices of commodities from their values or prices of production to the money commodity at the beginning of his investigation was only partly explained by his abstraction from market phenomena. There is no doubt, however, that he wished to locate the cause of crises without the complications inevitably imposed by such phenomena. In setting out his assumptions, he insisted that, 'The general conditions of crises, insofar as they are independent of *price fluctuations* (whether these are linked with the credit system or not) as distinct from fluctuations in value, must be explicable from the general conditions of capitalist production' (ibid., p. 515). Yet we have seen that crises are associated with significant price fluctuations.

While the deflation precipitated by overproduction may be understood as a straightforward operation of the laws of supply and demand, the inflation in the period leading up to a crisis is more elusive. Marx observed that:

> Crises are usually preceded by a general inflation in prices of all articles of capitalist production. All of them therefore participate in the subsequent crash and at their former prices they cause a glut in the market. The market can absorb a larger volume of commodities at falling prices, at prices which have fallen below their cost-prices, than it could absorb at their former prices. The excess of commodities is always relative; in other words it is an excess at particular prices. The prices at which the commodities are then absorbed are ruinous for the producer or merchant. (Ibid., p. 505)

In the third volume of *Capital*, Marx postponed the analysis of 'how far a falling rate of profit may coincide with rising prices' (1867/94, III, p. 231) to the discussion of the credit system, since, in his view, the key to inflation was the over-extension of credit in relation to productive capacity. This was also the point of departure for the post-Ricardian economists, who were interested in crises only insofar as they were connected with monetary behaviour. We therefore leave the world of metallic money, where the scope for inflation was limited – both in the long-run by the conditions of production and in the short-run by the pressure for conformity with those long-run conditions – and proceed to the more advanced though dramatically less stable world of fiduciary money and credit.

Part III

Currency and Credit

5 Introduction of Paper Currency

> Had every particular banking company always understood and attended to its own particular interest, the circulation never could have been overstocked with paper money. But every particular banking company has not always understood or attended to its own particular interest, and the circulation has frequently been overstocked with paper money.
>
> Adam Smith, *Wealth of Nations* (1776)

After the 'price revolution' of the sixteenth and seventeenth centuries, the next major episodes of British monetary history had as their central focus the role of fiduciary money and credit. The first of these, the 'bullion controversy', took place as a result of the Napoleonic war inflation at the end of the eighteenth and beginning of the nineteenth centuries; and the second, the 'currency–banking debate', was motivated by the increasingly cyclical character of economic activity towards the middle of the nineteenth century. These disputes were no longer between a pure exchange quantity theory of money on the one hand and classical value theory on the other. The law of monetary circulation had by this time been firmly established. Monetary requirements were determined by the 'supply side' of the equation of exchange, i.e., by the level of output and prices. The questions now raised were whether in a credit or fiduciary system the money supply could exceed (or fall short of) the normal requirements, and, if so, how this excess (or deficiency) was to be measured and what would be the consequences. The answers to these questions implied specific sets of policies.

The division among classical economists mirrored the division over the short-run effects of monetary disturbances in a metallic system. Indeed, it was generally accepted that the economic and analytical importance of the precious metals was not superseded by the development of credit and fiduciary money. The 'necessity of this order', according to Marx, was 'demonstrated theoretically by the fact that everything of a critical nature which Tooke and others hitherto expounded in regard to the circulation of credit money compelled them to hark back again and again to the question of what would be the aspect of the matter if nothing but metal were in circulation' (1867/94, II, p. 115). However, the emergence of a monetary role for valueless paper, once its relationship to a commodity money was no longer secured by legal convertibility, exposed the arbitrariness of Say's law and, as we shall see in the following chapters, consolidated the hold of quantity theory even when convertibility was restored.

By the time the Bank of England suspended cash payments in 1797, a body of principles on the role and behaviour of paper money had already been formed (Hollander, 1911). The collapse of Law's system led to considerable discussion, which culminated in Adam Smith's authoritative exposition of banking in the *Wealth of Nations*. It will be my intention in this chapter to retrace this eighteenth century discussion, whose participants laid the foundation for the classical analysis of currency and credit. As we shall see, three main propositions were to emerge with Smith's imprimatur. First, the view of Cantillon was accepted – as against that of Law and Steuart – that banking could not increase the quantity of capital but only its turnover. This accorded with the given output assumption of Say's law. Second, it was also established that paper money would not depreciate provided its total amount did not exceed the value of gold and silver that would otherwise have circulated at any given level of economic activity.

In other words, the validity of the monetary circulation law was not impaired by the introduction of credit or fiduciary money, though it was eventually deduced from experience that a 'principle of limitation' would have to be devised. This was the object of the third proposition, which stated, more contentiously, that the 'economic convertibility' of paper with metallic money could be maintained not only by enforcing legal convertibility but also by having banks adopt the practice of discounting 'real bills', i.e., securities backed by real assets. It became known as the 'real bills doctrine' (see Green, 1937, vol. 4, pp. 101–2) and was to be repudiated first by Henry Thornton and then by Ricardo and the Currency School, but ultimately rehabilitated as the 'law of reflux' by their Banking School opponents.

CREDIT AND FIDUCIARY MONEY

For the most part, eighteenth-century monetary theory was an attempt to define and classify new economic categories which had evolved with rapid industrialisation and the attendant growth of a modern banking system. I shall begin with credit and fiduciary money, whose point of difference was subsequently disregarded by economists in the nineteenth century at the cost of much analytical and practical confusion. This will allow us to investigate the specific role of credit in the production process and the conditions under which credit instruments circulate as money; and, in the next section, to outline the early development of the 'real bills doctrine', which served as a discretionary limitation operating on the supply of such instruments in the capital market.

In principle, the difference between fiduciary money and credit is clear (see Rist, 1940, pp. 34–43). One is a paper token which replaces, and represents, the monetary metals in the circulation process. The other, although it may function as a means of purchase, is not itself money in its aspect of means of payment; it is only a *legal claim to money*, an obligation which must still be discharged. As Steuart put it, 'real money' is simply coin, 'or a modification of the precious metals', which 'carries along with it its own intrinsic value'. Paper credit, or 'symbolical money', on the other hand, by which he meant 'Bank notes, credit in bank, bills, bonds, merchants' books', etc., is 'an obligation to pay the intrinsic value of certain denominations of money contained in the paper. . . . He who pays in coin, puts the person to whom he pays in the real possession of what he owed; and this done, there is no more place for credit. He who pays in paper puts his creditor in possession only of another person's obligation to make that value good to him: here credit is necessary even after the payment is made' (1767, I, pp. 314–5; II, p. 407).

The different nature of fiduciary money and credit reflected their separate historical and conceptual origins and gave rise to distinct laws of economic behaviour. The relegation of gold and silver to an apparently minor role in the financial system required new thinking about the application and development of classical value theory. The principles evolved in the context of metallic money might no longer operate with automatic effect; moreover, the form they took would depend crucially on the type of financial instruments in circulation and their relationship to the metallic base of the system. The sources of the categories of fiduciary money and credit in the early economic literature is therefore worthy of some mention, especially given the clarity with which they were delineated by some writers (Rist, 1940, ch. 1). This clarity was lost in the heat of the 'bullion controversy' and recovered only later by the leading figures of the Banking School.

To start with, the origin of *fiduciary money* may be traced to the divergence of the face value of coin from its real value, i.e., in the separation of the nominal weight of metallic money from its actual weight, due to clipping, alloying and natural wear and tear (Cannan, 1918, p. 46 ff.)

The function of coin as a medium of circulation was thus contradicted by its substance, which could no longer be equated with the commodities whose prices it was supposed to express.[1] The fact that such worn coin nevertheless continued to circulate as a symbol or token of its official content implied the possibility of its replacement by tokens composed of an entirely different material. Initially, silver, copper and other subsidiary metals of artificially decreed weight were substituted for gold in spheres such as the retail trade which combined small scale transactions with a rapid velocity of currency. Benjamin Franklin was one who noted the growing discrepancy between the intrinsic value of commodity money and its legal denomination:

> At this very time even the silver money in England is obliged to the legal tender for part of its value; that part which is the difference between its real weight and its denomination. Great part of the shillings and sixpences now current are, by wearing, become five, ten, twenty and some of the sixpences even fifty per cent too light. For this difference between the *real* and the *nominal*, you have no intrinsic value; you have not so much as paper, you have nothing. It is the legal tender, with the knowledge that it can easily be repassed for the same value, that makes three-pennyworth of silver pass for sixpence. (Franklin, 1836, II, p. 348)

The outcome of this historical tendency, however, was that inconvertible paper money could be issued by the state and acquire compulsory circulation within an area coterminous with its political sovereignty. Clearly, then, insofar as paper tokens were tokens of *value*, i.e., represented gold (or silver) in the process of commodity exchange, they were necessarily subject to the laws regulating the behaviour of metallic money. Under what circumstances their quantity may be said to conform to the amount of metal which would otherwise circulate is a problem we shall later have to confront. At this point, Berkeley's *Querist* could be answered in the affirmative: 'Whether the denominations being retained, although the bullion gone . . . might not nevertheless . . . a circulation of commerce [be] maintained?' (1750, p. 3).

Just as fiduciary money was derived from the function of money as a medium of circulation, so its role as a means of payment gave rise to *credit*. We must now consider the development of this category and the distinct character of the laws which govern its movement; this will take us beyond the simple circulation of commodities and money to the circulation process of capital.

Credit derived its original impetus as we found in the previous chapter, from the separation in time of the purchase and sale of commodities. A claim to money, or promise to pay, to be settled at some future date, was created in lieu of immediate payment: '*Confidence*, then, is the soul and essence of credit; and in every modification of it, we shall constantly find it built on this basis: but this confidence must have for its object a *willingness* and a *capacity* in the debtor to fulfil his obligations' (Steuart, 1767, II, p. 442). There was a measure of agreement among eighteenth century economists on the role of credit, although, as we shall see, different views were taken of its effects, and, in particular, of its relationship to the price level. Most of these early writers accepted that its fundamental role was to reduce the costs of circulation, both economising money itself, and by accelerating the turnover of capital and hence the process of reproduction as a whole.

To begin with, commercial credit arrangements, which set off one debt against another, might eliminate money from a wide variety of transactions, and restrict it in many others to the payment of a balance due. As Cantillon put it in his *Essai*:

> [T]hese exchanges by valuation seem to economise much cash in circulation, or at least to accelerate its movement by making it unnecessary in several hands through which it would need to pass without this confidence and this method of exchange by valuation. It is not without reason that it is commonly said Commercial Credit makes Money less scarce. . . . [T]he only real money needed for this commerce will be the balance which one owes to the other at the end of the year. Even then this balance may be carried forward to the next year, without the actual payment of any money. (1755, p. 141)

To the extent that these payments were concentrated in one place, money could be further economised by special institutions, such as the *virements*, or clearing house, in medieval Lyons. Cantillon again: 'If the clearings at Lyons in one of its four Fairs amount to eight millions of livres, if they are begun and finished with a single million of ready money, they are doubtless of great convenience in saving the trouble of an infinity of transports of silver from one house to another (ibid., pp. 311–13; see Postan, 1928). It was clear that the growing sophistication of the financial structure would have major implications for the level – and stability – of monetary velocity in the equation of exchange. A given sum of money could now facilitate a higher multiple of transactions within any defined time period.

Case for banking

The development of banking was the next logical step for economic theory, and it was one which, not surprisingly, corresponded with the historical sequence (Andréadès, 1935, pt III; Clapham, 1944, I, ch. 4). Our examination of the principles of banking in this chapter must begin with the eighteenth-century writers, for, having as their subject a credit structure in the early stages of its evolution under industrial capitalism, they were able to grasp these principles in their most elemental form.

The pioneer of modern banking was John Law, that 'reckless, and unbalanced but most fascinating genius' (Marshall, 1923, p. 41 fn.; also Schumpeter, 1954, p. 294 ff.), whose ideas and practical schemes constituted a point of reference for subsequent political economy. Fundamentally a mercantilist, he wanted an expansion of the nation's money supply and saw banking as the most potent means of bringing this about. In his *Money and Trade Considered*, he wrote: 'The use of Banks has been the best method yet practis'd for the increase of Money' (1705, p. 36). I shall return to Law and his practical proposals in the next section. Meanwhile, it may be noted that Cantillon, Law's arch-opponent, took a different view. Bank credit, he argued, like commercial credit, had its effect not upon the quantity of money in a country, but upon its velocity (1755, pp. 143, 301) – although in practice, 'an acceleration or greater rapidity in circulation of money in exchange, is equivalent to an increase of actual money up to a point' (ibid., p. 161).

Of course, when Law spoke of an increase of money, he meant an increase of *capital*; and it was this, among other 'splendid but visionary ideas', which Adam Smith then proceeded to counter with the classical notion of an independently given level of output: 'It is not by augmenting the capital of the country, but by rendering a greater part of that capital active and productive than would otherwise be so, that the most judicious operations of banking can increase the industry of the country' (1776, p;. 243, 245).[2] The role of credit in the banking system, according to Smith, was first of all to intermediate, that is, to convert 'dead stock', or capital which an economic agent was 'obliged to keep by him unemployed, and in ready money, for answering occasional demands', into 'active and productive stock' (ibid., p. 245). In this, he echoed Cantillon, who, while sharing to some extent Law's identification of money and capital, concluded that the proper function of banks was, 'to accelerate the circulation of money and to prevent so much of it from being hoarded as it would naturally be for several intervals' (1755, p. 305).

Second, the monetary metals were likewise seen by Smith as 'dead stock', which might substantially be replaced by paper, thus providing, in the words of the famous metaphor, 'a sort of waggon-way through the air'. The metaphor continued: 'The commerce and industry of the country, however, it must be acknowledged, though they may be somewhat augmented, cannot be altogether so secure, when they are thus, as it were, suspended upon the Daedalian wings of paper money, as when they travel about upon the solid ground of gold and silver' (1776, p. 246). Cantillon expressed the same idea even more cautiously, having just experienced the fiasco of Law's system: 'The Goldsmiths and public Bankers, whose notes pass current in payment, like ready money, contribute also to the speed of circulation, which would be retarded if money were needed in all the payments for which these Notes suffice' (1755, pp. 141–3). However, he did not refer to the additional economic advantages of a reduction in the proportion of social wealth set aside for the maintenance of the money material. Smith argued that, 'the substitution of paper in the room of gold and silver money, replaces a very expensive instrument of commerce with one much less costly, and sometimes equally convenient' (1776, p. 220). He was here adopting the position of Steuart, whose detailed account of banking was an undisguised attempt to rehabilitate the positive features of Law's approach.[3]

Steuart's case in his *Principles* for the more widespread use of credit, or what he called 'symbolical money', initially placed a particular emphasis on the expense saved by society. Since the constant circulation of coin 'insensibly wears it away', thus diminishing the 'real riches' of the country, it appeared desirable that the government should 'call in the metals and deposit them in a treasure' and should 'deliver, in their place, a paper-money having a security on the coin locked up'. While this treasure remained, according to Steuart, 'the paper circulated will carry along with it as real (though not so intrinsic) a value as the coin itself could have done'. Moreover, echoing Law, he maintained that the principal effect of expanding credit would be, 'to encourage consumption, and to increase the demand for the produce of industry' (1767, I, p. 330: see also Law, 1705, p. 102). Steuart's innovative discussion of money and finance, though perhaps ahead of its time, was far more influential than might be presumed from the dearth of acknowledgements in the writings of classical economists. The taint of mercantilism was still too strong for Smith and Ricardo, who quarried his work silently. Yet Marx and the Banking School made every attempt to restore Steuart to favour, just as Steuart himself had rescued Law from misinterpretation and neglect.

Fractional reserve

Steuart's classification of banking functions was a major step forward for monetary analysis. It recognised the value of fractional reserve banking and, for the purposes of our discussion, paved the way for the 'real bills doctrine'.[4] According to Steuart, there were three modes of lending in which banks could engage, given adequate cash reserves. (Their principles of limitation are the subject of the next section and following chapters). The first mode was 'private credit' which was 'established upon a security, real or personal, of value sufficient to make good the obligation of repayment both of capital and interest' (ibid., II, p. 471). In other words, bank notes could be advances upon a mortgage of property. This was the mode of issue favoured by the Bank of Scotland, given the agrarian character of the Scottish economy, and emphasised by Steuart as a lever of industrialisation. By means of private credit, he argued, 'solid property may be melted down' (ibid., p. 478) to satisfy the demand for money:

> Those nations, therefore, who circulate their metals only, confined industry to the proportion of the mass of them. Those who can circulate their lands, their houses, their manufacturers, nay their personal service, even their hours, may produce an encouragement for industry far beyond what could be done by metals only. And this may be done, when the process of industry demands a circulation beyond the power of the metals to perform. (Ibid., I, pp. 315–16)

The second type of lending was 'mercantile credit' which was 'established upon the confidence the lender has, that the borrower, from his integrity and knowledge in trade, may be able to replace the capital advanced, and the interest due during the advance, in terms of agreement' (ibid., p. 472). Here, notes were issued to discount commercial paper, e.g., bills of exchange. This was the central activity of the Bank of England, and it received the greater part of Smith's attention, especially in connection with the real bills doctrine. Steuart pointed out that its main object was 'to multiply circulation, and to furnish the industrious with the means of carrying on their traffic' (ibid., p. 483).

The third type of lending, 'public credit', was 'established upon the confidence reposed in a state, or body politic, who borrow money upon condition that the capital shall not be demandable; but that a certain proportional part of the sum shall be annually paid, either in lieu of interest, or in extinction of part of the capital; for the security of which, a permanent annual fund is appropriated, with a liberty, however, to the state to free itself at pleasure, upon repaying the whole' (ibid., p. 472; also, p. 600). In this case, the bank entered the market for government securities, thus helping to finance the public sector deficit. Notes were 'issued upon the faith of taxes to be paid within the year . . . [T]he collateral security of the state will serve to make up all deficiencies in the amount of taxes. No security, therefore, can be better than the notes of the bank of England, while government subsists' (ibid., pp. 530–1).[5]

This classification of banking functions was adopted explicitly by Smith and subsequent writers and was at least implicit in the accounts of Steuart's eighteenth century predecessors. The real points of contention were, first, the criteria on which loans were advanced, i.e., the nature of the collateral (especially in the case of mercantile credit), and, second, the extent to which the deposit base of the banking system could actually support a credit superstructure. Both had implications for a theory of price inflation, which encompassed a fixed level of output. The first point can be left to the following section, but a few words need to be said on the second. Only Cantillon made his view absolutely clear on the role of cash deposits in fractional reserve banking operations. He supposed that 100 000 ounces of silver were deposited at a bank in return for notes:

> In these circumstances the Banker will often be able to lend 90 000 ounces of the 100 000 he owes throughout the year and will only need to keep in hand 10 000 ounces to meet all the withdrawals. . . . [A]s fast as one thousand ounces are demanded of him in one direction, a thousand are brought to him from another. It is enough as a rule for him to keep in hand the tenth part of his deposits. (1755, pp. 299–301)

That is to say, lending had to represent a deduction from the cash in hand, up to a certain limit set by the reserve ratio.

The approach of Steuart and Smith, on the other hand, was more ambiguous. Steuart agreed with Cantillon that bank deposits in coin entailed a 'constant fluctuation of payments', which nevertheless left the greater proportion available for lending: 'By long practice in the trade, this sum of money becomes determinate: let us call it the *average-money* in the hands of the bank' (1767, II, p. 526). It was by no means clear, however, whether Steuart, or indeed Smith (1776, p. 221), conceived of this 'average-money' as a *fund* for redistribution, or as itself a *reserve base* for multiple credit expansion. If the latter, the bank in Cantillon's example (retaining the assumption of a 1:10 reserve ratio), would be able to issue notes up to a total value of 900 000 ounces of silver. This interpretation received support from two aspects of Steuart and Smith's discussion. In the first place, both envisaged that bank loans were extended solely in the form of notes; and, second, the reserve ratios they regarded as appropriate (1:3 and 1:5 respectively) were higher than would be the case if the note issue required one hundred per cent backing from, say, the 900 000 ounces of silver, and lower than if cash deposits were directly re-lent in the manner suggested by Cantillon. The development of this modern conception of fractional reserve banking – however hesitant – was an important motivation for the formulation of a real bills doctrine.

THE REAL BILLS DOCTRINE

In this section, I shall continue my examination of credit-money, at least insofar as it corresponds with that portion of the money supply constituted by bank notes, and trace the emergence of the real bills doctrine. This doctrine was the forerunner of the nineteenth century 'law of reflux', which will be considered in later chapters. The essence of the doctrine was that, provided notes were issued by the banking system on sound security, or 'real bills', which were nominal titles to a corresponding magnitude of value, their quantity had to conform in the long-run to monetary circulation requirements (see Green, 1937, vol. 4, pp. 101–2). These requirements were given, as we have seen, by output, (determined by the level of accumulation) and prices (calculated on the basis of the theory of value). Moreover, any short-run monetary excess associated with an inflation of commodity prices would be due not to overissue, but to 'overtrading' in the real economy.

The evolution of this Smithian orthodoxy had important implications for the positions taken in the later 'bullion controversy', where Ricardo and his followers firmly rejected the real bills doctrine in favour of a quantity theory account of the relationship between money and prices. Again, the origins of this controversy may be found in Petty (1899, I, p. 53), but I shall begin with the true pioneer of paper money, John Law. I shall then proceed to the opposition to this form of credit from Hume, the qualifications introduced by Cantillon, the defence of Law by Steuart and finally the elaborate exposition of the principles of note circulation by Smith.

Law is variously condemned and celebrated for having promoted either an erroneous theory of credit or a conceptual breakthrough which suffered from misapplication. Neither claim is completely untrue. Certainly, it has never been denied that Law's main theoretical contribution, *Money and Trade Considered*, is a classic in the history of banking. Taken together with the practical implementation of its central thesis in what became known as Law's 'system', it represents for several reasons a point of departure for eighteenth century political economy. As we have seen, Law was a mercantilist. He began his investigation by locating the cause of Scotland's economic backwardness in the 'great Scarcity of Money' (1705, p. 3; also p. 117) with which the country was afflicted. The confusion in his book, therefore, was less between money and credit than between money and *capital*.

According to Law, 'Domestick trade depends upon the Money. A greater Quantity employes more People than a lesser Quantity'. It was futile for governments to rely on legislation 'for Employing the Poor or Idle' without adequate money available to pay their wages. Law was driven to one conclusion: 'They may be brought to Work on Credit, and that is not practicable, unless the Credit have a circulation, so as to supply the Workman with necessaries; if that's suppos'd, then that Credit is Money, and will have the same effects, on Home, and Foreign Trade' (ibid., p. 13).[6]

Law's radical approach thus envisaged the creation of credit to make up the shortfall of metal. He rejected traditional mercantilist measures such as trade protection and exchange controls, although he did anticipate an expanded role for 'drawbacks' (state subsidies) once the money supply was sufficient to realise the productive potential of the economy. Moreover, following Petty (1899, I, p. 84 ff.), he delivered such a powerful indictment of devaluation and debasement of the standard as a means of augmenting the available stock of money that even his most fervent critics were disarmed.

Although the solution to the money shortage lay in the development of credit, Law did not place much faith in ordinary banking operations 'where the Money might be pledg'd, and Credit given to the Value, which past in Payments, and facilitat Trade' (ibid., p. 36). To start with, Law wanted a narrowing of the credit margin, i.e., fractional reserve banking. He gave the example of the Bank of Amsterdam:

> By the Constitution of this Bank, the whole Sum for which Credit is given, ought to remain there, to be ready at demand; Yet a Sum is lent by the Managers for a Stock to the Lumbar, and 'tis thought they lend great Sums on other occasions. . . . The certain good it does, will more than ballance the hazard, tho once in two or three years it failed in payment; providing the Sums lent be well secured: Merchants who had Money there, might be disappointed of it at demand, but the Security being good, and Interest allowed; Money would be had on a small Discount, perhaps at the Par. (Ibid., pp. 37–8)

Already we find Law expounding a rudimentary real bills doctrine: so long as loans were 'well secured', the bank reserve might be reduced to a fraction of its advances. Other examples given of this practice were the Bank of England and Bank of Scotland, whose recent suspension of payments was ascribed to an unfounded rumour that it planned to 'raise the money', i.e., devalue the unit in which the notes were denominated.

Law's system

Had the discussion ended at this point, it might still have been regarded as an acceptable account of banking procedures, albeit with a mercantilist flavour. But Law, while recognising the constraint set upon the note issue by the metallic reserve requirement, refused to be content with this state of affairs: 'Credit that promises a Payment of Money, cannot well be extended beyond a certain proportion it ought to have with the Money. And we have so little Money, that any Credit could be given upon it, would be inconsiderable' (ibid., p. 60; also, pp. 39, 58). It was Law's attempt to 'break through' the metallic barrier that gave him, in Marx's words, 'the pleasant character mixture of swindler and prophet' (1867/94, III, p. 441).

Since bullion, according to Law, was the key factor restraining economic activity, an alternative money would have to be found. Apart from the technical limitation imposed upon credit expansion by the reserve ratio, the precious metals suffered from a variety of 'defects', which made their demonetisation essential. Their main defect was their liability to changes in value. This was due to '[t]he Power the Magistrate has to alter the Money in its Denomination or Fineness' (ibid., p. 62), and second, to variations in demand and supply conditions. Law pointed out that silver coin had been debased by the state over at least the past century, and depreciated by the influx of American bullion, which increased the wealth only of its immediate recipients: 'When the Spaniards bring Money or Bullion into Europe, they lessen its value, but gain by bringing it; because they have the whole benefit of the greater Quantity, and only bear a share of the lesser value' (ibid., p. 76).

Thus Law came to his famous proposal to empower a commission to lend inconvertible notes on land security. Since these notes were available on the presentation of silver, and were related, at least initially, to the silver price of land, they would be equivalent to silver, while at the same time meeting the 'needs of trade':

> The Paper-money propos'd will be equal in value to Silver, for it will have a value of Land pledg'd, equal to the same Sum of Silver-money, that it is given out for. . . . This Paper-money, will not fall in value as Silver-money has fallen, or may fall: Goods or Money fall in value, if they increase in Quantity, or if the Demand lessens. But the Commission giving out what Sums are demanded, and taking back what Sums are offer'd to be return'd; This Paper-money will keep its value, and there will be as much Money as there is occasion, or imployment for, and no more. (Ibid., p. 89)

Here Law anticipated the operation of the nineteenth century law of reflux, that is, the return of superfluous notes to the issuer.

The commission, responding to public demand, had to issue notes to those who required them so long as their collateral was genuine: '[I]f the Commission do not give out Money when it is demanded, where good security is offer'd; 'tis a hardship on the Person who is refus'd, and a Loss to the Country: For few if any borrow Money to keep by them; and if employ'd it brings a Profit to the Nation, tho the Employer losses' (ibid., p. 90). It also had to receive deposits from those whose notes were in excess of their current requirements: 'If the Commission did not take back what Sums were offer'd to be return'd, it were a hardship on the Money'd Man, who has a Sum payed him, and does not know how to employ it; and the Quantity being greater than Demand for it, it would fall in value' (ibid.). Law clearly recognised that an overextension of credit-money might produce a fall in its value, and hence a rise in the level of commodity prices. However, he did not seem to be aware that excess issue might be the result of what Smith was to call 'overtrading', whereby not money but capital was borrowed without any reasonable prospect of recoupment. This, of course, obliged a bank to take restrictive action even if the original source of the problem was not within its control.

Despite the transformation at this time of land into an alienable commodity, its use as backing for the notes could not lead to the replacement of metal as the universal equivalent. As was shown by the implementation of Law's ideas by the Duke of Orleans, silver remained the standard by which the bank notes were judged. Initially, their redemption in specie was guaranteed, which meant that even temporary depreciation was impossible; indeed, confidence was such that the paper was at a premium.[7] The key factors in the subsequent collapse were the exchange of notes for the stock of the Mississippi company, a purely speculative venture fostered by the government; the suspension of cash payments as public confidence began to wane; the conversion of the *modus operandi* of the bank from credit to fiduciary issue, heralded by the change of name from the Banque Générale to the Banque Royale; and, finally, the breath-taking 50 per cent revaluation of the paper.[8]

Despite Law's exaggerated view of the power of credit, and the naivete of his proposal to demonetise silver, his positive analytical contribution outlived its less than successful application to the conditions of early eighteenth century France. He spelt out the major implication of the real bills doctrine, namely that 'good security' rather than legal convertibility should be the criterion for the issue of notes, whose quantity would be regulated by public demand. The initial impact of Law's System on the economy of France was beyond dispute. Steuart, for example, pointed to 'the surprising effects of Mr Law's bank established in France, at the time when there was neither money or credit in the kingdom'. Within two years, the 'superior genius of this man' had 'revived industry; he established confidence; and shewed to the world, that while the landed property of a nation is in the hands of the inhabitants, and while the lower classes are willing to be industrious, money never *can* be wanting' (Steuart, 1767, II, p. 497).[9]

Problems would only arise when it was not circulating media that were 'wanting' but real capital and banks were used to circumvent the process of production. Again, for Steuart, while credit might be 'no more than confidence', it was confidence which had to be established upon a 'solid foundation'; without a plan for the proper regulation of the 'huge fabric' of credit, schemes such as those of Law could come badly unstuck. Steuart's analysis was perhaps the most appropriate epitaph not just for Law's experiment but for the many like it which were to unfold in ensuing decades:

> When such a plan is once established, confidence will find a basis in the property of every individual who profits by it. When it is not established, credit will appear like a meteor: intelligent and crafty men will avail themselves of it, and dazzle the eyes of the public, with gilded schemes of opulence and prosperity: mankind will fly to industry, confidence will be established; but as there will be no method of determining the bounds of this confidence, the promoters of the scheme will profit of the delusion: confidence will vanish; and the whole will appear to have been a mystery, a dream. Is not this a representation of many projects set on foot since the beginning of this century? What were the South Sea's and Mississippi's but an abuse of confidence? Had

ever the *cause* of confidence been examined into, would ever such extravagant ideas have arrived at the height they did? (Ibid., pp. 438–9)

An 'anti-system'

There were several types of response to the collapse of Law's system. One was to abstract altogether from value and its development in the form of credit. As we saw earlier, this was the approach taken by the Physiocrats, who confined their analysis to material production, though within the sphere of landed property. Another response was simply to reject the development of a banking system, a view forcefully propounded by Hume. As inevitable as Hume's condemnation, however, was Steuart's defence not only of paper credit in general, but also of the particular form promoted by Law. Ultimately, it fell to Smith to isolate those aspects of Law's argument which were valid and to develop the principles of a modern credit structure.

To begin with, Cantillon provided the point of departure both for Physiocratic theory and for the analysis of Smith by emphasising the limited role of credit in the economy. Although he did not mention Law by name, almost every part of his exposition is directed against some or other feature of his System. Indeed, it would not be going too far to call the *Essai* an 'anti-System' (Rist, 1940, p. 73). Cantillon accepted that the major proportion of bank deposits could be re-lent upon a reserve adequate to meet withdrawals. But he refused even to contemplate loans in excess of this ratio, no matter how well secured. The proper function of a bank was to intermediate, i.e., to reduce the need for cash holdings by producers. It was simply not possible to eliminate cash altogether: 'Silver alone is the true sinews of circulation' (1755, p. 319). The metallic reserve remained for Cantillon the basis of the credit system. Furthermore, irrespective of lending criteria, excess issue of bank notes would lend to a commensurate price inflation and, in the subsequent retrenchment, a period of deflation:

> An abundance of fictitious and imaginary money causes the same disadvantages as an increase of real money in circulation, by raising the price of Land and Labour, or by making works and manufactures more expensive at the risk of subsequent loss. But this furtive abundance vanishes at the first gust of discredit and precipitates disorder. (Ibid., p. 311)

While Cantillon provided a vivid description of the fate of the Banque Royale, he did not consider whether notes could be overextended before the limit of the reserve ratio was reached, or, indeed, whether they might be incompatible with a stable price level beyond it. In other words, he gave no thought to the potential application of a real bills doctrine. He was mainly interested in the dangers of open market operations to prop up such schemes as those fostered by the South Sea Company:

> The excess bank notes, made and issued on these occasions, do not upset the circulation, because being used for the buying and selling of stock they do not serve for household expenses and are not changed into silver. But if some panic or unforeseen crisis drove the holders to demand silver from the Bank the bomb would burst and it would be seen that these are dangerous operations. (Ibid., p. 323)

If Cantillon took a more sceptical view than Law of the advantages of credit, Hume's attitude was hostile, though not unequivocal. Applying quantity theory to the 'counterfeit money' created by banks, he focused upon the inevitable rise in prices: '[T]o endeavour artificially to increase such a credit, can never be the interest of any trading nation; but must lay them under disadvantages, by increasing money beyond its natural proportion to labour and commodities, and thereby heightening their price to the merchant and manufacturer' (1752, p. 169). As a further consequence, the credit expansion would 'either banish a great part of those precious metals, or prevent their farther increase' (ibid., p. 189). Therefore, in order to 'cut off much of the dealings of private bankers and money-jobbers', Hume advocated a public bank which would be directed to maintain a 100 per cent reserve ratio: '[N]o bank could be more advantageous than such a one circulating coin, as is usual, by returning part of its treasure into commerce. . . . [T]he national advantage, resulting from the low price of labour and the destruction of paper credit, would be a sufficient compensation' (ibid., p. 169).[10]

By contrast, Steuart devoted a substantial part of his *Principles* to a study of credit; he presented a detailed defence of Law's system – at least as it was originally conceived – and a sharp rejoinder to Hume's *Essays*, which were 'neither more nor less than a project to destroy credit' (1767, II, p. 351). Having rejected the quantity theory interpretation of the connection between the price level and *metallic* money, Steuart now denied its application to paper credit. Again, much of his analysis was perceptive, but we shall find it lacking in precisely those elements which gave Smith's exposition its strength. Steuart managed to avoid the excesses of Law's grand design: he did not assimilate money and capital in this context, and, unlike Law, he laid down prudential requirements based upon a metallic reserve – as well as a real bills doctrine. The unsystematic nature of his presentation, however, makes one wary of attaching too much significance to individual propositions, and what follows must to some extent reorder his argument.

Lending criteria

Throughout the *Principles*, Steuart consistently emphasised the favourable effect of credit, and especially of a developed banking structure, upon economic activity. Credit performed two important operations: first, it activated hoards, redistributing existing coin to productive employments; and, second, it substituted for coin where the latter fell short of legitimate commercial needs. For Steuart, therefore, it was the role of government to 'facilitate circulation, by drawing into the hands of the public what coin there is in the country, . . . and [to] supply the actual deficiency of the metals, by such a proportion of paper-credit, as may abundantly supply the deficiency' (ibid., I, p. 326). Once such credit took the form of bank notes, or 'symbolical money', it was clear that the precious metals might be entirely replaced in commodity circulation. This had the immediate effect of saving the cost to society of the money material, a consequence later emphasised by Smith. The corollary, noted in the previous section, was that this operation would free resources and stimulate demand.[11]

In addition, Steuart accepted Law's idiosyncratic rationale for the demonetisation of the precious metals – their replacement by paper credit would fulfil his search for a unit of account of 'invariable value' (see above p. 44). As far as Steuart was concerned, the advantage of 'putting intrinsic value into that substance which performs the function of money of account' was compensated by the instability of that value due to variations in supply and demand. On the other hand, the advantage obtained from the stability of paper was compensated by 'the defect it commonly has of not being at all times susceptible of realization into solid property, or intrinsic value'. The solution, therefore, was to make paper money 'circulate upon metallic or land security' (ibid., II, pp. 419–20).

Steuart did not himself suggest a land bank along the lines mooted by Law, but he did treat land collateral as the foundation of the credit system. This was in contrast with Smith who, in reflecting more developed conditions of production, attached greater significance to lending on the security of commercial paper. Steuart was himself aware of this type of note issue and he advocated a rudimentary real bills doctrine which is worthy of examination, not least because it anticipated the main elements of Smith's presentation.

Steuart first attributed all bank advances in the form of notes to what he called banks of circulation, as opposed to banks of deposit which conducted book entry transfers. This was a wholly artificial distinction, as the author himself realised (ibid., p. 476). Nevertheless, it was adopted by Ricardo and the Currency School, and, once incorporated into the 1844 Bank Charter Act, became part of the legislative framework of British banking. The more substantial distinction was one we have already come across between private, mercantile and public credit, the three methods of lending by the banks of circulation (ibid., p. 471). Private credit, which was extended on the security of 'solid property', was given the responsibility of conducting 'the great national circulation' (ibid., p. 485). Land was identified as the primary component of such property, though Steuart added the rider that feudal burdens 'restricting the alienation of land-property, be dissolved' (ibid., 327; also, p. 475).

In this manner, bank notes issued on the basis of private credit fulfilled 'the mass of ready-money demands' (ibid., p. 496). If, however, the notes were superfluous to the needs of circulation, they would, according to Steuart, be 'realised' at the bank. By this he meant 'either the converting of it into gold and silver, which is the money of the world; or the placing of it in such a way as to produce a perpetual fund of annual interest' (ibid., p. 445); in the former case, the metals would be hoarded or invested abroad (ibid.). Given the possibility of notes returning on banks for payment, Steuart recommended an adequate specie reserve, although, '[n]othing but experience can enable them to determine the proportion between the coin to be kept in their coffers, and the paper in circulation' (ibid., p. 497). Thus, the reserve performed a dual function; in addition to meeting domestic obligations it had also to be available to liquidate international debts.[12]

Steuart rejected contraction of the note issue as a measure to accompany an external gold drain. So long as collateral was offered, the bank was obliged to accommodate the demand for money: 'Now if the bank, from a terror of being drained of coin, should refuse to issue notes upon new credits, for the demands of domestic circulation; in this case, I say, they fail in their duty to the nation, as banks, and hurt their own interest' (ibid., p. 502). The collateral had, of course, to represent real value; otherwise, it was not just a 'circulating equivalent' that the bank lent but *capital*: 'When paper is issued by a bank for no value received, the security of such paper stands upon the original capital of the bank alone' (ibid., p. 480). Since capital in the form of specie would quickly be exhausted if the bank were to persist with such advances, Steuart concluded that, 'the solidity of a bank which lends upon private security, does not so much depend upon the extent of their original capital, as upon the good regulations they observe in granting credit' (ibid., p. 482). This applied equally to mercantile credit. Steuart's formulation here touched upon the essence of the real bills doctrine.

Clearly, if bank lending was to take place exclusively upon the security of property in existence at the time of the loan, merchants and manufacturers would have little access to it. Steuart therefore advocated a secondary banking system which would discount commercial paper such as bills of exchange. Invoking the principles previously developed under the head of private credit, he pointed out that, 'Credit therefore must have a *real*, not an *imaginary* object to support it; . . . although I allow that in all operations of *mercantile* credit, there must be something left to chance and accident; yet this chance must bear a due proportion to the extraordinary profits reasonably to be expected from the undertaking' (ibid., p. 439). This strikingly modern view could hardly be described as reckless, even if there was more than a hint of complacency: 'The greatest risk the bank runs, is in discounting bad bills', but it acquired 'so perfect a knowledge' of its clients' business that the likelihood of default was kept to a minimum (ibid., p. 531).

The bank was in continuous receipt of cash deposits, of which only a small proportion was required to meet the flow of withdrawals. A considerable, and, in the long-run, stable, quantity of bullion was therefore available for mercantile credit. As we have seen, Steuart called this the 'average-money' of the bank. It made no difference whether the loan was advanced in notes or coin, for, so long as it was restricted to real bills, it simply fulfilled the needs of trade and could not be characterised as excessive: '[T]o this I repeat again, because of the importance of the subject, that notes issued to support the demand of circulation can never return upon the bank, so as to form a demand for coin; and if they do return, it must be in order to extinguish the securities granted by those who have credit in the bank' (ibid., p. 507). This was the key proposition of Steuart's analysis in the context of our inquiry. Bank lending governed by real bills criteria *could not act upon prices in the long-run*; rather, it passively adjusted to legitimate commercial needs.

The main defects of Steuart's approach were, first, his failure to determine the long-run position from a classical standpoint, and, second, his refusal to consider short-run overexpansion due to excess demand in the real economy, i.e., 'overtrading'. Although Steuart made some progress in identifying the main features of the real bills doctrine, his approach was ultimately limited by a demand and supply framework. He was therefore unable to distinguish the long-run from the short-run – both were governed by the *same* principles. Smith was the first to advance the doctrine on the basis of classical political economy.

Smith's new orthodoxy

Smith provided the authoritative interpretation of the real bills doctrine, and prepared the ground for the Tooke-Fullarton law of reflux. Marx called his views on paper money 'original and profound' (1859, p. 168; cf. Schumpeter, 1954, p. 367; Vickers, 1975). These were both a synthesis and a development of previous ideas; indeed, the mark of Steuart was evident in the argument, but never acknowledged. This argument was concentrated in the chapter on money as a 'branch of the general stock' in Book II of the *Wealth of Nations*, which could be appealed to for support by both sides of the subsequent 'bullion controversy'. It is well then to have a clear picture of its analytical content.

First, as we have already seen, the role of bank credit, according to Smith, was to increase not the quantity of capital but only its turnover (1776, pp. 245–6). Output was fixed by the level of accumulation, which for all the classical economists included the speed of its turnover. Credit had the effect both of reducing the magnitude of reserve funds which economic agents needed to hold, and, of allowing the money material itself – treated as an element of circulating capital and an unproductive portion of the social wealth – to be displaced by paper (ibid.). Bullion might thus be confined to the role of a bank reserve, and, in an example given by Smith, 'the whole circulation' could be 'conducted with a fifth part only of the gold and silver which would otherwise have been requisite' (ibid., p. 221).

With the growing tempo of industrialisation, Smith, unlike Steuart, gave predominance to commercial security over land security as a basis for bank lending, although he appreciated the impetus transmitted by the latter to Scotland's less developed economy.[13] He followed Steuart, however, in arguing that the overissue of notes could not take place if they were advanced upon 'real' bills of exchange, i.e., those 'drawn by a real creditor upon a real debtor', as opposed to 'fictitious' bills, i.e., those 'for which there was properly no real creditor but the bank which discounted it, nor any real debtor but the projector who made use of the money' (ibid. p. 239; also p. 231).

When a banker discounted fictitious bills, the borrowers were clearly 'trading, not with any capital of their own, but with the capital which he advances to them' (ibid.). When, on the other hand, real bills were discounted, bank notes were merely substituted for a substantial proportion of the gold and silver which would otherwise have been idle, and therefore available for circulation (ibid., p. 231; see Hobson, 1913, p. 76 and *passim*). The quantity of notes was thus equivalent to the maximum value of the monetary metals that would circulate in their absence at a given level of economic activity: 'The whole paper money of every kind which can easily circulate in any country never can exceed the value of the gold and silver, of which it supplies the place, or which (the commerce being supposed the same) would circulate there, if there was not paper money' (ibid., p. 227).[14]

This important development of the classical circulation law applied to credit and fiduciary money alike, with the difference that in the latter case overissue in the short-run might result in a *permanent* depreciation of the paper. Credit-money, on the other hand, which was exchanged for real bills could never be in long-run excess: 'The coffers of the bank, so far as its dealings are confined to such customers, resemble a water-pond, from which, though a stream is continually running out, yet another is continually running in, fully equal to that which runs out; so that, without any further care or attention, the pond keeps always equally, or very near equally full' (ibid., p. 231). Under these circumstances, Smith maintained, an increase in the money supply could have no effect on prices; indeed, the analogy with the initial replacement of the precious metals by paper money was complete:

> The increase of paper money, it has been said, by augmenting the quantity, and consequently diminishing the value of the whole currency, necessarily augments the money price of commodities. But as the quantity of gold and silver, which is taken from the currency, is always equal to the quantity of paper which is added to it, paper money does not necessarily increase the quantity of the whole currency. (Ibid., p. 249.)[15]

It was only in the short-run that, for Smith, bank notes could become superfluous to requirements. This was attributed not to overissue by the banks themselves, but rather to a level of demand for credit by the non-bank public whose nominal value was not matched by the real or potential value of output: 'The over-trading of bold projectors . . . has been the original cause of this excessive circulation of paper money' (ibid., p. 231).[16] Provided the notes were convertible, then, in accordance with his analysis of the metallic system, Smith maintained that only a determinate sum could remain in the 'channel of circulation' alongside gold and silver: 'Whatever, therefore, is poured into it beyond this sum cannot run in it, but must overflow' (ibid., p. 222). With the level of output independently fixed, it was clear that the 'annual produce cannot be immediately augmented by those operations of banking' (ibid., p. 221); yet Smith nowhere even considered the possibility of a short-run transitional depreciation of paper and bullion together, which would be reflected in a a corresponding rise in the market prices of commodities (see Rist, 1940, p. 89). Any excess notes were thought simply to return upon the banks for gold and silver, which would then 'be sent abroad, in order to seek that profitable employment which it cannot find at home', thus freeing resources for 'carrying on a new trade; domestic business being now converted into a fund for this new trade' (ibid., p. 222).

On the other hand, if the bank notes were *inconvertible*, Smith recognised, as we shall see, that they might depreciate *permanently* in relation to *all* commodities, including bullion (ibid., p. 252). A drain of bullion from the banks therefore necessarily indicated an overextension of credit-money in the form of convertible paper. Smith further argued that banks could not remain passive in this situation:

> A banking company which issues more paper than can be employed in the circulation of the country, and of which the excess is continually returning upon them for payment, ought to increase the quantity of gold and silver which they keep at all times in their coffers, not only in proportion to this excessive increase of their circulation, but in a much greater proportion; their notes returning upon them much faster than in proportion to the excess of their quantity. (Ibid., p. 228)

It was therefore the role not of government but of the banks themselves to regulate the note issue with a view both to their profitability and to the danger of insolvency; indeed, Smith's somewhat complacent hypothesis was that the general interest of stable monetary management would be best served merely by each individual bank pursuing its 'own particular interest' (ibid., p. 229). He concluded with Law's reckless scheme as fresh in his memory as more recent malpractices: 'Upon every account, therefore, the attention of government never was so unnecessarily employed, as when directed to watch over the preservation or increase of the quantity of money in any country' (ibid., p. 330).

To summarise, then, the quantity of paper money – whether credit or fiduciary in character – that could circulate without incurring depreciation was not permitted to exceed the value of the gold and silver which would otherwise have circulated at the same level of economic activity. The case of fiduciary money will be examined shortly. Credit-money, with which we have been concerned in this section, would 'automatically' conform to the above criterion so long as it was issued on the basis of real bills, i.e., titles to value currently in existence or in the process of creation. At any given level of velocity and output, therefore, the supply of paper money in long-run circulation would depend upon the price level. Only in the short-run would excess demand drive up market prices through the vehicle of credit. Although the eighteenth-century writers did not investigate this short-run phenomenon – sometimes known as a 'credit-inflation' – in any depth, it became a central issue in the currency–banking debate, which I discuss at a later stage.

6 Theory of the Fiduciary System

> There is no point more important in issuing paper money, than to be fully impressed with the effects which follow from the principle of limitation of quantity.
>
> Ricardo, *Principles of Political Economy* (1817)

In the previous chapter, I have examined the development of eighteenth century monetary analysis. The period began with the inflationary collapse of Law's System and ended with Smith's succinct presentation of classical doctrine in the *Wealth of Nations*. The suspension of cash payments by the Bank of England in 1797 following the outbreak of the Napoleonic war opened a new phase of price inflation – or, more precisely, several distinct phases – and rekindled theoretical debate. This inflation was accompanied by a rise in the market price of bullion over its mint price, i.e., a depreciation of paper currency in terms of the monetary standard, a phenomenon which could not have existed when convertibility was enforced by law. The central problem was to explain the appearance of a premium on bullion, and to find a principle whose practical implementation would restore and maintain 'economic convertibility', thus ensuring that the bank notes conformed to the laws of metallic currency I have already outlined. It was not surprising, therefore, that the first decade of the nineteenth century should have been, in Marx's words, 'hardly more prolific of war bulletins than of monetary theories' (1859, p. 81).

The debate surrounding the Bullion Report of 1810 is now associated almost exclusively with Ricardo's formidable contribution. Indeed, there can be little doubt that his 'exposition of the theory of the currency was that upon which the more scientific part of the controversy turned' (Tooke, 1838/57, IV, p. 100). Yet it should not go unremarked that this controversy was initially shaped, and the battle lines drawn, in a series of pamphlets by writers such as Walter Boyd, John Wheatley and Lord King (see Hollander, 1911; Viner, 1937).

Most prominent among them was Henry Thornton, whose *Inquiry into the Nature and Effects of the Paper Credit of Great Britain* may be seen as a bridge between the monetary orthodoxies of the eighteenth and nineteenth centuries. Indeed, it would not be going too far to say that the appearance of this important but largely forgotten work in 1802 'marks the beginning of a new epoch in the development of monetary theory' (Hayek, Introduction to Thornton, 1802, p. 36). Thornton's book is the subject of the first section of the present chapter. Its immediate purpose was to defend the Bank of England against the charge of overissue, rightly attributing the depreciation of notes to specific and temporary factors; yet it rejects the real bills doctrine as a long-run principle of limitation under conditions of inconvertibility in favour of direct regulation by the monetary authorities. I shall argue that this latter principle, while clearly relevant to a fiduciary system, had little application to the credit-money of the Bank Restriction. This is exemplified by the contradiction in Thornton's analysis between his abstract quantity theory on the one hand and his concrete interpretation of the actual events on the other.

In the second section of this chapter, it will be shown that Ricardo was able to overcome this contradiction – to the advantage of quantity theory – as a result of his consistent adherence to Say's law. In effect, however, he too conducted an analysis not of bank notes advanced upon loan, but of a fiduciary issue. As Rist points out:

> This use of forced paper currency . . . is the origin of all the ambiguities and controversies in the years following the Napoleonic wars. The confusion between bank-notes and money, between credit instruments and standard money, . . . was considerably strengthened. All the efforts which Tooke was to make twenty years later to distinguish between paper money and bank-notes were met by the affirmation that the forced paper currency issued by the Bank of England differed from the ordinary bank-note in one respect only; its non-convertibility into bullion. The misunderstanding arose out of the special conditions in which forced currency was operated in England; that is probably the chief reason why the correct theory of bank-notes and credit encountered so many obstacles in that country. (1940, p. 132)

The confusion of credit with a forced currency persisted even when convertibility was restored in 1821; it was expressed in the 'currency principle', which, as we shall see, was presented as a simple extension of the Ricardian view. For Ricardo himself, however, it was only when the link with commodity money was *severed* that the 'value' of the monetary unit became wholly dependent upon its quantity. In his analysis, the classical theory of value retained its practical validity, but in a new guise. Ricardo's principle of limitation which, like Thornton, he championed in opposition to the prevailing real bills doctrine, was an attempt to approximate the value of commodity money by means of direct quantitative control. This was the strict application of a short-run quantity theory, irrespective of the modifying economic circumstances called into play by Thornton. We shall find, as did Ricardo's opponents, that the mere recitation of these circumstances was not a sufficient basis upon which to mount a challenge to the 'classical monetary orthodoxy'. Lacking a theory of output, these opponents were unable to offer an alternative account of the relationship between money and the price level.

THORNTON'S PAPER CREDIT

At the time of the Bank Restriction, Smith's monetary views had become firmly established as the conventional wisdom of bankers and economists. The quantity of paper money of any kind, it was contended, ought not to exceed the value of gold and silver which would otherwise circulate in its absence at the same level of velocity, output and prices. This much at least of Smith's analysis was to be upheld by Ricardo, and later by the Banking School and Marx. Smith was, of course, primarily concerned with bank notes, or credit-money freely convertible into specie. Under these circumstances, as we have seen, lending on the security of real bills formed both a necessary and a sufficient long-run check against overissue by the bank. Furthermore, in the short term, it acted as a stabilising force, correcting any deviation of the note issue from normal circulation requirements.

The onset of war, however, precipitated a suspension of convertibility which put the real bills doctrine in dispute. Smith offered little explicit guidance on the behaviour and regulation of *inconvertible* bank notes. For him, the problem simply did not arise. Convertible notes were 'equal in value to gold and silver money; since gold and silver money can at any time be had for it' (1776, p. 249). There was no possibility, therefore, of a long-run depreciation either of notes in relation to specie or of notes and specie taken together; an increase in the quantity of paper money, all other things being equal, would merely signify the replacement of an equivalent amount of the precious metals.

Smith allowed two exceptions to this rule. The first was where the bank notes contained an 'optional clause', i.e., a clause making redemption conditional or extending the time for compliance by the bank. In this case, Smith formed the opinion that, 'Such a paper money would, no doubt, fall more or less below the value of gold and silver, according as the difficulty or uncertainty of obtaining immediate payment was supposed to be greater or less; or according to the greater or less distance of time at which payment was exigible' (ibid., p. 425).

The second exception was fiduciary money, i.e., 'government paper' with forced currency, of which the North American colonies provided an example. Given that bullion remained the monetary standard, its rate of exchange with the paper indicated whether or not the latter had retained its value in circulation. According to Smith, 'A positive law may render a shilling a legal tender for a guinea . . . But no positive law can oblige a person who sells goods, and who is at liberty to sell as he pleases, to accept of a shilling as equivalent to a guinea in the price of them' (ibid., p. 251). He was thus aware of the role of fiduciary money and of the fact that it could depreciate against the metallic standard; he even referred to the 'quantity of paper' as one factor determining its relationship to the standard (ibid., p. 251).[1]

Smith did not, however discuss the criteria of fiduciary issue in any greater depth, nor did he anticipate the 'hybrid' currency created by the Bank Restriction – legal tender credit-money – which I shall come to in a moment. What he did emphasise was that no amount of depreciation by inconvertible paper would alter the value of the monetary metals or the proportion in which they exchanged with commodities: 'A paper currency which falls below the value of gold and silver coin does not thereby sink the value of those metals, or occasion equal quantities of them to exchange for a smaller quantity of goods of any other kind'. The relationship of exchange depended ultimately upon 'the proportion between the quantity of labour which is necessary in order to bring a certain quantity of gold and silver to market, and that which is necessary in order to bring thither a certain quantity of any other sort of goods' (ibid., pp. 252–3).[2] This account of depreciation was an essential component of the classical analysis of paper money, though, of course, it tells us nothing about the nature of the money – whether credit or fiduciary in character – nor about the cause of depreciation.

The problem of monetary depreciation was presented squarely with the Bank Restriction, when a general inflation of commodity prices reflected a sharp divergence in the market price of bullion from its mint price. Many interpretations were published at this time, but none stood out so much as those of Thornton and Ricardo – though the former was overshadowed by the latter just as Steuart had been by Smith in previous decades. Despite important differences, they comprised the intellectually decisive contributions to the Bullionist case against the supposed adequacy of the real bills doctrine to prevent overissue of an inconvertible currency. As we shall see, Ricardo developed this case, together with Smith's preliminary specification of the monetary circulation law as it applied to paper, into the classical theory of the fiduciary system. Thornton, on the other hand, was not so much concerned with doctrinal consistency – certainly not with Say's law – and attempted to distinguish at least formally the credit money of the Restriction period from fiduciary money. He was to become one of the authors of the Bullion Report, along with Francis Horner and the redoubtable William Huskisson (see Green, 1937, vol. 2, pp. 699–700).

Thornton's reputation was established by his work on *Paper Credit*; indeed, it has been called 'the clearest and sanest book which had up to then been written on monetary theory' (Horsefield, 1941/44, p. 24).[3] Thornton recognised that the inconvertible notes of the Restriction period were not given forced currency by the state to meet its expenses, but were advanced *on loan* by the Bank of England to accommodate the needs of business. His aim was merely to show that long-run overextension of the notes had become a *possibility*, and, furthermore, to absolve the Bank from precisely that charge by ascribing the contemporary inflation to short-run 'real' factors. However, the argument he employed led eventually to an assimilation of credit to the operation of a fiduciary system – even if he himself did not pursue it to the degree, or with the relentless logic, found in Ricardo's writings (see Peake, 1978). His approach found favour with Malthus, whose criticisms of Ricardo's theory of inflation anticipated their famous dispute over deflation and the possibility of a 'general glut'.[4]

In the remainder of the first half of this chapter, we shall find that Thornton's revision of the Smithian orthodoxy under conditions of inconvertibility entailed an abandonment of earlier classical propositions. The reintroduction of these propositions into the framework of monetary analysis by Ricardo is discussed in the next section. Here, I shall begin with Thornton's characterisation of the role of credit and then proceed to his determination of the amount that can circulate as money, his comprehensive study of the consequences of overissue, and his re-evaluation of the status of the real bills doctrine.

Money and credit

In his Introduction to *Paper Credit*, Thornton pointed out that his original intention was 'merely to expose some popular errors which related chiefly to the suspension of the cash payments of the bank of England and to the influence of our paper currency on the price of provisions'. In the course of his investigation, however, questions arose which had not been given a satisfactory treatment by previous writers. Hence, the work 'assumed, in some degree, the character of a general treatise' (1802, p. 67). Horner's review, which subsequently became as influential as the book itself, understandably found it a cause for complaint, 'that it did not receive in every respect the form, as it contains the substance, of a general treatise' (1957, p. 30). Obscurity of exposition was another attribute which Thornton shared in large measure with Steuart. Still another was their adoption of a supply and demand approach to price formation; while Thornton was no mercantilist, his argument made little attempt to incorporate the developments in classical theory.

Before we assess the implications of this retrogression, let us first establish Thornton's view of the nature of credit. Here he was in almost complete accord with the eighteenth-century economists. Credit, Thornton affirmed, was not money but an 'engagement to pay', though it might perform the role of circulating medium (ibid., pp. 76, 92). Money was fundamentally a commodity and acted as a universal measure of value: 'The precious metals, when uncoined (or in the state of bullion) are themselves commodities; but when converted into money they are to be considered merely as a measure of the value of other articles' (ibid., p. 81). The main effect of credit was that it 'spares the use of the expensive article of gold'. If a merchant was obliged to give 'ready money' in return for goods, 'he must always have in his hands a very large stock of money; and for the expence of keeping this fund (an expence consisting chiefly in the loss of interest) he must be repaid in the price of the commodities in which he deals'. He would avoid this charge by buying on credit, 'that is to say, by paying for his goods not by money, but by the delivery of a note in which he promises the money on a future day' (ibid., p. 76). Indeed, the function of the notes themselves could be served, '[m]erely by the transfer of the debts of one merchant to another, in the books of the banker' (ibid., p. 101).

The greater sophistication of the credit structure in Thornton's day enabled him to provide a more advanced description than his predecessors of the variety and scope of credit instruments and of an increasingly centralised banking system with the Bank of England as lender of last resort. He reiterated that these instruments (bills of exchange and promissory notes), 'not only spare the use of ready money; they also occupy its place in many cases. . . . [T]hey evidently form, in the strictest sense, a part of the circulating medium of the kingdom' (ibid., pp. 91–2). There was no difference *in principle*, therefore, between commercial paper and the notes issued by banks, 'which purport to be exchangeable for money; and which, through the known facility of thus exchanging them, may circulate in its stead; a part only of the money, of which the notes supply the place, being kept in store as a provision for the current payments' (ibid., p. 90). Both forms of paper credit were capable of circulating as money; the only difference between them lay in the magnitude of their velocity. In Thornton's estimation, the total value of bank notes was considerably less than that of bills, but as would be expected from their more general character, their velocity was several times greater. This fact he explained by what would now be called 'liquidity preference', a point which will be amplified in our later discussion of interest.[5]

It was on the grounds of the velocity differential between notes and bills that Thornton objected to Smith's definition of monetary circulation requirements. Let us recall the important argument in the *Wealth of Nations*, that the supply of paper money in long-run circulation could not exceed the value of the gold and silver for which it was substituted, or which, 'the commerce being supposed the same', would circulate in the absence of paper money. Furthermore, it was held by Smith and his forerunners in the classical tradition, that the volume of monetary metals was dependent upon their own value and the aggregate value of transactions, i.e., upon the sum of prices of circulating commodities. Thornton's misinterpretation of the former proposition followed from his failure to understand, or even to acknowledge, the latter.

Thornton argued that the amount of paper money would not 'bear a regular proportion to the quantity of trade and payments' (ibid., p. 94), because it was composed of media which circulated at different speeds. Since bills as well as notes were included in the definition of the money supply, it would, according to Thornton, have to be enlarged beyond the amount of specie that would otherwise circulate. Even if that did not occur, variation over time in the velocity of particular credit instruments, or indeed of metallic money, was said to make the requisite quantity of circulating media indeterminate: '[Smith] appears, in short, not at all to have reflected how false his maxim is rendered . . . both by the different degrees of rapidity of circulation which generally belong to the two different classes of paper of which I have spoken, and also of the different degrees of rapidity which may likewise belong to the circulation of the same kinds of paper, and even of the same guineas, at different times' (ibid., pp. 95–6).

The answer to Thornton's charge was quite simple. Smith was not so unrealistic as to have thought that the amount of paper money was equivalent to the specie that would *actually* have circulated had the paper not existed. In supposing a given state of commerce, like most classical economists, he also assumed that velocity was given in the long-run, without which the point of the comparison would have been lost. The quantity of paper, therefore, was commensurate with the total value of the gold and silver which notionally circulated – all other things being equal. That the money supply – whether paper or metallic – was theoretically determinate was a principle which had to be resuscitated by Ricardo. It was at least accepted in practice by Thornton, who regarded the convertibility of paper and gold as an economic law, irrespective of legal enforcement: '[G]old coin is to be viewed chiefly as a standard by which all bills and paper money should have their value regulated as exactly as possible' (ibid., p. 111). If paper money depreciated in relation to gold, i.e., if the market price of bullion rose above its mint price, did this mean that there was too much paper in circulation? This seemed to be the implication of Smith's analysis; let us now see how Thornton developed it in the context first of a 'mixed currency' of inconvertible notes and coins, and then of a currency consisting only of notes.

Output response

Smith, it will be remembered, maintained that a definite amount of paper money was required to fill the 'channel of circulation'. Any additional sum would not be able to run in it, but would have to 'overflow'; since this sum was too valuable to lie idle, it would be sent abroad to find 'profitable employment'. Now, if the superfluous money consisted of paper, it could not go abroad. Instead, it would displace an equivalent amount of gold and silver from circulation, and this would be the sum exported. Thornton modified Smith's account of monetary 'overflow' by alluding to two 'intermediate' phenomena:

> There seems to be only two modes in which we can conceive the additional paper to be disposed of. It may be imagined either, first, to be used in transferring an encreased quantity of articles, which it must, in that case, be assumed that the new paper itself has tended to create; or, secondly, in transferring the same articles at a higher price. (Ibid., p. 235)

While Thornton anticipated Ricardo, as we shall see, in identifying the price response as the short-run mechanism by which an expulsion of specie from domestic circulation took place, the projected response of output was clearly inconsistent with the classical assumption of fully utilised capacity. Credit expansion could only affect output up to a certain point by accelerating the turnover of capital; beyond that point, the creation of new productive capital was a prerequisite to increasing the level of economic activity. Thornton recognised that paper credit formed no part of the real capital of a country, and that this capital could not be enlarged by it.[6] Indeed, he readily conceded that even if bank loans appeared to the customers to represent 'new capital', this would be an illusion, 'for it does not occur to them that the commerce or manufactures of any other individuals can be at all reduced in consequence of this encrease of their own' (ibid., p. 236).

Having thus assumed full capacity utilisation, irrespective of the existence of 'antecedently idle persons', i.e., unemployment of labour, he could not now assert that a redistribution of capital by means of credit would be capable of raising output above the level commensurate with past accumulation. Nevertheless, he proceeded to endorse and apply Hume's earlier dictum – ignored by Smith and denied by Ricardo – that monetary growth would be 'favourable to industry' before a price adjustment could take full effect (ibid., p. 238 and *passim*). Moreover, he found equally acceptable Steuart's counterclaim that the price adjustment would be offset to the extent not only that commodities were purchased from abroad (ibid., p. 238 fn.), but also that this increased domestic output absorbed the superfluous paper: '[T]he new circulating medium will, in this manner, create for itself much new employment' (ibid., p. 237).

A further implication of the adjustment process – which was not considered by Hume, Steuart or Smith and was dismissed by Ricardo – was an actual increase of capital by means of what we would now call 'forced saving'.[7] Here a rise in prices following excessive monetary expansion might not be matched by an increase in worker's wages, thus leading in turn to lower consumption and an 'augmentation of stock'. While this implication at least had the merit of being consistent with a rise in the level of output, it was clearly incompatible with the original supposition that credit did not augment capital but was merely the 'instrument' by which it was 'distributed with convenience and advantage among the several members of the community' (ibid., p. 237). The source of Thornton's error may be found earlier in a comment upon Smith's characterisation of the function of credit. He declared: 'Whether the introduction of the use of paper is spoken of as turning dead and unproductive stock into stock which is active and productive, or as *adding* to the stock of the country, is much the same thing' (ibid., p. 176 fn., emphasis in original). The error is repeated in an assessment of Law's System (ibid., p. 239 fn.) and finally repudiated, probably under Ricardo's influence, in a parliamentary debate on the Bullion Report in 1811 (ibid., p. 353).

Price response

We have now considered Thornton's postulation of an output response to overextension of the note issue. His casual approach to Say's law was not to be used to advantage by any of Ricardo's opponents, whose case was presented scrupulously within the classical framework. Thornton's discussion of the price response, on the other hand, was drawn upon by the Ricardian school to explain the process by which the volume of notes was restored to its long-run magnitude. Here, Thornton was right to take issue with Smith, who did not, as we have already seen, show how the 'medium of prices' acted to trigger the import and export of gold in an open economy (ibid., pp. 203–4). He pointed out, by contrast, that the circulation could 'never be said to be over full'; monetary expansion drove up the level of market prices, which then gave employment to a greater volume of circulating media: 'This advanced price of goods is the same thing as a reduced price of coin; the coin, therefore, in consequence of its reduced price, is carried out of the country for the sake of obtaining for it a better market' (ibid., p. 205).

At this stage the assumption was made that the currency comprised coin in addition to notes. Should notes be overextended, coin would be displaced from the currency in equal measure, and, when added to the stock of bullion, would correspondingly lower its value in the market. This depreciation of bullion and paper together was the same as that which occurred under a convertible regime, with the difference that in the one case overissue was limited by the bank's metallic reserve, whereas in the other, as we shall see, once coin was exhausted, the paper could continue to depreciate against bullion as well as against other commodities. Although this latter, purely 'nominal', depreciation might be permanent,[8] the rise in commodity prices associated with a fall in the value of a mixed currency was viewed as a short-run transitory phenomenon:

> The general and permanent value of bank notes must be the same as the general and permanent value of that gold for which they are exchangeable, and the value of gold in England is regulated by the general and permanent value of it all over the world; and, therefore, although it is admitted that a great and sudden reduction [or increase] of bank notes may produce a great local and temporary fall [or rise] in the price of articles (a fall [or rise], that is to say, even in their gold price, for we are here supposing gold and paper to be interchanged), the gold price must, in a short time, find its level with the gold price over the rest of the world. (Ibid., p. 119 fn.)

The manner in which domestic prices adjusted to world prices was straightforward. Coin initially depreciated along with paper not only against the mass of commodities but also against bullion, whose market price rose above its mint price. Here it was necessary, Thornton wrote, 'to consider coin as sinking below its proper and accustomed price' (ibid., p. 200). This was the signal that profit might be gained from melting down the coin for export, or for reselling to the Bank of England. A situation might then arise where the Bank bought gold at a premium in order to replenish the stock of coin, only to find that individuals were melting it just as rapidly for resale at a profit. This situation would be unsustainable for any length of time: 'The one party will be melting and selling, while the other is buying and coining . . . The bank, if we suppose it, as we now do, to carry on this sort of contest with the melters, is obviously waging a very unequal war; and even though it should not be tired early, it will be likely to be tired sooner than its adversaries' (ibid., p. 147).

Whether the excessive note issue was the cause or effect of inflation depended, according to Thornton, upon the 'permanence' of the departure both of the market price of bullion from its mint price and of the value of circulating media from the point consistent with equality in the foreign exchanges: '[S]o far as they *permanently* stand above that point, it is the enlarged and too great quantity of notes of the Bank of England which is to be considered as the cause of the high price of goods rather than the high price of goods which is to be taken to be the cause of the enlarged quantity of notes of the Bank of England' (ibid., p. 221). What Thornton meant by the term 'permanently' was explained in a footnote as "such a degree of permanence as may serve to shew that the fall of our exchanges, and the rise in the price of bullion, are not referable to any extraordinary and passing event, such as that of one or even two bad harvests; for these may not unfairly be termed temporary circumstances, though their influence may extend over a period of one or two years' (ibid., p. 221 fn.).[9]

We shall see in the next section that Ricardo rejected this distinction between permanent and temporary price variations, attributing *all* such changes to a 'redundant currency'. Thornton, on the other hand, maintained that it was precisely the influence of specific and temporary phenomena which accounted for the inflation of the early restriction era and that the gold drain associated with an unfavourable balance of trade would cease with the payment of the increased import bill. He enumerated these 'real' phenomena as follows:

That the bullion price of some British articles has lately been much encreased, and that the bullion price of all, or of almost all, has in some degree risen, are facts which cannot be doubted. But that this enhancement is to be charged to an increase of paper, is not equally to be admitted; for it is plain that other causes have powerfully operated, namely, a state of war, new taxes, and two bad harvests, which, by raising the price of bread, have in some degree lifted up that of labour, and of all commodities. Our prices may have also been partly augmented by the enhancement of the cost of raw materials brought from other countries. (Ibid., p. 263)[10]

The evidence bore out this interpretation. Thornton's apparent change of mind in the Bullion Report, which focused upon monetary expansion by the Bank of England, was due to the fact that by the end of the decade the currency was no longer mixed, but *consisted wholly of inconvertible paper*. Indeed, it was only under such conditions that a premium on bullion could become 'permanent', in the sense that there was no tendency at work to eliminate it.

A managed currency

In any case, at the time of writing *Paper Credit*, Thornton regarded it as misconceived to restrict the supply of notes, even if by such action it were possible to stem the outflow of gold. He argued: 'The idea which some persons have entertained of its being at all times a paramount duty of the Bank of England to diminish its notes, in some sort of regular proportion to that diminution which it experiences in its gold, is, then, an idea which is merely theoretic' (ibid., p. 116). Indeed, in developing his concept of a managed currency, Thornton foreshadowed many of the propositions to be associated later with the Banking School. These propositions, as we shall see, directly confronted the Ricardian approach to financial management, especially the form it was to take in the hands of its professed adherents in the Currency School.

To begin with, bank notes were only one form of credit, and, although the Bank had by that time established effective control over the whole domestic issue, there was nothing to prevent other credit instruments outside its control from expanding to take their place. The directors of the Bank, observed Thornton, 'have now, by their exclusive power of furnishing a circulating medium to the metropolis, the means of, in some degree, limiting and regulating its quantity; a power of which they would be totally divested, if, by exercising it too severely, they should once cause other paper to become current in the same manner as their own' (ibid., pp. 115–16).

Furthermore, a contraction of the note issue, to the extent that any immediate effect was achieved, would depress economic activity – the counterpart of the output response to excess credit. Thornton repeatedly emphasised that it must be asked 'whether the bank, in the attempt to produce this very low price, may not, in a country circumstanced as Great Britain is, so exceedingly distress trade and discourage manufactures as to impair . . . those sources of returning wealth to which we must chiefly trust for the restoration of our balance of trade, and for bringing back the tide of gold into Great Britain' (ibid., p. 152; also ch. 4). However realistic this prognosis, it was again inconsistent, as Ricardo was later obliged to point out, with the classical assumption of a given output.

More to the point was Thornton's argument, dismissed by Ricardo, that the foreign exchanges would ultimately return to normal without any assistance from the monetary authorities, provided that the original cause of disruption was a transitory event: '[T]he favourable effect which a limitation of bank paper produces on the exchange is certainly not instantaneous, and may, probably, only be experienced after some considerable interval of time; it may, therefore, in many cases, be expected that the exchange will rectify itself before the reduction of bank paper can have any operation' (ibid.). Supposing that the Bank of England did succeed in reducing the note issue in conformity with the export of gold, Thornton went on to show that the deficiency of circulating media might be made up not only by new money substitutes but also by an internal demand for gold in addition to the pre-existing external demand. This was another reason why a passive stance by the Bank was considered more appropriate: '[I]t may be the true policy and duty of the bank to permit, for a time, and to a certain extent, the continuance of that unfavourable exchange, which causes gold to leave the country, and to be drawn out of its own coffers: and it must, in that case, necessarily encrease its loans to the same extent to which its gold is diminished' (ibid.).[11]

An adequate reserve was essential for the pursuance of a policy of accommodation: 'The bank, however, ought generally to be provided with a fund of gold so ample, as to enable it to pursue this line of conduct with safety to itself, through the period of an unfavourable balance; a period, the duration of which may, to a certain degree, be estimated though disappointment in a second harvest may cause much error in the circulation' (ibid., pp. 152–3; also, pp. 111–12). Ricardo, by contrast, had little to say on the subject of reserve management (see Deane, 1978, pp. 51–3).

To reiterate, the convertibility of gold and silver remained an economic law even when it was not legally stipulated. This convertibility was not in danger of infringement in the long-run, according to Thornton, if a divergence of the market price of bullion from its mint price and a corresponding fall in the foreign exchanges were due to short-run influences. In general, therefore, the note issue would conform to the behaviour of a metallic currency. For practical convertibility to be 'permanently' infringed, the money supply had to be overextended by the Bank; and we may add that this was only possible once coin had been totally withdrawn from circulation and the Bank refused to introduce any more. Under these circumstances, contended Thornton, the authorities acquired a justification, indeed a duty, to *operate directly upon the quantity of notes*. At this point, credit, whose distinct character was previously stressed, was treated as though it were merely a fiduciary issue.

Thornton challenged the central component of the anti-Bullionist position – the real bills doctrine – relied upon by the Bank directors and most of their supporters (see Fetter, 1965, pp. 40–2). Lacking the theoretical acumen of their antagonists, the anti-Bullionists badly overstated their case; they held not only that the real bills doctrine was valid under conditions of inconvertibility, but that, provided there was compliance by the Bank, overissue simply could not take place, irrespective of the level of interest rates. Their error, Thornton claimed, lay in 'imagining that a proper limitation of bank notes may be sufficiently secured by attending merely to the nature of the security for which they are given' (ibid., p. 244). If the Bank, by discounting real bills, financed an excessive demand which resulted in an increased price level, how, he asked, was a 'natural tendency' of limitation to take effect (ibid., p. 251 ff.)? The full nominal value of the loan might be punctually repaid to the Bank and the bills extinguished, but to the extent that notes were depreciated, the Bank had made a transfer of capital from its reserves to its customers just as surely as though a proportion of the bills were fictitious.

Thornton, concluded, therefore, that the note issue had to be 'regulated by a principle which is not even connected with the question of the opulence of the borrowers at the bank, or of the nature of the bills discounted'. Certainty of payment was no longer the material factor:

> But in what manner is the payment to be affected? It will be made either in notes furnished by the Bank of England itself, or else in gold

> supplied by the same company, which notes and gold the bank must take care to render interchangeable for each other; and this is only to be done by keeping down their quantity, and thus maintaining their value. (Ibid., p. 228)

Generally, in a credit system, as will be shown in the next chapter, it was the role of the rate of interest to act as the lever of restraint. Thornton, despite his theoretical preference for this instrument, nevertheless advocated that the Bank should directly control the quantity of notes in circulation, given the interest rate ceiling imposed by the Usury Law. He argued that the needs of commerce did not constitute an effective principle of limitation once we 'consider this question as turning principally on a comparison of the rate of interest taken at the bank with the current rate of mercantile profit' (ibid., p. 254). This argument was true, however, only in those exceptional circumstances which justified an increase in the rate of interest above the legal ceiling, namely at the initial stages of an inflationary process which encouraged a shift of funds from productive investment to speculation (ibid., p. 254). Otherwise, under normal conditions, as we have seen, the demand for circulating media expressed in real bills did form an adequate safeguard against overissue, since only a strictly circumscribed amount would be required to extend the process of social reproduction.

In sum, Thornton was at least aware of defects in the quantitative method of monetary control, which were later to be given detailed attention by the Banking School. In particular, he recognised that bank notes were only one element of the credit-system, and their reduction could lead either 'to the creation of some new London paper, or possibly to some new modes of economy in the use of the existing notes . . .' (ibid., p. 119 fn.). Moreover, to the extent that this reduction had an immediate impact upon firms which required ready money, it might precipitate a fall in industrial output. Ricardo did not even discuss these possibilities, first because he treated the note issue as fiduciary money rather than as a component of credit, and, second, because output was fixed by assumption.

Thornton's conclusion suggested broad policy guidelines for a central bank, which would steer a pragmatic course between Smith's real bills doctrine and Ricardo's mechanical application of classical quantity theory. He was the first to advocate what might now be called a managed currency. This was designed to take account of the growing sophistication of financial instruments on the one hand and the volatile and crisis-prone character of industrialisation on the other. A nation's currency, in Thornton's view, should be permitted to 'vibrate only within certain limits', while meeting the legitimate needs of the non-bank public.[12] It was a view which scarcely survived the rigid formulations of the ensuing 'bullion controversy'.

OVERISSUE AND LIMITATION

We have seen that Thornton's rejection of the real bills doctrine in favour of quantitative regulation of the note issue implied the substitution of a principle of limitation appropriate to a fiduciary system for one appropriate to credit. This was thought justified by the suspension of convertibility and imposition of interest rate ceilings, which together introduced the possibility of a permanent depreciation of paper against gold. Whereas Thornton nevertheless attributed the price inflation of the Bank Restriction to 'real' short-run factors – at least in the initial stages – we shall find in this section that Ricardo *always* explained inflation which accompanies a divergence of the market price of bullion from its mint price (and a fall in the foreign exchanges) by the overissue of paper money.[13] He therefore joined Thornton in treating direct monetary control rather than specific lending criteria as the means of ensuring price stability; but he also founded this principle of limitation upon classical postulates – especially Say's law – which entailed important revisions to Thornton's argument (see Peake, 1978).

In what follows, I shall first examine Ricardo's theory of paper money, noting its application by the mid nineteenth-century Currency School to a system of convertible bank notes. The refutation of the currency principle by the Banking School and by Marx will then be anticipated; they affirmed the validity of Ricardo's theory in the context of a fiduciary system, but, as will be demonstrated in the next chapter, they found it inapplicable to a credit system, regardless of legal convertibility.

Our discussion of Ricardo's monetary writings will start where the earlier analysis of metallic currency broke off. The initial task for Ricardo was to define the circulation requirements of paper money, i.e., how much was needed to circulate the mass of commodities. Only then was it possible to address the question of overissue and thus to evaluate the respective merits of the real bills doctrine and of direct monetary control in the maintenance of economic convertibility. Smith, as we have seen, had established the quantity of paper money necessary for circulation by reference to metallic currency. Thornton, on the other hand, missed the point of this approach, since unlike Smith, he displayed no real interest in the problem of value and distribution. It was left to Ricardo to reintegrate monetary theory into the classical framework (Deane, 1978, p. 57).

First, Ricardo determined the requisite supply of money in a metallic system, all other things being equal, by its own value as a commodity (1951/58, I, p. 352; also III, pp. 52–3; IV, p. 55). This was the law of monetary circulation, to which I have already given considerable attention. Second, he was prepared to advocate the replacement of gold and silver in the exchange sphere by paper – even inconvertible paper – provided only that it was issued in the same amount i.e., the amount prescribed by the value of the metal which was to become the monetary standard:

> On these principles, it will be seen that it is not necessary that paper money should be payable in specie to secure its value; it is only necessary that its quantity should be regulated according to the value of the metal which is declared to be the standard. If the standard were gold of a given weight and fineness, paper might be increased with every fall in the value of gold, or, which is the same thing in its effects, with every rise in the price of goods. (Ibid., p. 345)[14]

It is this application of the circulation law to paper money with which I shall be concerned in the remainder of this chapter. Ricardo was preoccupied for much of his life, as we have seen, with the notion of an 'invariable' standard or measure of value. Although in his later writings, this notion was clearly connected with the development of his value theory, it began simply as a wish for a monetary standard immune to the fluctuations in commodity prices. Even as late as his *Proposals for an Economical and Secure Currency* (1816), Ricardo maintained that, 'A currency may be considered as perfect, of which the standard is invariable, which always conforms to that standard, and in the use of which the utmost economy is practised' (ibid., IV, p. 55). Steuart had promoted paper money itself as just such a standard (ibid., p. 59), but, in refuting this idea, Ricardo demonstrated that, for specific historical and institutional reasons, gold had become the standard by which the value of the paper was necessarily judged (ibid., III, pp. 65–70). Although he himself would have preferred a *silver* standard – being 'much more steady in its value' (ibid., IV, p. 63) – he conceded that the value of gold, despite it susceptibility to the same fluctuation as any other commodity; was 'for short spaces of time . . . tolerably fixed' (ibid., III, p. 64 fn).[15]

The proper quantity of paper money was therefore ensured by its economic convertibility with gold irrespective of any legal requirement: 'The issuers of paper money should regulate their issues solely by the price of bullion, and never by the quantity of their paper in circulation' (ibid.,

IV, p. 64). Hence Ricardo concluded in the *Principles* that, 'A currency is in its most perfect state when it consists wholly of paper money, but of paper money of an equal value with the gold which it professes to represent' (ibid., I, p. 361). The fact of convertibility would be attested to by the correspondence of the market price with the mint price of bullion and by the equality of foreign exchanges (ibid., III, pp. 72–4). A rise in the market price over the mint price and a fall in the exchanges indicated both the depreciation of paper money (ibid., IV, pp. 62–3), and, as we shall now discover, its overissue in relation to long-run circulation needs.

Although, from a theoretical viewpoint, Ricardo recognised that legal convertibility was not strictly necessary to prevent depreciation, in practice he regarded it as essential: 'Experience, however, shews that neither a State nor a Bank ever have had the unrestricted power of issuing paper money, without abusing that power: in all States, therefore, the issue of paper money ought to be under some check and control; and none seems so proper for that purpose, as that of subjecting the issuers of paper money to the obligation of paying notes, either in gold coin or bullion' (ibid., I, p. 356).

Ricardo's discussion of *convertible* bank notes closely followed Smith, though incorporating some of Thornton's modifications. Since the equivalence of notes with gold was guaranteed, they *could not* be issued in a greater quantity than the value of the coin which would otherwise have circulated. Any attempt to exceed this sum would precipitate a return of notes for specie, a depreciation of both paper and metallic currency, and the subsequent export of superfluous bullion. Ricardo made the following observation on the Bank of England in his *High Price of Bullion*:

> The Bank might continue to issue their notes, and the specie be exported with advantage to the country, while their notes were payable in specie on demand, because they could never issue more notes than the value of the coin which would have circulated had there been no bank. If they attempted to exceed this amount, the excess would be immediately returned to them for specie: because our currency, being thereby diminished in value, could be advantageously exported, and could not be retained in our circulation. These are the means . . . by which our currency endeavours to equalize itself with the currencies of other countries. (Ibid., III, p. 57)

Ricardo went on to show that if the Bank persisted in returning their notes into circulation, 'every guinea might be drawn out of their coffers'. Hence,

> The Bank would be obliged . . . ultimately to adopt the only remedy in their power to put a stop to the demand from circulation, till they should have increased the value of the remainder to that of gold bullion, and, consequently, to the value of the currencies of other countries. All advantage from the exportation would then cease, and there would be no temptation to exchange bank-notes for guineas. (Ibid., p. 59)[16]

Whereas Thornton criticised Smith's failure to refer to the depreciation of currency prior to its 'overflow' from domestic circulation, Ricardo treated this short-run mechanism as implicit in the presentation of long-run relationships in the *Wealth of Nations*. Throughout his monetary writings, Ricardo laid claim to the Smithian legacy, either replicating his ideas or extending them to new fields. One such field was, of course, the behaviour and regulation of *inconvertible* paper money. Here Ricardo also found Thornton both an instructive authority and counterfoil for the development of his own approach. On the one hand, he drew upon Thornton's analysis of the connection between the money supply and the price level, and, on the other, revised the analysis to the extent necessary to make it consistent with Say's law (Sayers, 1953).

Inconvertible paper

It will be recalled that Thornton was primarily concerned in *Paper Credit* with a 'mixed currency' of gold coin and inconvertible bank notes. Ricardo agreed with him that an overextension of notes under these conditions had the same effect as under conditions of convertibility, provided only that the degree of excess was no greater than the amount of coin in circulation. First Horner and then Blake and Huskisson had argued that this overextension of notes would increase only the 'paper' or 'currency' price of commodities, but not their 'bullion price'. Ricardo, in an important footnote to the third edition of *High Price of Bullion*, demonstrated on the contrary that:

> This would be true at a time when the currency consisted wholly of paper not convertible into specie, but not while specie formed any part of the circulation. In the latter case the effect of an increased issue of paper would be to throw out of circulation an equal amount of specie; but this could not be done without adding to the quantity of bullion in the market, and thereby lowering its value, or, in other words, *increasing the bullion price of* commodities. (Ibid., p. 64 fn.)

It was therefore the melting down of coin displaced by paper in circulation and its addition to the existing stock of bullion which depressed the market value of the currency as a whole and correspondingly increased the bullion price of commodities. Again, as a result, the mining of gold would be cut back until its market value coincided with the intrinsic value given by its cost of production; or, to characterise the process in terms of Ricardo's international specie-flow doctrine, bullion would be exported in exchange for commodities until its value was equalised with bullion in the rest of the world.[17]

The nature of the problem changed, however, when the currency consisted *entirely* of inconvertible paper. This was the situation when Ricardo entered the controversy in 1809, and it goes some way towards explaining Thornton's decision to favour the resumption of cash payments in the Bullion Report of the following year. An excess note issue would have no other effect, according to Ricardo, than to 'raise the *money* price of bullion without lowering its *value*, in the same manner, and in the same proportion, as it will raise the prices of other commodities' (ibid.; see also p. 211). In other words, despite the depreciation of paper money, the 'bullion price' of commodities was unaltered. Consequently, the deterioration of the foreign exchanges 'will only be a *nominal*, not a *real* fall, and will not occasion the exportation of bullion' (ibid.). Ricardo's emphasis upon the proportionality of the domestic price adjustment to changes in the money supply indicated his adherence to the 'classical dichotomy' and thus distinguished his own approach from that of Thornton: 'If the Bank were restricted from paying their notes in specie, and all the coin had been exported, any excess of their notes would *depreciate the value of the circulating medium in proportion to the excess*' (ibid., p. 91, emphasis added).

Pursuing the logic of Say's law, Ricardo reiterated the objection he first made in the context of a metallic system to the possibility of an output response to monetary expansion, either directly by means of an increased level of demand or indirectly through a fall in the rate of interest (see Fetter, 1965, p. 43). Only greater capital accumulation resulting from higher savings could have any effect in raising the level of output; and he had found no convincing proof 'that additions to the paper currency would be the cause of accumulation of capital' (ibid., III, p. 333). When this view was put to the House of Lords Committee on the Resumption of Cash Payments in 1819, there was the barest hint of a qualification:

> State what in your Judgement are the Effects on Agriculture, Commerce, and Manufactures of a superabundant Issue of Paper? – Under some

> Circumstances *it may derange the Proportions in which the whole Produce of Capital is divided*, between the Capitalist and the Labourer; but in general I do not think it even affects those Proportions. It never I think increases the Produce of Capital. (1951/58, V, pp. 445–6, emphasis added)

Under continued questioning, Ricardo conceded that, 'by affecting the Proportions into which Produce is divided, [monetary overissue] may *facilitate the Accumulation of Capital in the Hands of the Capitalist*; he having increased Profits, while the Labourer has diminished wages. This may sometimes happen, but I think seldom does' (ibid., emphasis added). In other words, the lagged response of wages to price inflation may give rise to 'forced saving', a notion we struck previously in Thornton's *Paper Credit*.

As we shall see in the next chapter, Ricardo applied the same principles to credit, which he termed 'fictitious capital'. Although it would not enlarge the quantity of real capital, it might increase its rate of turnover *up to a certain point* and hence the volume of production per unit of time. The assumption that ran through his work, however, was that this point had been reached and that, with velocity and output constant, a system of inconvertible bank notes therefore took on the character of a fiduciary system (Viner, 1937, p. 243). That is to say, the Bank of England might now issue notes to any sum whatever, for they would simply depreciate and raise the general price level in a commensurate degree. (The potential fluctuations in the money rate of interest, which I shall also consider in the following chapter, were treated as strictly temporary and did not materially affect the present analysis.)

An analogy was drawn by Ricardo between the issues of the Bank and the output of a new gold mine:

> If instead of a mine being discovered in any country, a bank were established, such as the Bank of England, with the power of issuing its notes for a circulating medium; after a large amount had been issued, either by way of loan to merchants, or by advances to Government, thereby adding considerably to the sum of the currency, the same effect would follow as in the case of the mine. The circulating medium would be lowered in value, and goods would experience a proportionate rise. (Ibid., III, pp. 54–5)[18]

In both cases, monetary expansion reduced the value of the unit of account, though, in the case of gold, the depreciation could only be permanent to the extent that its new value reflected an increase in productivity. Expansion of inconvertible paper, on the other hand, could be continued *indefinitely*, as we now find, creating a cycle of overissue, depreciation and price inflation – without any self-correcting mechanism.

Ricardo combined Smith's definition of monetary circulation requirements with Thornton's insight that, in the absence of legally enforced convertibility, the Bank's claim merely to be satisfying the 'wants of commerce' was no guarantee of convertibility in practice, or of what we have called economic convertibility (ibid., p. 194). Since the circulation could never be 'overfull', excess paper had to be retained at a lower value in the same manner, according to Ricardo, as *forced currency* issued by the state. By this term, he pointed out to critics of the Bullion Report, 'is meant only that the restriction bill enables them to keep in circulation an amount of notes . . . greater than they could maintain but for that measure'; he continued: 'It is this surplus sum which I consider as producing the same effects as if it were forced on the public by a Government Bank. The plea that no more is issued than the wants of commerce require is of no weight; because the sum required for that purpose cannot be defined' (ibid., p. 215).[19]

More specifically, the real bills doctrine was dismissed as a principle of limitation for paper money with forced currency: 'The refusal to discount any bills but those for *bona fide* transactions would be as little effectual in limiting the circulation; because, though the Directors should have the means of distinguishing such bills, which can by no means be allowed, a greater portion of paper currency might be called into circulation, not than the wants of commerce could employ, but greater than what could remain in the channel of currency without depreciation' (ibid., p. 219). Those advocating reliance upon the real bills doctrine did their case little good by pretending that depreciation was impossible whatever the level of interest rates.[20] This apparent denial of the actual course of events on the part of the Bank of England and its supporters allowed Ricardo to escape with his equally 'unrealistic' but logically consistent assumptions. Credit money issued by the Bank was likened to fiduciary money issued by the state in the sense that both might be expanded indefinitely: 'If, indeed, any power in the state have the privilege of increasing the paper currency at pleasure, and be at the same time protected from the payment of its notes, there is no other limit to the rise of the price of gold than the will of the issuers' (ibid., p. 226).[21]

Ricardo's policy conclusions were straightforward. Since, in his view, the basic cause of the rise in the market price of bullion over its mint price, and of the corresponding level of inflation, was the overissue of paper money, the only remedy – indeed the only effective principle of limitation – was an assertion of *direct control* over the note issue by the Bank. The arguments of the anti-Bullionists made little headway, though it became increasingly clear that, 'in the divergence between the paper and the gold, it was the gold that, by increased demand departed from the paper, and not the paper by increased quantity from the gold' (Tooke, 1838/57, I, p. 158). The line of action recommended by Ricardo to the monetary authorities during the period of restriction was seen as a preliminary step to the ultimate resumption of specie payments:

> If the Bank directors had kept the amount of their notes within reasonable bounds; if they had acted up to the principle which they have avowed to have been that which regulated their issues when they were obliged to pay their notes in specie, namely, to limit their notes to that amount which should prevent the excess of the market above the Mint price of gold, we should not have been exposed to all the evils of a depreciated, and perpetually varying currency. (Ibid., p. 95)[22]

Ricardo later proposed a transfer of responsibility for the note issue from the Bank of England to a state-controlled 'national bank' – confining the former only to commercial lending (ibid., IV, pp. 271–300).[23] A wholly artificial distinction between the functions of 'circulation' and 'deposit' was derived from Steuart and found its way into the ill-conceived 1844 Bank Charter Act, whose provisions and limitations I shall address in the next chapter. For the moment, it is sufficient to note that the impact of Ricardo's theory on events was greater than the impact of events on his theory.

Theory and evidence

It was clear, in the prevailing circumstances of the Bank Restriction, that Ricardo's diagnosis and cure for monetary overissue had little practical value, though no one could doubt their relentless consistency with classical assumptions.[24] As I have earlier indicated, the inflation of the Restriction period was due to a multitude of short-run factors (such as poor harvests, war subsidies and the Blockade Decrees), and the discount of the notes against gold was caused not by the Bank's imprudence but rather by the demand for means of payment for external transactions. Having assembled the evidence, Morgan concludes that:

> [A]lmost all the major [price] changes are associated with important non-monetary factors; either inflationary budgets, a rising cost of living

> due to bad harvests, exchange depreciation due to artificial payments, or commercial speculation consequent on the development of new markets. We have also seen that there is little correlation between price movements and the notes or advances of the Bank, and that, so far as this correlation exists there is a marked tendency for accommodation to follow prices. Contemporary critics, with the notable exception of Tooke, attacked the Bank for having actively caused the price rise. But if this was so, surely we ought to find some trace of it in the statistics, instead of which the fact that the note issue always increases after price rises suggests that the Bank played a passive role. If we disabuse our minds of 'quantity theory' notions, this seems the more likely sequence. (1965, pp. 46–7)[25]

Yet Ricardo held throughout his career, first, that, so long as the note issue conformed to the monetary standard, its quantity would be governed in the long-run by the level of prices and output; second, that any excessive increase in this quantity would have no 'real' consequences, but simply alter to a proportionate extent the domestic price level; third, that a rise in commodity prices which was accompanied by an equivalent disparity between the market price and mint price of bullion had to be the result of an increase in the quantity of paper money; and, fourth, that the depreciation of paper against bullion and the corresponding price inflation could only be rectified by monetary contraction of the part of the Bank of England.[26]

These propositions all had a common point of reference, namely their consistency with Say's law, and – by implication – the dichotomy between the 'real' and monetary sectors of the economy. The first proposition, which applied to all types of paper currency, was derived from Smith. The second was directed against Thornton's failure to comply with Say's law in his analysis of overissue. The third and fourth propositions, however, which were accepted less tentatively by Thornton in the Bullion Report and subsequent speeches than in his early book, were flawed. They required that credit money be assimilated in its nature and role to the functioning of a fiduciary system. This gave rise to a complete misconception not only of the transitory supply and demand factors at work in the inflationary process of the Restriction era, but also of the appropriate practical response by the authorities.

Even if the fixed output and velocity assumptions were to be accepted, contraction of the note issue by the Bank of England might lead not to a reduction in the price level as Ricardo had asserted, but rather to *disintermediaton* by borrowers, i.e., switching into forms of credit outside the banking system. Paper money of the Restriction was issued by the Bank *on loan*, not by the state to meet its expenses, and hence the primary determinant of quantity was not the 'will of the issuers' but the demand of the non-bank public. However, in his evidence of March 1819 to the House of Commons Committee on the Resumption of Cash Payments, Ricardo repeated his view that 'one of the evils attending a paper currency not convertible, is, that it encourages over-trading, and leads us into some of those difficulties into which we should not be plunged, if our paper were corrected by the issuers of the metals'. As he once more explained, 'it appears so to me, because men rely more confidently on renewing the discounting of their bills' (ibid., V, pp. 397–8).

The following exchange with the committee revealed the extent of Ricardo's refusal to countenance any discrepancy between this hypothesis and the actual state of the economy:

> Are you aware that there is at present a considerable stagnation in trade, and that there has been a great reduction of prices in consequence? – I have heard so; but I am not engaged in trade, and it does not come much within my own knowledge. (Ibid., pp. 384–5)

It was common ground that this stagnation had been accompanied in the preceding fifteen months by a substantial monetary contraction; yet the market price of gold was *higher than before*. The committee put it to Ricardo that this fact was 'somewhat inconsistent' with his theory, whereupon he resorted to dogmatic assertion: 'It does not in the least shake my confidence in the theory, being fully persuaded that such an effect must have followed, if it had not been counteracted by some of those causes to which I have already adverted' (ibid., p. 376).[27]

When the committee asked what were the causes which had 'practically operated to countervail the effect of this reduction in the circulating medium', Ricardo again replied: 'The facts are not sufficiently within my knowledge to give any plausible explanation of them; but I am persuaded that there are other causes, besides the mere amount of paper, which will so operate, and I therefore infer, that some of them have now been acting' (ibid.). Nevertheless, if the committee imagined that they had discovered a flaw in Ricardo's theory, they were certainly not able to offer an alternative. Ricardo's answers may have been less than persuasive, but they were logically watertight:

> Then supposing the bank to make a further reduction, beyond the present amount of their issues, might not the operations of the same causes prevent the good effects to be expected from that reduction?

> *It is quite possible but I do not think it probable.*
>
> Have the goodness to state why you think it probable that the same causes that must have operated to produce that effect in the former case, should not continue to produce it in the case assumed?
>
> *Because, in commerce, it appears to me that a cause may have operated for a certain time without our being warranted to expect that it should continue to operate for a much greater length of time; and being fully persuaded that a reduction in the quantity of such a commodity as money must either raise its value, or prevent its falling in value, I am sure that a reduction of the quantity of currency, provided it be sufficient in degree, will operate in raising its value, whatever countervailing causes may contribute to oppose it.* (Ibid., pp. 376–7)

Even though the economy was already in recession, therefore, Ricardo maintained that, so long as the market price of gold persisted above its mint price, the note issue was excessive and, in the present case, had to be reduced to lower prices by 'about five or six per cent' (ibid., pp. 385). Most commentators would now share Viner's judgement that Ricardo 'could very rarely interest himself in the immediate and transitory phases of an economic process sufficiently to trace it in detail through its successive stages, and he frequently confined his analysis to the end results either passing over without mention or even denying the existence of the intermediate stages' (1937, pp. 139–40). However, these commentators fail to recognise that it was not so much Ricardo's lack of interest in short-run phenomena as the interpretation he placed upon them which marked out his analysis. This interpretation followed 'automatically', as I have argued, from the absence of a theory of output in classical economics.

In contradistinction to Ricardo's analysis, the relative stability of the note issue during the Restriction period established a *prima facie* case for regarding the real bills doctrine as a sound – though not infallible – instrument of policy under normal circumstances. As Tooke pointed out in his *History of Prices*: 'The rule by which the Bank directors professed to be, and were in the main, guided, viz. the demand for discount of good mercantile bills, not exceeding sixty-one days' date, at the rate of five per cent per annum, did, with the necessary policy of government in periodically reducing the floating debt within certain limits by funding, operate as a principle of limitation upon the total issues of the Bank' (1838/57, I, p.159).[28] There was no unchecked inflationary expansion, despite the Usury Law and despite the *possibility* – highlighted by Thornton but foolishly denied by the Bank directors – that excess demand for credit might if met, depreciate the currency. We shall see in the next chapter that th real bills doctrine was later defended more effectively by the Bankin School than it was by the anti-Bullionists, who, it was painfully obvious were no match for Ricardo's debating skills. In this chapter, coverage o the Banking School will be confined to their view of fiduciary money.

Banking School

The Banking School economists were as committed as Ricardo, if no more so, to the legal convertibility of bank notes. Indeed, during the in quiry into the resumption of cash payments in 1819, Thomas Tooke, wh was to become a leading figure in this group, opposed Ricardo's sugges tion in the so-called 'ingot plan' to make notes payable in *bullion* in fa vour of a return to payment in *coin*. He argued in evidence to the Hous of Lords Committee on Resumption that:

> A Circulation so saturated with Paper would be liable to Abuse, and t Suspension of the Check of partial Convertibility, on lighter Ground than if the Currency consisted of Coin and of strictly convertible Pape And, taken in a general point of view, it must be admitted, that a basis o so frail a Material, resting so exclusively on Credit and Confidence, i exposed to the Danger of frequent Derangement, and in some conceiv able Cases to total Destruction'. (Cited in Ricardo,1951/58, V, p. 362

Tooke and the Banking School accepted the classical law of monetar circulation and, like Ricardo, wished to apply it to a system of pape currency. They were concerned, however, in their dispute with the Cur rency School, that a theory of fiduciary money was being employed t explain the behaviour of credit. Tooke constantly referred to the dange of 'confound[ing] bank notes strictly convertible into coin, with a compul sory and inconvertible paper money' (1844, p. 19; also 1838/57, IV p. 171). I shall examine the Banking School interpretation of the behaviou of credit instruments such as bank notes in the next chapter; here I ar interested primarily in their characterisation of a fiduciary issue or, a Tooke called it, a 'government compulsory paper' (see Laidler, 197 Rist, 1940, p. 187 ff.; Sayers, 1960).

Like Ricardo, Tooke recognised that, '[d]epreciation is not an essenti element in variations of the value of an inconvertible paper'; but he de parted from Ricardian doctrine in the following deduction from this in tial premise: '[N]or is depreciation always a necessary consequence c inconvertibility' (ibid., p. 70 fn.)[29] What mattered, according to the hypothesis he finally devised in his *Inquiry into the Currency Principle* (1844), was not so much the absence of legal convertibility as the 'manner or purpose of the issue' (ibid., p. 68; also Fullarton, 1844, p. 67 and *passim*). If this crucial point of difference between credit and fiduciary money – which was embryonic even in eighteenth century thought – was overlooked by Ricardo, then his position was at least explicable on the grounds of internal consistency, despite its more obvious external failure to come to terms with the direction of causation between money and prices during the Restriction period.

The Currency School, however, went further than Ricardo, applying the theory of a fiduciary system and its associated principle of limitation to bank notes which were by that time *legally convertible into coin.* As Tooke pointed out: 'An increase or diminution of the amount of bank notes is evidently considered . . . by the professed adherents of the doctrine of the currency principle . . . to be analogous, in the effects on markets, to alternations in the quantity of a government compulsory paper; or, in other words, they consider that prices in such cases are under a direct influence from, and affected in the same manner by, variations in the amount of bank notes in circulation, which they designate indiscriminately as paper money' (ibid.).[30]

Tooke conceived of fiduciary money as paper issued by the government which was 'inconvertible and compulsory current' and usually in payment for the personal expenditure of the sovereign, public works and buildings, the salaries of civil servants and the maintenance of military and naval establishments. Although this is not the place to consider the Banking School's 'law of reflux', it may be noted, with Schumpeter, that there was 'a very material difference between the case of bank credit which does, and the case of government paper money which does not, "flow back" automatically' (1954, p.731). Fiduciary money was therefore seen as an *element of demand* which, if extended beyond the point given by past accumulation – and hence the level of output – would tend inevitably to depreciate in value. The assumption of Say's law was shared by the Banking School with the prevailing monetary orthodoxy, despite their theoretical advance in other respects.

Tooke was in as little doubt about the criteria and consequences of the overissue of specifically fiduciary money as was Ricardo in his discussion of inconvertible paper in general:

> It is quite clear that paper created and so paid away by the Government, not being returnable to the issuer, will constitute a fresh source of

> demand, and must be forced into and permeate all the channels of circulation. Accordingly, every fresh issue beyond the point at which former issues had settled in a certain rise of prices and of wages, and a fall of the exchanges, is soon followed by a further rise of commodities and wages, and a fall of the exchanges; the depreciation being in the ratio of the forcibly increased amount of the issues. (Ibid., pp. 69–70)[31]

Tooke went on, like Smith, to resolve demand simply into revenue 'under the head of rents, profits, salaries, and wages, destined for current expenditure' (ibid., p. 71). Although, on this point, Marx was to correct him,[32] he supported the main thrust of Tooke's monetary analysis and employed it in his account of the business cycle.

John Fullarton, a surgeon, traveller and sometime banker, whom Marx included among 'the best writers on money' (1867/94, I, p. 129 fn.), defended Tooke against his powerful critics and at the same time staked a well argued claim to Ricardo's intellectual heritage on behalf of the Banking School (see Green, 1937, vol. 2, pp. 433–4). His *Regulation of Currencies* (1844) is a neglected yet 'penetrating tract', according to Gregory, and 'perhaps the most subtle and able production emanating from the Banking School' (Introduction to Tooke, 1838/57, I, p. 81).

The discussion of fiduciary money, however, was inevitably a weak point of the book, lacking the force of the analysis of credit. Here, Fullarton attempted a similar comparison to that of Ricardo with the effect of a gold mine: 'The process by which the redundant issues of an inconvertible government paper act upon prices, is exactly analogous to that which is set in motion by an increase of the productive power of the mines' (1844, pp. 62–3). While this comparison might have a limited short-run validity under strict assumptions, it would by no means generally be the case. As Hobson demonstrated in the context of later gold discoveries:

> The evidence as to the disposal of the new gold suggests . . . that the initial force is exerted in the shape of a demand for the larger volume of credit, and that this demand draws into the banks of the countries where it is operative the requisite amount of gold to sustain it. Thus the increased quantity of money appears in response to a demand for it. (1913, p. 52)

Fullarton at least possessed a clear understanding of the differences between a fiduciary issue and credit. The intention behind the gold mine analogy was to highlight the dangers of such an issue, but it showed instead the constraints placed upon his analysis – and upon that of Tooke and Marx – by the fixed output assumption of Say's law. This necessarily implied a 'quantity theory of money' in a fiduciary system, even if as we shall see shortly, there are crucial points of difference with commodity money.

Although Fullarton had forgotten his own perfectly sound analysis of the metallic system in the rush to nail his colours to a 'Ricardian' mast, he did make an important practical distinction between state expenditure covered by taxation and what is now called deficit spending:

> It is in the discretion of the issuing authority, either to limit the employment of the notes which it sends out to the purposes of a temporary advance in anticipation of taxes, or to issue them for all purposes of state expenditure without making any provision to secure their return. In the former case, there will be no permanent addition to the circulation, nor any power of purchase obtained which would not sooner or later have been obtained through taxation alone. In the latter, the issuing authority will be placed nearly in the same position with the merchant returning with his double cargo of gold and silver from El Dorado. It will have invested itself with a power, only limited in the first instance by its own discretion, of competing in the market for every article of which the government or the host of individuals receiving pay from government may chance to stand in need; and there is no channel, through which the notes which it issues can ever return. There exists therefore every condition necessary to a depreciation of the paper and a rise of the nominal prices of commodities. (Ibid., p. 63)

Inflation was thus not an inevitable consequence either of an inconvertible paper currency or of state spending, but only of spending which was not covered – at least potentially – by tax revenues. While it is not my intention to stray into the field of public finance, it may be recognised that this was a bold statement for its time and attracted considerable vilification from supporters of the currency principle. This was in spite of Fullarton's scrupulous commitment to legal convertibility and his repeated attempts to distance himself from Thomas Attwood and the spokesmen for Birmingham manufacturing interests, who wanted an immediate return to inconvertible paper and a devaluation of the monetary standard (Fetter, 1965, p. 179).[33] Protest as he might, Fullarton was depicted widely as 'another John Law' with designs on turning the Bank of England into a Banque Royale.[34] We shall come back to the ideas and practical proposals of the Banking School in the following chapter.

Marx's 'quantity theory'

Marx premised his argument in support of the Banking School upon a clear distinction between fiduciary money and credit. In the course of a lengthy discussion in his *Critique of Political Economy*, he showed that tokens of value – including paper money – did not come about 'by arrangement or state intervention' but rather evolved more or less 'spontaneously' from the separation effected by constant use and debasement between the 'real weight' of coins and their 'nominal weight' (1859, pp. 107–18; also 1867/94, I, pp. 125–7).[35] Fiduciary money was seen as 'an advanced form of the token of value, and the only kind of paper money which directly arises from metallic currency or from simple commodity circulation itself'; on the other hand, '[c]redit money belongs to a more advanced stage of the social process of production and conforms to very different laws' (ibid., p. 116).

The classical law of monetary circulation still applied to the fiduciary system, but it assumed a different form; once the state issued notes in various denominations, it followed that:

> Insofar as [the notes] actually take the place of gold to the same amount, their movement is subject to the laws that regulate the currency of money itself. A law peculiar to the circulation of paper money can spring up only from the proportion in which that paper money represents gold. Such a law exists; stated simply, it is as follows: the issue of paper money must not exceed in amount the gold (or silver as the case may be) which would actually circulate if not replaced by symbols. (1867/94, I, p. 128)

Marx repeated his observation that the quantity of gold which the circulation could absorb 'constantly fluctuates about a given level'; but the fact that, in any given currency, it 'never sinks below a certain minimum easily ascertained by actual experience' facilitated the substitution of a paper currency. If, however, this paper was issued to *excess*, it would not have any 'real' effects; it would, according to Marx, simply depreciate proportionately:

> If the paper money exceed its proper limit, which is the amount in gold coins of the like denomination that can actually be current, it would, apart from the danger of falling into general disrepute, represent only that quantity of gold, which, in accordance with the laws of the cir-

culation of commodities, is required, and is alone capable of being represented by paper. If the quantity of paper money issued be doubled what it ought to be, then, as a matter of fact, £1 would be the money-name not of 1/4 of an ounce, but of an ounce of gold. The effect would be the same as if an alteration had taken place in the function of gold as a standard of prices. (Ibid.)[36]

At this level of analysis, it could be said that Marx accepted a 'quantity theory of money' similar in outward appearance to Ricardo's short-run adjustment mechanism in a metallic system. The differences which marked out the system of fiduciary money, however, were crucial: first, there was no limit to the extent of depreciation; and secondly, no mechanism existed to restore the paper to its previous value. Kuhne argues that, in this context, 'Marx recognised the quantity theory as only a tautological formula, for *ceteris paribus* implies the velocity of circulation of money to be constant' (1979, p. 340). This is true, but it misses the point. The point is that Marx shared with the classical economists the Say's law assumption of a given level of output. Consequently, any unwarranted extension of a fiduciary issue could have no other effect than to devalue the unit of account.

Indeed, Marx explicitly opposed the idea that the state might actually create wealth just because it 'seems now to transform paper into gold by the magic of its imprint'. Of course, it could issue a theoretically unlimited amount of notes, but what it could not do was maintain their value: '[T]his power of the State is mere illusion. It may throw any number of paper notes of any denomination into circulation but its control ceases with this mechanical act. As soon as the token of value or paper money enters the sphere of circulation it is subject to the inherent laws of this sphere' (1859, p. 119).[37] The opposite view had been put in its most extreme form by one of Proudhon's disciples, Alfred Darimon, who, in his *De la Réforme des Banques* (1856), announced a plan to augment the capital of France through deliberate and far-reaching monetary expansion. Marx's response in the *Grundrisse* was mocking: 'The bank would not have increased the wealth of the nation through a stroke of magic, but would merely have undertaken a very ordinary operation to devalue its own paper' (1973, p. 122).[38] The common thread running through all of Marx's monetary writings was that convertibility into gold and silver, i.e., money as a produced commodity, was 'the practical measure of the value of every paper currency denominated in gold and silver, *whether this paper is legally convertible or not*' (ibid., p. 132, emphasis added).

In the final analysis, it must be concluded, neither Marx or the Banking School added substantially to Ricardo's own theory of fiduciary money; their contribution was simply to demarcate its functions more accurately and, of course, to deny its application to the inconvertible notes of the Bank Restriction. These notes were issued *on loan* and were thus subject to the principles not of a fiduciary system but of credit, including the 'law of reflux', which constituted the main focus of the Banking School investigation. As we shall see in the next chapter, these principles could have served as the cutting edge of their contribution to debate, but for their adherence to Say's law. This assumption, by confining the Banking School account of the credit system within narrow bounds, also inevitably affected their account of a fiduciary issue, where, as Marx put it, 'all the laws governing the circulation of real money seem to be reversed and turned upside down' (1859, p. 121). Significantly, however, the economists of the Banking School were not among those whose vision of the credit system was restricted to paper money with a legal rate of exchange; such economists, Marx observed, 'must misunderstand the inherent laws of monetary circulation' (ibid., p. 122). The case of the Currency School, to whom I now turn, was only the most striking example of this approach.

7 Theory of the Credit System

> [W]ith the development of the credit system, capitalist production continually strives to overcome the metal barrier, which is simultaneously a material and imaginative barrier of wealth and its movement, but again and again it breaks its back on this barrier.
>
> K. Marx, *Capital*, III (1867/94)

The debate between the Currency and Banking Schools in the mid nineteenth century gave rise to important developments in the theoretical analysis of inflation and business cycles in the context of an increasingly sophisticated credit system. Indeed, Marx spoke of the 'economic literature worth mentioning since 1830' as resolving itself 'mainly into a literature on currency, credit and crises' (1867/94, III, pp. 492–3). The 'bullion controversy' in the early part of the century was addressed, as we have seen, almost exclusively to the operation of a fiduciary system; hence, the resumption of cash payments by the Bank of England in 1821 was the first occasion for any real advance in the theory of *credit* since Adam Smith. In this chapter, I shall begin with the concept of 'fictitious capital' and the determination of the rate of interest, and then attempt to deduce the laws governing the behaviour of credit instruments and their connection with economic activity and prices.

The inflation of the Bank Restriction was, according to the prevailing orthodoxy, a direct and inescapable consequence of excessive monetary expansion. As we found in the previous chapter, the adoption of Say's law and stable velocity as underlying assumptions by Ricardo and his followers prevented them from taking into account less prosaic reasons for the inflation, which included harvest failures, war subsidies and the Napoleonic blockade. The real events were drawn to his attention without effect. Moreover, from a theoretical viewpoint, he was criticised for superimposing a theory of *fiduciary* money on a credit system. Bank notes were not issued at will by the state, but advanced on loan to meet commercial needs. If the notes were fiduciary money, Ricardo would have been correct in his characterisation of their relationship to the price level. Fiduciary money only *represents* gold in the circulation process and is depreciated to the extent of its overissue. The depreciation persists until the quantity is reduced, for there are no self-correcting tendencies as in the case of convertible paper.

The fact that the notes of the Restriction period were not forced currency but credit responding to the demand of the non-bank public was excluded from Ricardo's consideration by assumptions established in the context of metallic currency. He treated the notes as though they were fiduciary because output and velocity were independently given. The possibility of disintermediation, when the authorities tried to contract the note issue, was therefore also excluded. The fixed velocity assumption implied that the rest of the spectrum of credit would shrink commensurately with the notes. In fact, as the Banking School was to demonstrate, credit instruments simply expanded in their place. The anti-Bullionist opposition to Ricardo was analytically weak. They did not directly attack the confusion of money with credit, and they relied on an overstated real bills doctrine. More fundamentally, however, they did not challenge Say's law, and their alternative approach therefore remained incomplete. While not overcoming this limitation, the Banking School arguments against the currency principle were superior.

The resumption of specie payments on the advice of Ricardo and the Bullionist spokesmen did nothing to eliminate price instability from the market economy. In fact, the experience of subsequent decades showed not only that periodic crises were an inherent feature of industrialisation, but that their scale and intensity had increased rather than diminished. In 1825 and 1836, phases of vigorous expansion ended with an adverse balance of payments, gold drain from the Bank of England and an inflationary collapse into recession (see Andréadès, 1935, p. 248 ff.). The Currency School – a new orthodoxy which Morgan (1965) describes as the 'heirs of the Bullion Report' – attributed the recurrent dislocation to excessive monetary growth. The convertibility of bank notes was no longer seen as a sufficient safeguard against overissue and consequent depreciation. First, James Pennington and Thomas Joplin and then, more prominently, Robert Torrens, S. J. Loyd (later Lord Overstone) and G. W. Norman argued that rules would have to be devised to make the paper currency fluctuate as though it were metallic, in other words to replicate the 'automatic' operation of Ricardo's international specie-flow mechanism. This implied regulation of the note issue by the monetary authorities in strict conformity with the foreign exchanges; the export and import of bullion was treated as an index of monetary excess or deficiency and thus of the value of notes (see Viner, 1937, ch. 5; Daugherty, 1942/43; Fetter, 1965, ch. 6).

The genesis of the currency principle was summed up by Marx as follows:

> The commercial crises of the nineteenth century, and in particular the great crises of 1825 and 1836, did not lead to any further development of Ricardo's currency theory, but rather to new practical applications of it. It was no longer a matter of single economic phenomena – such as the depreciation of precious metals in the sixteenth and seventeenth centuries confronting Hume, or the depreciation of paper currency during the eighteenth century and the beginning of the nineteenth confronting Ricardo – but of big storms on the world market, in which the antagonism of all elements in the bourgeois process of production explodes; the origin of these storms and the means of defence against them were sought within the sphere of currency, the most superficial and abstract sphere of this process. The theoretical assumption which actually serves the school of economic weather experts as their point of departure is the dogma that Ricardo had discovered the laws governing purely metallic currency. It was thus left to them to subsume the circulation of credit money or bank-notes under these laws. (1859, p. 182)

The currency principle was given practical effect by the Bank Charter Act of 1844, which set the pattern of the UK financial system for almost a century (Horsefield, 1944). The Act's main provision split the Bank of England into two separate departments. A banking department was to handle the deposit business, while an issue department absorbed the note issue of the country banks and made any expansion of the note issue beyond a statutory minimum of £14 million conditional upon an equivalent increase in its bullion reserve. This legislative prescription was rejected by the Banking School, which Morgan calls 'the heirs to the opposition to the Bullion Report, but the opposition as it might have been rather than as it was'. The long-run determination of aggregate monetary requirements by nominal output – the 'supply side' of the equation of exchange – was common ground in the debate. The real point at issue was rather the *short-run* behaviour of the variables (Viner, 1937, p. 221).

Whereas the Currency School adopted Ricardian quantity theory and applied it to a credit system made up of convertible bank notes, the Banking School took the alternative view of metallic circulation and tried to develop a theory specific to credit. The accomplishments of the Banking School – especially of Tooke, Fullarton and James Wilson – were hailed not only by Marx but also by J. S. Mill, who gave their position the stamp of his authority (Deane, 1978, p. 58). By that time, however, the currency principle had become firmly entrenched as the new monetary orthodoxy. As before, in the analysis of metallic and fiduciary money, the failure of the critics to dispose of the Say's law assumption which underpinned this orthodoxy allowed it to dominate banking theory and practice until the formulation of a 'principle of effective demand' in the next century.

FICTITIOUS CAPITAL AND INTEREST

In previous chapters, I have traced the development of the classical theory of money at the level both of simple commodity circulation, and less extensively, of capital accumulation. The theory had as its point of departure the surplus approach to value and distribution, from which it was detached only at the cost of arbitrariness and even incoherence. We have also seen that a law of monetary circulation was found to define the circulation requirements of metallic and paper money – albeit in distinctive ways – and their relationship to the price index in the equation of exchange. To the extent that we have touched upon the accumulation of capital, it has been 'real' capital which has concerned us; it will be necessary in our analysis of credit, however, to take into account the concept of 'fictitious' capital as well, which similarly entered into the formation of the general rate of profit. This separate category of capital denoted not value as such but only *titles to value* – existing either in fact or merely as *potential* value – whose origin was the credit transaction.[1] It could accumulate alongside real capital, and might even circulate from time to time in the form of money; yet it obeyed very different economic laws (see Hilferding, 1910, pt II).

The essential nature of fictitious capital, and the part it played in the credit system, was clearly conveyed by Tooke in his *Inquiry into the currency principle*. There, he began by explaining that, '[c]redit, in its most simple expression, is the confidence which, well or ill-founded, leads a person to entrust another with a certain amount of capital, in money, or in goods computed at a value in money agreed upon, and in each case payable at the expiration of a fixed term'. This capital was *real* capital; and, as Tooke went on to point out, where it was lent in *money*, whether in bank notes or a cash credit, 'an addition for the use of the capital of so much upon every 100 l is made to the amount to be repaid'. This 'addition' – a charge for tying up the capital of another – was of course, the *interest* on that capital; its magnitude depended upon factors to be examined in a moment. It applied also to *goods*, 'the value of which is agreed in terms of money'; in that case, 'the sum stipulated to be repaid includes a consideration for the use of the capital and for the risk, till the expiration of the period fixed for payment'. The *fictitious* capital was constituted by the '[w]ritten obligations of payment at fixed dates [which] mostly accompany these credits'; and 'the obligations or promissory notes after date being transferable, . . . [the lenders] . . . are most enabled to borrow or to buy on lower terms, by having their own credit strengthened by the names on the bills in addition to their own' (1844, p. 37).[2]

The secondary market for commercial paper acted, therefore, as a lever to promote multiple credit expansion – and, correspondingly, the accumulation of fictitious capital. Marx observed that:

> With the development of interest-bearing capital and the credit system, all capital seems to double itself, and sometimes treble itself, by the various modes in which the same capital, or perhaps even the same claim on a debt, appears in different forms in different hands. The great portion of this 'money-capital' is purely fictitious. . . . All connection with the actual expansion process of capital is thus completely lost. (1867/94, III, pp. 466, 470)

The accumulation of fictitious capital could theoretically proceed at an exponential rate; it seemed to be limited only by the scope of lending activity, and within certain boundaries, the terms on which lending took place. Yet the level of *output* would ultimately remain unaffected. We have already seen that eighteenth-century authors were at one in their view that the proliferation of credit could not alter the quantity of capital, but only its speed of turnover; they saw the role of credit as being solely to *redistribute* capital so that it could be used most productively. The classical economists of the nineteenth century, whatever their other differences, also held this view, due to their shared acceptance of Say's law. Just as the 'classical dichotomy' reflected the separation they effected between the 'real' economy on the one hand and purely monetary phenomena on the other, so they used it to differentiate the accumulation of fictitious capital, which could have no such influence in the long-run (see Cramp, 1962, ch. 2).

The only point at issue here among economists, as in the question of a price response, was whether any *temporary* deviation of output could occur. The position of Ricardo was unambiguous and entirely consistent with his account of inflation. During his presentation of evidence to the House of Lords Committee on the Resumption of Cash Payments in 1819, the following exchange took place:

> State what in your Opinion is the Difference between that State of Things, in which a Stimulus is given by fictitious Capital arising from an Over-abundance of Paper in Circulation, and that which results from the regular Operation of real Capital employed in Production?
>
> I believe that on this Subject I differ from most other People. *I do not think that any Stimulus is given to Production by the Use of fictitious Capital*, as it is called. (1951/58, V, p. 445, emphasis added)

In other words, the position was analogous with monetary overissue, where, as we have seen, no effect was produced on the level of output; there might, however, be a limited 'forced saving' response due to a temporary alteration in the distribution of income (ibid., p. 446; see above ch. 6).

In addition, it was argued, an excess of fictitious capital could depress the money rate of interest in the short-run process of price adjustment. This aspect of the adjustment process had been spelt out earlier by Ricardo to the same hearing of the Lords Committee: 'Reduction or Increase of the Quantity of Money always ultimately raises or lowers the Price of Commodities; when this is effected, the Rate of Interest will be precisely the same as before; it is only during the Interval, that it, before the Prices are settled at the new Rate, that the Rate of Interest is either raised or lowered' (ibid., p. 445).[3] This was, at one level, merely a restatement of the classical dichotomy, but it reflected a theory of interest which had evolved as part of the surplus approach to value and distribution.

The 'classical theory of interest' was preserved in its popular form by the Lord's Committee itself: 'Are we to understand that, when Money is lent, Capital is advanced, and that Interest only can be affected by the Abundance of Scarcity of real Capital, combined with the Opportunity of employing it?' Ricardo concurred: 'Precisely so; Money is only the Medium by which the Borrower possesses himself of the Capital which he means ultimately to employ' (ibid.). Yet Ricardo, in this exchange, was selling his analysis short. In his desire to uphold a short-run quantity theory of money, he obscured the role played by the general rate of profit, which he had earlier identified in the *Principles* as determining the rate of interest in the *long-run* (Sayers, 1953; Hollander, 1979). I intend to look at Ricardo's theory of interest more closely in a moment. It should first be noted that it was only the 'popular' aspect of his theory which was adopted by the Currency School and was thereafter to become a cornerstone of the 'classical monetary orthodoxy'. The disturbing connotations of the surplus approach persuaded them to develop instead the notion of a 'natural rate of interest', which would be wholly dependent upon the supply and demand for real capital. There would be no question in this approach of a 'deduction' from profits or from a surplus of any kind (Cassel, 1903, p. 32).

It will thus be seen that just as the Currency School modified Ricardo's quantity theory to ensure its application to a system of convertible bank notes, so they revised his theory of interest to underpin their concession to supply and demand analysis. Although the Banking School did not subscribe to this theory of interest, they had nothing to put in its place beyond empirical observation. Indeed, they pronounced themselves unconcerned with the theoretical aspects of the discussion.[4] It was left to Marx to indicate the direction an alternative approach might take by resurrecting fruitful eighteenth-century ideas, though he was unable to offer a complete solution (Panico, 1980).

Marx began, with Ricardo, from the premises of the surplus approach; he, too, insisted on the absolute separation between the accumulation of real and fictitious capital. Not only was 'the actual accumulation of industrial capitalists . . . accomplished, as a rule, by an increase in the elements of reproductive capital itself', but fictitious capital might accumulate 'at the expense of both the industrial and commercial capitalists' since 'in the unfavourable phases of the industrial cycle the rate of interest may rise so high that it temporarily consumes the whole profit of some lines of business' (1867/94, III, p. 502). It is to the determination of the rate of interest in classical and Marxian analysis that we must now turn in order to evaluate its connection with the variables in the equation of exchange.

Money and competition

We have already touched upon the notion of 'interest-bearing capital', which may be defined as capital lent in the form of money or commodities with a charge for its use over a fixed period. This capital was therefore itself a 'commodity', but, as Marx pointed out, a 'commodity *sui generis*' (1867/94, III, p. 339), with interest serving as its price.[5] Hume was generally credited with discovering the factors governing the rate of interest, though, as we shall see, they had been presented two years earlier in an anonymous work by Joseph Massie (Roll, 1973, pp. 120–1; Schumpeter, 1954, p. 327 ff.)

In his essay, 'On Interest' (1752), Hume wished to refute the view of Locke that the interest rate was dependent upon the quantity of money; apart from anything else, this view cut across his interpretation of price behaviour, which has previously been examined at some length. He argued instead that the rate of interest was determined by the 'demand for borrowing', on the one hand, and the available 'riches to supply that demand', on the other – that is to say, by demand and supply – and, ultimately, by the amount of 'profits arising from commerce'. High interest and high profits were both seen as the expression 'of the small advance of commerce, and industry, not the scarcity of gold and silver', since it was evident that, 'we really and in effect borrow [a stock of labour and commodities], when we take money upon interest'. Conversely, low interest and low profits 'are both originally derived from that extensive commerce, which produces opulent merchants, and renders the monied interest considerable' (1752, pp. 177–82).

At a certain stage in the accumulation process, according to Hume, 'there must arise rivalships among the merchants, which diminish the profits of trade at the same time that they increase the trade itself'; the result of this competition was to 'induce the merchants to accept more willingly of a low interest'. Nevertheless, Hume was not concerned ' to inquire which of these circumstances, to wit, *low interest* or *low profits*, is cause, and which the effect', since they 'both arise from an extensive commerce, and mutually forward each other'. Indeed, he concluded in a famous passage that:

> [I]nterest is the barometer of the state, and its lowness is a sign almost infallible of the flourishing condition of a people. . . . Those who have asserted, that the plenty of money was the cause of low interest, seem to have taken a collateral effect for a cause; since the same industry, which sinks the interest, commonly acquires great abundance of the precious metals. (Ibid., p. 181)

Massie's pamphlet, *An Essay on the Governing Causes of the Natural Rate of Interest* (1750), was critical not just of Locke but also of Petty, who similarly ascribed variations in the rate of interest to monetary factors: 'It appears . . . that Mr Locke attributes the Government of the natural Rate of Interest to the Proportion which the Quantity of Money in a Country bears to the Debts of its inhabitants one amongst another, and to the Trade of it; and that Sir William Petty makes it depend on the Quantity of Money alone; so they only differ in regard to Debts. . . .' (1750, pp. 18–19). Massie's main contribution was to show for the first time that, on the contrary, the rate of interest was fundamentally determined by the rate of profit.[6]

The terms in which Massie conducted his investigation were as follows:

> [T]he Equitableness of taking interest, depends not upon a Man's making or not making Profit by what he borrows, but upon its being capable of producing Profit if rightly employed. It cannot therefore be difficult to determine what the natural Rate of Interest immediately depends on; for, if that which Men pay as Interest for the use of what they borrow, be a *Part of the Profits* it is capable of producing, *this Interest must always be govern'd by those Profits*. (Ibid., pp. 46–7, emphasis added)[7]

The day to day calculation of interest was settled for Massie by competition in the financial market. Asking himself, 'what proportion of these Profits do of right belong to the Borrower, and what to the Lender', he answered: '[T]his there is no other Method of determining, then [sic] by the Opinions of Borrowers and Lenders in general; for Right and Wrong in this Respect, are only what common Consent makes so' (Ibid., p. 47).[8]

By the time Adam Smith wrote, he could brush aside Locke's interpretation (shared by Law and Montesquieu) of the rate of interest and its magnitude as having been 'so fully exposed by Mr Hume that it is, perhaps, unnecessary to say anything more about it' (1776, p. 273). Smith, however, was able to place his own theory of interest in the context of the classical approach to value and distribution (Rist, 1940, p. 126; Schumpeter, 1954, p. 720). To begin with, the quantity of actual or potential interest-bearing capital in a country was regulated 'by the value of that part of the annual produce which, as soon as it comes either from the ground, or from the hands of the productive labourers, is destined not only for replacing a capital, but such a capital as the owner does not care to be at the trouble of employing himself' (ibid., p. 271). In other words, real capital was not created but merely redistributed by credit; moreover, this operation became the function of a separate class in society: 'As such capitals are commonly lent out and paid back in money, they constitute what is called the *monied interest*. It is distinct, not only from the landed, but from the trading and manufacturing interests . . .' (ibid., emphasis added).[9]

Although money could serve as an instrument for transferring capital, and for the repayment of loans, it was not itself part of the capital stock:

> A capital lent at interest may, in this manner, be considered as an assignment from the lender to the borrowers of a certain considerable portion of the annual produce; upon condition that the borrower in return shall, during the continuance of the loan, annually assign to the lender a smaller portion, called the interest; and at the end of it a portion equally considerable with that which had originally been assigned to him, called the repayment. Though money, either coin or paper, serves generally as the deed of assignment both to the smaller and to the more considerable portion, it is itself altogether different from what is assigned by it. (Ibid., p. 272)[10]

Again, since the rate of interest was proportionate to the rate of profits, it would tend to fall as 'competition between different capitals . . . sinks the profits of stock' (ibid., also I, ch. 9).

Interest and prices

While Ricardo eventually abandoned Smith's theory of profit, he accepted the proposition, whose authorship he ascribed to Hume, that, 'the rate of interest is not regulated by the abundance or scarcity of money, but by the abundance or scarcity of that part of capital, not consisting of money . . . [viz.] by the profits on the employment of capital' (1951/58, III, pp. 88–9). This proposition was central to Ricardo's first pamphlet, *High Price of Bullion*, and was developed in the *Principles*. There he made it clear that the rate of interest was 'ultimately and permanently governed by the rate of profit', although it might be 'subject to temporary variations from other causes' (ibid., I, p. 297).

In the *High Price of Bullion*, Ricardo trenchantly repudiated the idea that an increased supply of bank notes could permanently lower the rate of interest; this would 'attribute a power to the circulating medium which it could never possess'. He maintained that:

> Banks would, if this were possible, become powerful engines indeed. By creating paper money, and lending it at three or two per cent under the present market rate of interest, the Bank would reduce the profits on trade in the same proportion . . . [N]o nation, but by similar means, could enter into competition with us, we should engross the trade of the world. To what absurdities would not such a theory lead us! (Ibid., p. 92)[11]

It was only during the 'interval' prior to the influence of expansion on prices that the rate of interest might be affected: '[I]nterest would, during that interval be under its natural level; but as soon as the additional sum of notes or of money became absorbed in the general circulation, the rate of interest would be as high, and new loans would be demanded with as much eagerness as before the additional issues' (ibid., p. 91). In other words, a low rate of interest was not the cause of high prices, as the Currency School was later to allege. The sole cause of inflation, according to Ricardo, lay in monetary expansion. This was treated as an entirely separate phenomenon.

Ricardo held fast to his basic position in the *Principles*,[12] and, as we have seen, pressed it upon the inquiry into the resumption of cash payments shortly thereafter. It was adopted by the Currency School, though only in a form so revised as to constitute a different principle. Apart from positing a causal relationship between low interest rates and inflation, this 'Ricardian orthodoxy' identified a 'natural rate' of interest which was given by the demand and supply of real capital and to which was counterposed a 'market rate', expressing the daily fluctuations in the money market.

While the Banking School attempted to confront this orthodoxy, their lack of success in establishing an alternative theory of interest mirrored the shortcomings of their opposition to quantity theory. For example, in his *Inquiry into the Currency Principle*, Tooke began by reaffirming the dependence of the rate of interest upon the 'abundance' or 'scarcity' of 'disposable capital', and pointed to the confusion which arose when the term 'value of money' was employed indiscriminately 'to signify both value in exchange for commodities and value in use of capital' (1844, pp. 76–7).[13] Instead of refuting the concept of a 'natural rate' of interest, which was to be Marx's approach (as we shall discover in the following section), Tooke simply avoided any reference to it and attached importance only to the market rate, or the Bank rate to the extent that it was independently determined. His opposition to the currency principle in this context was confined to a rebuttal of the argument that, 'a low rate of interest is calculated to raise prices, and a high rate to depress them' (ibid., p. 77). This argument was premised upon the effect an enhanced 'facility of borrowing' would have on the money supply and hence, in accordance with classical quantity theory, on the price level (Rist, 1940, pp. 222–5).[14]

Ricardo himself had never suggested that interest rates would have any such effect on the money supply. Indeed, as we have just noted, the causation in his analysis ran in precisely the opposite direction. Tooke was able, however, to show why the effect proposed by the Currency School was far from being inevitable, or even likely. To begin with, the greater volume of bank notes might not be demanded, and, if they were, might not be spent:

> The truth is, that the power of purchase by persons having capital and credit is much beyond anything that those who are unacquainted practically with speculative markets have any idea of. The error is in supposing the *disposition* or *will* to be co-extensive with the power. The limit to the motive for the exercise of the power is in the prospect of resale with a profit. (Ibid., p. 79)[15]

Whereas, in the metallic system, a hoarding mechanism might have come into play, here this mechanism took the form of a decision not to use a borrowing facility to the fullest available extent. The contention that such a facility acted as a 'stimulus' to borrowing and speculation carried no weight with Tooke. Unless there was 'a laxity of regard to security or repayment by the lender', the mere existence of a low interest rate was not a significant factor in motivating speculative activity; this was 'seldom if ever entered into with borrowed capital, except with a view to so great an advance of price, and to be realized within so moderate a space of time, as to render the rate of interest or discount a matter of comparatively trifling consideration' (ibid., p. 82).[16] Tooke did not stop there (see Wicksell, 1935, pp. 99–100; Laidler, 1972, p. 178). He maintained that a fall in the rate of interest would tend – in the long-run – to *reduce* commodity prices, since it could be seen as 'equivalent to or rather constitut[ing] a diminution of the cost of production' (ibid., p. 81). This highly original view – the reverse of the causation implied by the currency principle – was derived from recent evidence which Tooke expertly paraded.[17] It would be through the 'competition of the producers', he concluded, that the lowered cost of production would 'inevitably cause a fall of prices of all the articles into the cost of which the interest of money entered as an ingredient' (ibid.). Although Tooke did not construct a theory of interest which would rival the orthodox interpretation of the Currency School, he succeeded in making his more limited point '[B]oth the currency theory, and the money market theory, that is, on the one hand, the theory which connects prices with bank notes, and, on the other hand, the theory which connects them with the rate of interest are equally in error' (ibid., p. 85).

'Natural' rate of interest

Marx's analysis of credit was pursued largely in a series of manuscripts which were subsequently edited and published by Engels in the third volume of *Capital*.[18] In these manuscripts, he was able to go considerably further than Ricardo or Tooke (see Panico, 1980). Having introduced interest-bearing capital in its most primitive form as usury and as it evolved in the modern credit system, Marx turned his attention to the nature and magnitude of interest. He affirmed the classical view – founded by Massie – that the general rate of profit was 'to be regarded as the ultimate determinant of the maximum limit of interest' (1867/94, III, p. 360; see Hilferding, 1910, p. 100). In the short-run, the rate of interest oscillated according to the various phases of the industrial cycle; and, in the longer term, it had 'a tendency to fall quite independently of the fluctuations in the rate of profit', due to the extensive accumulation of money capital in the more advanced countries and also to the evolution of the credit system.

The 'average rate of interest' was therefore no more than that – the calculation of an average amid mutually compensating variations. The Currency School's idea of a 'natural rate of interest' was something else. Marx commented:

> The average rate of interest prevailing in a certain country – as distinct from the continually fluctuating market rates – cannot be determined by any law. In this sphere there is *no such thing as a natural rate of interest* in the sense in which economists speak of a natural rate of profit and a natural rate of wages. . . . Wherever it is competition as such which determines anything, the determination is accidental, purely empirical. (Ibid., p. 363, emphasis added)

The competition in the money markets, as Massie had long ago discovered, was between the lenders and borrowers of 'loanable capital' over their respective shares of the profit, which, after all, could be produced only once.[19] Marx explained further that the reason 'why the limits of a mean rate of interest cannot be deducted from general laws . . . lies simply in the nature of interest. It is merely a *part of average profit*' (ibid., p. 364, emphasis added).[20] The contrast with the determination of the rate of profit was of crucial importance:

> Two entirely different elements – labour power and capital – act as determinants in the division between surplus value and wages, which division essentially determines the rate of profit; these are functions of two independent variables, which limit one another; and it is their *qualitative difference* that is the source of the *quantitative division* of the produced value. . . . [T]he same occurs in the splitting of surplus value into rent and profit. Nothing of the kind occurs in the case of interest. Here the *qualitative differentiation* . . . proceeds rather from the purely *quantitative division* of the same sum of surplus value. (Ibid.)

Nevertheless, although there was no law to set down the limits of the average rate of interest, it 'appears as a uniform, definite and tangible magnitude in a quite different way from the general rate of profit' (ibid., p. 365).[21] Indeed, the perpetually fluctuating market rate of interest existed at any moment as a 'fixed magnitude', like the market price of commodities, 'because in the money market all loanable capital continually faces functioning capital as an aggregate mass, so that the relation between the supply of loanable capital on the one side, and the demand for it on the other, decides the market level of interest at any given time. . . . On the other hand, the general rate of profit is never anything more than a tendency, a movement to equalise specific rates of profit' (ibid., p. 366). Money capital, more clearly than industrial capital, manifested itself 'as essentially the common capital of a class', since, with the growth of a modern credit system it 'assumes the nature of a concentrated, organised mass, which, quite different from actual production, is subject to the control of bankers, i.e., the representatives of social capital' (ibid., p. 368).

Marx drew heavily upon the increasing amount of available empirical data to disprove the Currency School notion that the rate of interest was established by the demand and supply of *real* capital.[22] This notion was, of course, an essential precondition for their further proposition, which I shall examine in the next section, that variations in the price level were a function of specifically monetary movements – even, or especially, in a credit system. Marx cited, for example, the evidence of J. G. Hubbard, former governor of the Bank of England, to the House of Commons Select Committee on the Bank Acts in 1857. Hubbard stated that not only in the ten years 1834–43 but also in 1844–53, 'movements in the bullion of the Bank were invariably accompanied by a decrease or increase in the loanable value of money advanced on discount'; moreover, 'the variations in the prices of commodities in this country exhibit an entire independence of the amount of circulation as shown in the fluctuations in bullion at the Bank of England' (cited in ibid., p. 551).

Marx used this evidence to refute Overstone's identification of the demand for loanable (money) capital with the demand for real capital, which was nothing more than a cloak for his quantity theory interpretation of the mid nineteenth-century business cycle:

> Since the demand and supply of commodities regulate their market prices, it becomes evident here how wrong Overstone is in identifying the demand for loanable money capital (or rather the deviations of supply therefrom), as expressed by the discount rate, with the demand for actual 'capital'. The contention that commodity prices are regulated by fluctuations in the quantity of currency is now concealed by the phrase that discount rate fluctuations express fluctuations in the demand for actual material capital, as distinct from money capital. (Ibid.)

Marx then turned his attention to the Currency School's international specie-flow doctrine, which was simply a wider application of quantity theory. He insisted, by contrast, that gold movements, to the extent that they altered the relationship between the demand and supply of money capital, merely affected the rate of interest. While it would be wrong to see this hypothesis as a return to the viewpoint of Petty and Locke – since the gold was not just money but *capital* – it did entail a clear rejection of the Currency School determination of the interest rate by capital in the form of commodities, i.e., real capital: '[A] decrease in the quantity of gold raises only the interest rate; and if not for the fact that the fluctuations in the interest rate enter into the determination of cost-prices, or in the determination of demand and supply, commodity prices would be wholly unaffected by them' (ibid.).[23]

Although Ricardo was more scrupulous than Overstone and the Currency School in differentiating money capital from real capital, Marx's argument suggested that any change in supply and demand conditions affecting the former would not just influence the rate of interest during an 'interval' before a corresponding price response, but would do so for as long as those conditions persisted. The only rate of interest which mattered was the 'market rate', since no such thing as a 'natural rate' could exist; and this market rate – or, more accurately, the spectrum of rates for commercial paper – was exclusively dependent upon *competition in the money market*, that is to say upon the currently prevailing relationship between demand and supply of money capital.

Marx had thus moved far beyond either Ricardo or Tooke, while adopting elements of their respective accounts. From Ricardo, he inherited the determining role of the general rate of profit; and from Tooke, he gained a perceptive account of the relationship between interest and prices. It has been argued (Panico, 1980, pp. 174–5) that Marx's discussion of the factors affecting the determination of the rate of interest foreshadowed the analysis in Keynes's *General Theory* (1936).[24] To the extent that this was so, it only went to highlight the damaging effect on the history of classical economics of the absence of a theory of output. This was the one element that might have completed its investigation into the relationship between prices and money.

In practice, according to Marx, the authorities could only vary the rate of interest through their control of the Bank rate by changing the relationship between the demand and supply of money capital, an operation whose success was determined mainly by the stage of the business cycle when it was attempted.[25] Indeed, it was this cycle, not the authorities, which primarily governed fluctuations in the market rate of interest. The authorities had to be content with at best a marginal impact; though, at the crucial turning point from prosperity into recession, they would acquire the power either to alleviate business conditions by accommodating 'distress borrowing' or to make them worse by pursuing a 'tight money' policy (Daugherty, 1942/43, p. 141; Kuhne, 1979, pp. 350–3).

What concerned the Banking School, as we shall see in a moment, was that interest rate fluctuations would be artificially exaggerated by the regulatory framework championed by the Currency School; even without this framework, however, the periodical overaccumulation of money capital sowed the seeds of its own destruction, forcing up the market rate of interest. As Fullarton put it:

> From more recent events, indeed, one would almost be tempted to suspect, that a *periodical destruction of capital has become a necessary condition of the existence of any market rate of interest at all.* And, considered in that point of view, these awful visitations, to which we are accustomed to look forward with so much disquiet and apprehension, and which we are so anxious to avert, may be nothing more than the natural and necessary corrective of an overgrown and bloated opulence, the *vis medicatrix* by which our social system, as at present constituted, is enabled to relieve itself from time to time of an ever-recurring *plethora* which menaces its existence, and to regain a sound and wholesome state. (1844, p. 165, initial emphasis added)[26]

CREDIT CONTROL AND LAW OF REFLUX

The origin of the currency principle may be found in a memorandum drafted by James Pennington for the Political Economy Club in the wake of the 1825 crisis (Viner, 1937, p. 224 ff.; Fetter, 1965, pp. 130–2). Until that crisis, with its attendant financial panic, the controversy over the resumption of cash payments had largely died down; and the clamour for a fiduciary issue on the part of the Birmingham 'little shilling men' no longer had any resonance in parliament or the country. In April 1826, Pennington was asked, probably by Tooke, to make a contribution to the continuing discussion of the issue of bimetallism. This he did, but ended his memorandum with a reference to damaging monetary fluctuations, which were once again a matter of public concern, and hinted at a possible solution: 'Are there, then, no means to be found, of preventing those alterations of excitement and depression – of extravagant expectation and disappointed hope – but in the exclusive employment of so expensive medium of interchange of gold, and the suppression of paper? The difficulty which this question implies, is not insuperable' (cited by Fetter, 1965, pp. 130–1).

Huskisson replied a year later in the following terms: 'This, for a long time, has appeared to me one of the most important matters which can engage the attention of the legislature and the Councils of this country. The subject is certainly intricate and complicated; but the too rapid contraction of paper credit (I speak of it in the largest sense) at another, is unquestionably an evil of the greatest magnitude' (ibid., p. 131; see Green, 1937, vol. 2, pp. 699–700). He requested that Pennington come forward with practical suggestions as to how these fluctuations could be minimised, whereupon the latter submitted a second memorandum in August 1827. Although not mentioned by name, the dominating influence of Ricardo, who had died three years earlier, was apparent in this memorandum. Pennington began with the now familiar assertion that credit and fictitious capital could have no effect upon the level of output, but could only modify its 'direction'. In his own words, 'when the Bank of England increases or lessens its outstanding paper, by an augmentation or diminution of its advances upon securities bearing interest, no extraordinary exchange of commodities for money, or of money for commodities, with other countries, necessarily takes place. The capital and labour of the country remain unaltered, but an artificial direction is given to both' (ibid.).

Pennington argued, first, that the note issue ought to be concentrated in the Bank of England (unlike Ricardo, he did not favour a new institution for this purpose); second, that the securities of the Bank should be kept 'even'; and, third, that, as a consequence, the quantity of 'paper money' could be made to vary in conformity with the Bank's holdings of bullion:

> If the the Bank of England were the sole issuer of paper money or if the country banks were, in all cases, directly, and immediately, controlled by the bank, the means of preventing this source of unintended mischief would be obvious and easy. Nothing more would be necessary than that the bank should constantly hold a fixed amount of the same unvarying species of securities. If its outstanding liabilities amounted, at any particular time, to £26 000 000, and if, against these, it held £18 000 000 of government securities, the action of the foreign exchange would necessarily turn upon the gold: at one time the bank might have six, at another ten, and at another time eight millions of treasure; and in all cases, its paper would contract and expand according to the increase or diminution of its bullion. (Ibid., pp. 131–2)

No sooner had Pennington announced his plan for monetary control than J. Horsley Palmer, governor of the Bank of England, independently formulated what became known as the 'Palmer rule'. This obliged the Bank, when the circulation was 'full' (that is, when the exchanges were on the point of becoming unfavourable, to maintain a specie reserve equal to about one third of notes and deposits. Every alteration in the latter, 'excepting under special conditions', then had to match the ebb and flow of specie. Despite their superficial resemblance, the Palmer rule – by encompassing deposits as well as the note issue and by confining itself to the liabilities of the Bank of England, instead of suppressing the country bank circulation – fell far short of Pennington's more radical proposal. Nevertheless, it reflected the consensus immediately after 1825, which was nothing if not pragmatic (Daugherty, 1942/43, pp. 143–5).

From the long-run perspective, the classical law of monetary circulation was generally accepted; but as far as short-run events were concerned, it was the outlook of Thornton not Ricardo which prevailed in practice at this time (Feavearyear, 1931, p. 229 ff.). Without openly reviving the real bills doctrine, the Bank allowed itself more discretion than hitherto in determining lending criteria and its response to exchange rate movements. As Fetter remarks, 'it was still possible for the Bank in the long-run to accept the Ricardian view that credit policy and prices controlled exchange rates, but in the short-run to act on the anti-Ricardian view that the exchange rates were the result of influences independent of prices, and in large part independent of Bank policy' (ibid., p. 150).

However, the Bank was not without its critics, who, following a new crisis in 1836, elevated Pennington's ideas to the status of an economic law, thereby provoking what became known as the currency–banking debate. The main spokesman for these critics, at least in the initial stages of the debate, was Robert Torrens. The fact that the Palmer rule had survived unscathed through the Bank Charter investigation of 1832 did not deter him from advocating a year later in parliament strict regulation of the note issue *alone* in accordance with the Bank's specie holdings. When the easy credit of 1834–36 culminated in bank runs and economic recession, Torrens grasped his opportunity. In his influential pamphlet, *A Letter to the Right Honourable Lord Viscount Melbourne* (1837), he reiterated Pennington's argument, and his own parliamentary contribution, making a sharp distinction between 'circulating money', under which head he included both notes and coin, and 'credit money', which covered only bank deposits and cash credits (1837, pp. 5–6). It was the overriding duty of the Bank, therefore, to make the supply of notes and coin comply with fluctuations in the specie reserve.

A pragmatic reply followed from Palmer, but Torrens's case was taken up in turn by Loyd, Samson Ricardo and Norman. While none of their pamphlets added anything new to the discussion, they all highlighted the need as they saw it for a complete separation of the note issuing and deposit business of the Bank of England.[27] Their persistence was rewarded in 1844 with Sir Robert Peel's Bank Charter Act; now the critics could don the mantle of orthodoxy and leave the role of opposition to the Banking School, whose contribution was referred to by Marx as the 'newer English writings about circulation – the only branch in which real new discoveries have been made' (1973, p. 883).

The currency–banking debate

It has been said that the currency principle is easy to describe 'because it formed an intelligibly connected set of ideas', whereas Banking School views were 'far from constituting a coherent or unified theory' (Daugherty, 1942/43, p. 246). There is sufficient truth in this remark to justify a preliminary summary of the rival positions in the debate; and if, in addition, greater weight is placed upon Banking School views, then this will not merely reflect the present writer's evaluation of their inherent merits but will also compensate for their comparative neglect in the literature.[28]

To begin with, both sides in the debate recognised the importance of theorising the laws of metallic circulation as a precondition for the analysis of paper currency. The entire Currency School case for monetary control rested upon the assertion that the note issue would not by itself emulate the behaviour of a metallic system. Despite legal convertibility it might depart at least temporarily – and even indefinitely in some accounts – from the amount and value of the metallic money which would otherwise have circulated. In practice, therefore, economic convertibility could only be ensured by quantitative intervention of the part of the authorities. Torrens summarised their position in the *Letter to Lord Melbourne* as follows: 'It is universally admitted by persons acquainted with monetary science that paper money should be so regulated as to keep the medium of exchange, of which it may form a part, in the same state, with respect to amount and to value, in which the medium of exchange would exist, were the circulating portion of it purely metallic' (ibid., p. 29).

We shall see that Banking School criticism took three main lines. First, starting from the assumption that legal convertibility necessarily implied economic convertibility, they pointed out that any discrepancy between the note issue and a purely metallic system arose from the Currency School's erroneous theory of metallic circulation rather than from the supposed autonomy of the notes. Second, any effect on prices attributed to bank notes could not be denied to a range of financial assets excluded by the Currency School from their definition of money. Third, bank notes were in any case not money but credit, and therefore could be overissued, though the credit structure as a whole might be extended beyond the limits of real accumulation by 'speculation and overtrading'. I shall discuss these lines of criticism in turn, beginning with a brief resume of the metallic system.

Many commentators, including Morgan (1965), and Fetter (1965), have treated the Currency School as the great 'innovators', while the Banking School were content simply to defend the status quo. However true this may have been of their practical proposals, it is certainly not a valid assessment of their respective theoretical positions. The Currency School retained not only the long-run framework of classical economics, but also, uncritically, the short-run analysis of deviations associated with Ricardo and the Bullionists. As we have seen, this approach at least had the merit of logical consistency. Having subscribed to the saving–investment identify of Say's law, they felt bound to accept a constant velocity assumption as well (Schumpeter, 1954, p. 702). The inevitable corollary was the quantity theory of money, which was central to the Currency School vision of metallic circulation – and hence of the credit system.

They went considerably further than Ricardo and the Bullionists, however, in applying the theory of a fiduciary system not just to inconvertible bank notes but also to notes *convertible at will* into a given weight of gold. Whereas during the Bank Restriction the note issue was at least liable to depreciation against bullion, the whole point of restoring cash payments was, according to Ricardo, to make such depreciation impossible. The Currency School tried to account for the changed institutional setting by arguing that, although convertible paper could not *permanently* depreciate, it might do so for significant periods of time – that is to say for as long as the overissue persisted. This superficially attractive distinction was meaningless, however, because no tendency operated to reestablish *economic* convertibility in this scheme (Laidler, 1972, p. 179). The notes could be placed at a discount more or less indefinitely, motivating both an internal run on the bank for gold and an external drain. Since there was no theoretical limit to this process, the Currency School concluded that legal convertibility was put at risk by excessive monetary growth and that restraint would have to be enforced by reforms to the statutory framework of banking.

Their reasoning proceeded in two stages. To begin with, international equilibrium was assumed to prevail; all variables in the equation of exchange corresponded with their normal positions. An influx of bullion into one country then represented an equivalent expansion of its domestic money supply, which in turn proportionately devalued the unit of account and raised the general price level. That was the first stage. Next, forces came into operation which encouraged the import of commodities and the export of bullion until both money supply and price were restored to their normal magnitudes. This traditional specie-flow doctrine was then applied to an economy whose money supply included bank notes. In the first stages, an influx of bullion was a signal to the financial system to increase correspondingly its discounts and hence expand the note issue. When the rise in domestic prices brought the second stage into effect, the authorities were required to contract the paper circulation in line with the drain of bullion. The process also applied in reverse. The note issue was therefore susceptible to departures from the self-correcting movement of metallic currency, and had to be regulated in accordance with externally imposed criteria, namely the movement of bullion into and out of the country (Viner, 1937, p. 261 ff).

The Banking School – especially the formidable duo of Tooke and Fullarton – deployed a range of arguments against the currency principle.[29] The most effective in practice was simply the fact of disruption to industry and trade resulting from its strict implementation. They won Marx's approval through their recognition both of the inevitability of periodic crises and of the futility of monetary 'cures' enforced by ill-conceived legislation. Moreover, their theoretical assault on the currency principle was far-reaching. They agreed that the note issue ought to comply with the behaviour of a metallic currency, but insisted that with free convertibility it *could not do otherwise*. Fullarton put it most forcefully:

> As a general principle . . . the increase or decrease of circulation of bank-notes, from whatever cause it may proceed, ought to correspond with the increase or decrease which a currency of metallic coin would exhibit under the same circumstances. But I go further than this: *I contend, that there not only ought to be such correspondence, but that there always is*. . . . [I]t is only from the intervention of some such arbitrary and empirical system of restraint as is now projected, that this conformity runs any risk of being disturbed. (1844, p. 27, emphasis added; see also Wilson, 1859, pp. 37–43)

The idea that bank notes might fluctuate autonomously reflected, as we shall see, a misunderstanding of the nature of credit and its point of difference with money; but it stemmed fundamentally from an underlying perception of the working of a metallic system. While the Banking School largely shared the Currency School's long-run classical analysis, which I have examined in an earlier chapter, they parted in their configuration of the short-run adjustment mechanism.[30] The central thrust of their argument was directed against quantity theory; and, like Smith, their rejection of the fixed velocity assumption allowed them to provide an account of monetary disturbances which corresponded more closely with reality. The progress made by the Banking School, however, was gained at the expense of internal consistency; for, by accepting the Say's law assumption of full capacity utilisation, they could explain concrete conditions only by going beyond the limits of existing classical doctrine.

Gold drains

Our discussion of the Banking School approach must begin with the international specie-flow mechanism described earlier. Tooke was convinced by the empirical data as much as by any theoretical preconceptions that the assumption of constant velocity was an abstraction which impeded a proper understanding of cause and effect in a world of metallic money.[31] It was clear to him that bullion was held not only for luxury consumption, but also in the form of reserve funds to discharge trade and other obligations. The operation of these 'hoards' served to invalidate the quantity theory interpretation of bullion movements:

> If, therefore, we take into account the magnitude of the stock necessarily imported, partly for the consumption of plate in this country, and partly for that abroad, and of the amount required as available funds for the adjustment of international balances, it may not be deemed an extravagant supposition that there might occasionally be under a perfectly metallic circulation fluctuations within moderately short periods, to the extent of at least five or six millions sterling in the import and export of bullion, perfectly extrinsic of the amount or value of the coin circulating as money in the hands of the public, and *perfectly without influence on the general prices of commodities*, as equally without general prices having been a cause of such fluctuations. (1844, pp. 13–14, emphasis added)[32]

In other words, the authorities would not be justified in attempting to expand or contract a circulation comprised of bank notes on the assumption that such action ensured conformity with metallic currency. This was not the end of the matter. The Currency School further maintained that a gold drain would ultimately exhaust the most extravagant hoard unless its basic cause was eliminated, by which they meant the overissue of bank notes. The response of the Banking School carefully differentiated between the various types of external drain, assigning to them causes other than monetary excess. Fullarton, for example, observed that: 'Different drains are of different intensity, and are more or less difficult to be dealt with, according to the difference of circumstances in which they may have originated, or by which they are attached. But each has its natural termination, in the spontaneous cessation of the causes which gave rise to it' (ibid., p. 151).

This is not to say that the Banking School refused to acknowledge the existence of drains associated with an overextension of the credit structure as a whole. What they did argue, as we shall see later, was that such occurrances could not be prevented; and that their effects were best alleviated by official passivity – or at most discretionary restraint – rather than statutory ceilings on the note issue (Tooke, 1844, pp. 115–17; Fullarton, 1844, pp. 153–66). In any case, an outflow of bullion was more usually due to less intractable events, such as harvest failure, whose effect on the balance of payments obviously ceased with the liquidation of debts for subsequent corn imports. Since a metallic reserve existed for precisely that purpose, it struck the Banking School as irrational that monetary contraction should be decreed at just the point when the needs of domestic circulation were greatest.

In one of the most eloquent passages in his *Regulation of Currencies*, Fullarton found 'nothing at variance with economic principles' in the duty of the Bank of England 'to advance . . . the funds indispensable for the public relief, postponing their reimbursement till the ordinary course of industry shall have had time to repair the deficiency'. He went on: 'The Bank of England stands, as it were, in the place of a vast national granary, to which, in seasons of famine, the community is entitled to resort for succour.' When the banks, by issuing notes to meet legitimate demands, 'contribute to fill up some part of the vacancy left by the action of the exchange on the circulation of the Bank of England, I consider, that they are merely fulfilling their part in the general plan, and following with the most perfect exactness the analogies of a metallic currency' (ibid., pp. 151–2).

Fullarton concluded that a bad harvest always led to some suffering, but at least a 'poor and half civilized community' would part with a proportion of its accumulated savings of gold and silver to make up for this temporary loss. Such a simple and obvious remedy was not possible under the new Bank Charter Act:

> But under our artificial system, nothing of this kind, it seems is to be permitted. To the single object of preserving a certain arbitrary proportion between the treasure in the coffers of the Bank of England and that portion of the circulating credit of the country which has been dignified with the name of money, all other considerations are to give way. . . . The people are told, indeed, in nearly so many words, that . . . they have nothing to do but to starve. And this, then, is to be the brilliant result of all our refined devices – the utmost that science can do for the perfect regulation of our monetary system. (Ibid.)[33]

The currency principle only half survived this onslaught. Although endlessly repeated as official doctrine, it did not prove so resilient in practice (Andréadès, 1935, p. 331 ff.). Whenever the pressure on the Bank of England became intense in subsequent years, the provisions of Peel's 1844–5 legislation were relaxed. That the currency principle survived at all was due to two factors. First, Bank mismanagement, not to say impotence, in the fact of recurrent economic crises fuelled public demands for tighter formal controls; and, second, the analysis of the Currency School, by contrast with that of the Banking School, appeared to be logically watertight. Following in the shadow of Ricardo's contribution, they excluded the very possibility of hoarding and dishoarding from the problem they wanted to solve; even so, the failure of every attempt to give their abstract principle immediate practical application – the 'Ricardian vice' – was not thought to detract from the validity of the principle itself.[34]

The Banking School, on the other hand, could not substitute a quantity effect for a price effect without disposing of the assumption of constant velocity, and, more fundamentally, the assumption of full capacity utilisation. The two seemed logically interconnected in the minds of the Currency School theorists. Nor was the Banking School successful in maintaining that an unfavourable balance of payments was due to any cause other than excessive monetary expansion. Their attempt to distinguish gold drains resulting from an overextension of credit and drains resulting from, say, a bad harvest may have been empirically correct, but it was ultimately futile in the climate of opinion generated by the prevailing monetary orthodoxy. They were therefore obliged to pursue their critique of the currency principle beyond metallic circulation into the labyrinth of credit.

Concept of money

Before going further, let us briefly recapitulate. There was agreement on both sides of the currency–banking debate about the need for bank notes to correspond to the quantity and value of the monetary metal which would otherwise have had to circulate. Since legal convertibility suggested that *by definition* the notes must comply with metallic circulation, it fell to the Currency School to prove that they could differ. Their argument rested upon a view of the working of a metallic system the Banking School refuted. Strictly speaking, the outcome of this exchange might have been sufficient to conclude the debate. Yet, for reasons just given, the Banking School was obliged to theorise the behaviour of credit; that was the true nature of bank notes, which, as the Banking School never tired of pointing out, could only be advanced *on loan* to meet commercial requirements.

The Currency School, on the other hand, like Ricardo, treated the note issue as analogous to *fiduciary money* i.e., inconvertible tokens given forced currency by the state. The profound implications of their failure to distinguish money and credit will be elaborated shortly. I shall now focus simply on their concept of money – in the sense of circulating media – which was defined to include bank notes but *omit* a range of financial assets which were equally qualified to perform a monetary role (Laidler, 1972, p. 142–3). The importance of this definition was explained by Tooke as follows: '[B]y arriving at a conclusion as to what part of the various forms of paper credit should be considered exclusively as money or currency, conferring *a power of purchase*, some criterion or test might be found of the influence of one of the principal elements upon which not only the state of trade and credit, but also general prices depend; it being assumed that commodities, although liable in each particular instance to be influenced by circumstances affecting the supply and demand, are more or less under a direct influence from variations in the quantity of money or currency' (1844, pp. 67–8).

Whereas the Banking School therefore placed the emphasis on the overall level of aggregate demand – the spectrum of liquidity – rather than the form in which this demand was exercised, the Currency School attributed demand exclusively to the volume of notes and coin, which consequently became the object of scrutiny and control (Schumpeter, 1954, pp. 702–5). While this line of approach may not have been an *inevitable* consequence of Say's law, it was seen as highly compatible, especially when a constant velocity assumption was also integral to the approach (Viner, 1937, p. 248).

Forms of credit other than bank notes which could logically act as circulating media were categorised not as money by the Currency School but as 'money substitutes', which influenced velocity rather than quantity. Since, however, velocity was externally given, money substitutes were assumed to bear a stable relationship to notes and coin, and hence to be incapable of fluctuating independently. Notes and coin became a 'proxy' for the spectrum of financial assets – a monetary base – which alone constituted the operative factor in price movements.[35] Later, bank deposits were included in this narrow measure, but the principle remained the same. An arbitrary spread of assets was defined as money and any actual or potential circulating media outside this definition were neutralised by assumption.

The Banking School reintroduced the distinction between money and credit, refusing to accept these supposed implications of Say's law. Having rejected the constant velocity assumption, they were able to make two telling points against the currency principle. The first related to the definition of the 'money supply', and the second to its actual behaviour. To start with, according to the Banking School, there was no difference in character between the note issue and other demand liabilities of the banking system. As credit instruments, both were equally able to serve as circulating media; and it therefore followed that to attribute to one the description of money, and hence the power to raise prices, was to assign the same qualities to the other (Viner, 1937, p. 222; Daugherty, 1943/44, p. 149).

The case for counting deposits (or cheques) as part of the money supply was first established by Pennington, and developed by Tooke: '[M]y argument . . . is to show that, as instruments of exchange, cheques, or the deposits on which these are founded, answer the purposes of money, and more conveniently in most cases; and that therefore whatever influence may be ascribed to bank notes, whether on prices, or on the rate of interest, or on the state of trade, cannot be denied to cheques or to their substratum, deposits payable on demand' (ibid., p. 25; see also Mill, 1873, p. 326).

Tooke then further extended the category to include commercial paper outside the banks, such as bills of exchange (ibid., pp. 26–33). All these instruments represented a mass of purchasing power which dwarfed the note issue, and, as the evidence showed, *compensated* its short-run movements rather than keeping in step. Fullarton, too, examined in detail the vast reservoir of circulating media outside the Currency School definition of money, and maintained that, 'the same action on prices which you attribute to the occasional excesses of circulation of notes, over which you profess effectual means of control, must be exercised in a far greater degree by the excessive use of other forms of credit, which perform precisely the same offices in exchange that are performed by the notes, but probably to ten times the extent, and which are wholly beyond the reach of control or limitation' (1844, p. 40). Since the material factor was not the 'mere existence' of the notes but the state of underlying demand, the consequences of the transaction were in no way dependent upon the credit instrument employed (Rist, 1940, p. 203 *et seq.*).[36]

Fullarton went on to demonstrate that the functions of bank notes could adequately be performed by any number of alternative devices; indeed, there was no reason in principle why the note circulation could not be wholly *displaced* without significant economic dislocation: 'Why, the whole bank-note circulation of this country might be turned tomorrow into a system of book-credits transferable by cheque, or all our banking accounts might be commuted, on the contrary, for promissory notes, and in neither case would the course of monetary transactions be essentially disturbed or altered. On this simple and undeniable proposition, indeed, I should be content to rest my whole argument' (ibid., p. 41; see also pp. 48–9). Fullarton presented the example of Ireland at the turn of the century, where the spontaneous introduction of IOUs made up for a deficiency of small denomination circulating media. How much simpler would it be in an advanced country like England, he concluded, with its developed financial structure, to nullify any doctrinaire restriction of the note issue, 'the small change of credit, the humblest of the mechanical organisations through which credit develops itself' (ibid., p. 51; see Feavearyear, 1931, p. 248).

Once velocity was no longer assumed to be fixed, not only could it be shown that a shortage of bank notes was offset by other circulating media, but an explanation emerged for the fact that price movements bore no necessary relationship to the total purchasing power represented by credit. Again the operative factor in the actual employment of credit was the extent of demand, which was determined by Tooke as follows:

> That it is the quantity of money, constituting the revenues of the different orders of the State, under the head of rents, profits, salaries, and wages, destined for current expenditure, that alone forms the limiting principle of the aggregate of money prices, the only prices that can properly come under the designation of general prices. As the cost of production is the limiting principle of supply, so the aggregate of money incomes devoted to expenditure for consumption is the determining and limiting principle of demand. (1844, p. 123)

It was a mistake, according to Tooke, to suppose that the 'will' necessarily matched the power of purchase (ibid., p. 79; see also Mill, 1873, p. 322).

Fullarton in turn showed that this mistake was linked to a mechanical identification of the money supply with the total volume of available credit. Using an approach which anticipated liquidity preference – and built upon Thornton's earlier observations – he argued that so long as bank notes met the current needs of circulation, interest-bearing paper would 'accumulate for the most part in the hands of the capitalist'. For this reason, he went on, 'the amount of bills of exchange at any given time in existence can never . . . be anything like a correct measure of the power they are exerting in the currency'. The same applied to the category of bank deposits: '[W]hile dormant, it is nothing more than credit in the abstract; it only becomes currency when brought into action.' Nor were bank notes themselves exempt: 'In as far as prices and exchanges are concerned, the notes accumulated as a reserve in a banker's drawer can exercise as little influence as the gold which is still in the ore' (1844, p. 43).

Fullarton therefore regarded 'these various forms of circulating credit . . . rather as an element of monetary power than as in itself money, as a vast and inexhaustible *fund* of potential currency' (ibid., p. 44). Paucity of data made it impossible to calculate the degree to which this monetary power was utilised at a given time. Although it was 'the fashion of the day, to attach an inordinate degree of importance to the periodical returns of the bank-note circulation', these could only serve to a limited extent as 'an index of the state of commercial credit'. While they were useful for certain purposes, it was a 'palpable delusion' to suppose that such statistics 'supply anything like a comprehensive view of the amount or value of monetary dealings, or furnish data from which any one can determine the scale of prices, or predict the revolutions of exchange' (ibid., pp. 44–5). The Banking School thus came to the modern conclusion that a narrow measure of money was arbitrary as an indicator of the active money supply, let alone the totality of financial assets, and was both theoretically unsound and economically damaging as a target of policy.[37]

Reflux law

So far in our discussion the Banking School have not only gone some way towards disproving the theory of metallic circulation underlying the currency principle, but they have also clarified the definition of the money supply itself and the place of bank notes in that definition. I now turn to their distinction between fiduciary money and credit in the spectrum of liquidity; and, in attempting to resolve the question of cause and effect in the inflationary process, I shall examine the law of reflux which Fullarton called 'the great regulating principle of the internal currency' (1844, p. 68; see esp. Schumpeter, 1954, pp. 730–1; Fetter, 1965, pp. 187–92; Laidler, 1972, pp. 173–4).

Fiduciary money, as we have seen in the previous chapter, was a means of payment whose quantity could be varied *at will* by the state. While depreciation was not an *inevitable* characteristic of such forced currency, overissue would result in it representing proportionately less metallic value than indicated by its denomination. Bank notes, on the other hand, were a species of credit, and if issued on adequate security, were *not liable to overissue*. The Banking School emphasised that the volume of notes in circulation could not be increased at will by the authorities, but only in response to the demand of the non-bank public (Tooke, 1844, p. 122).

This crucial difference between fiduciary money and bank notes was explained by Tooke as consisting 'not only in the limit prescribed by their convertibility to the amount of them, but in the *mode of issue*'. He argued that:

> [Bank notes] are issued to those only who, being entitled to demand gold, desire to have notes in preference; and it depends upon the particular purposes for which the notes are employed, whether a greater or less quantity is required. The quantity, therefore, is an *effect, and not a cause of demand*. A compulsory government paper, on the other hand, while it is in the course of augmentation, acts directly as an *originating*

> *cause on prices and incomes*, constituting a fresh source of demand in money, depreciated in value as compared with gold, but of the same nominal value as before. (Ibid., pp. 70–1, emphasis added; see also Fullarton, 1844, ch. 3 and Wilson, 1859, pp. 48, 51–2, 57–8)

An advance of bank notes did not *add* to the money supply, therefore, but merely changed its *composition*, allowing the substitution of one financial asset for another in the hands of the public. Excess notes returned automatically to the bank 'in the shape of deposits or of a demand for bullion' (ibid., p. 60). This was one aspect of the law of reflux. It was also stated by Wilson, founder of the *Economist*, in his *Capital, Currency and Banking*: 'The public do not . . . retain notes in their possession beyond what the convenience of trade requires, and, therefore, if issued in excess of that quantity, and, if convertible, a portion would be instantly returned upon the issuers' (1859, p. 58). The law was endorsed in similar terms by Marx in his analysis of credit: 'The quantity of circulating notes is regulated by the turnover requirements, and every superfluous note wends its way back immediately to the issuer' (1867/94, III, p. 524).[38] Thus it was clear to the Banking School that the note issue was dependent on the state of demand. Since demand, as these economists defined it, in turn reflected the sum of prices consumers were 'able and willing to pay', the causal relationship postulated by the currency principle was reversed (Schumpeter, 1954, p. 710). The money supply in a credit system did not determine, but was determined by, commodity prices in the short-run as well as the long-run. In Tooke's words, 'the prices of commodities do not depend upon the quantity of money indicated by the amount of bank notes, nor upon the amount of the whole of the circulating medium: but . . . on the contrary, the amount of the circulating medium is the consequence of prices' (ibid., p. 123; see also Fullarton, ibid., p. 100).

Tooke's conclusion was strengthened by a further aspect of the law of reflux, which was based upon the real bills doctrine. This held that economic convertibility could be ensured not only by a legal right to exchange notes for specie but also by maintaining a balance between the notes advanced on loan and those returned to the bank at maturity. A measure of equilibrium between these two flows could be achieved by lending on 'real bills', i.e., commercial paper which represented a real or (within a given timescale) potential sum of values. Fullarton presented this aspect of the law of reflux in a celebrated passage:

> New gold coin and new conventional notes are introduced into the market by being made the medium of *payments*. Bank notes, on the

> contrary, are never issued but on *loan*, and an equal amount of notes must be returned into the bank whenever the loan becomes due. . . The banker has only to take care that they are lent on sufficient security, and the reflux and the issue will, in the long run, always balance each other. . . . [I]t is not so much by convertibility into gold, as by the regularity of the reflux, that in the ordinary course of things any redundance of the bank-note issues is rendered impossible. (1844, pp. 64–7; also p. 207)[39]

The impossibility of overissue referred, of course, to the *monetary circulation*. Notes simply took the place of an equivalent amount of coin. The Banking School did not deny that the *credit structure as a whole* could be overextended and that this might accommodate an increase in the general level of prices (see pp. 373, 383); but they refuted the idea that an excessive issue of bank notes was responsible for inflation – or indeed the business cycle itself – an idea which Marx pointed out 'completely identifies *monetary turnover* with *credit*, which is economically wrong' (1973, p. 123).[40]

The main drawback of the law of reflux as a principle of limitation, as we have seen in previous chapters, was a practical one. There were times when banks found it virtually impossible to differentiate, in Smith's use of the terminology, between 'real' and 'fictitious' commercial paper. This was seen as a problem which could not entirely be avoided under any method of regulation; it could only be guarded against by prudent banking, adequate reserves and, ultimately, by Bank of England intervention as the lender of last resort.[41]

A further objection of a more theoretical kind to the law of reflux was that borrowers might not require notes provided by a bank for more than a fraction of the period allowed for repayment of the debt. In the time remaining, therefore, the money supply would be excessive to circulation needs and the unit of account would be depreciated in proportion to the extent of redundancy (O'Brien, 1975, p. 158). The Banking School had a ready answer to this criticism. As Wilson pointed out, any superfluous notes would either be invested in interest-bearing assets, or be used, 'through the medium of a banker or bill-broker', to discount the bills of other economic agents, hence contracting the money supply in the same degree as would have been the case had the excess been returned to the bank in the first place: 'It is quite clear that in this way no larger quantity of notes could be kept out than the purposes of currency actually required; for the moment a man held notes for which he had no use, he would with them intercept some interest-bearing securities on their way to the bank, and, while other notes were flowing in, in repayment of bills or loans falling due, he would to that extent prevent further reissues' (ibid., p. 29; see also Fullarton, ibid., pp. 95–7).[42]

As soon, however, as inconvertible paper was lent to the government on irredeemable securities, any excess would be mirrored in a commensurate depreciation of the monetary unit: 'The State creates paper money at will but cannot withdraw it from circulation; the banks do not create credit instruments at will, but can withdraw them by ceasing to renew credits' (Rist, 1940, p. 213). While the Banking School successfully disposed of the constant velocity assumption, their refusal to challenge the assumption of full capacity utilisation fostered a deep scepticism of state-regulated fiduciary money: 'In practice, therefore, we conceive such a principle far too dangerous for one instant to encourage' (Wilson, ibid., p. 30).

Business cycle

For the main protagonists of the currency–banking debate, the operation of credit could only be understood, and practical measures devised, in the context of the business cycle. Indeed, according to Schumpeter, 'their work succeeded in setting on foot what may be described as a new analysis of "the" business cycle' (1954, p. 743). This became more rather than less pertinent with the passing of the Bank Charter Act, which embodied the principle of the Currency School. In the words of Clapham:

> While the champions fought with pen and ink, a surge of trade that was influenced by many other things than currency, well or ill regulated, was moving up with power towards its crest: when the Act was little more than three years old its value and their opinions would be tested by events. (1944, II, p. 185)

In what follows, I shall concentrate attention on the Banking School and Marx, as the main innovators of *theory* in the debate.

Although the Banking School did not attempt to analyse the accumulation of *real* capital, their discussion of *money* capital (of which fictitious capital was a component), and its relationship to the price level, represented a significant achievement. In the course of the cycle, according to Tooke, the growth phase was characterised by low interest rates and a strong demand for loans, as investment opportunities were taken up. In this phase, bank notes were used to circulate *revenue* rather than *capital*, whose redistribution was effected largely by book entries, etc., since cash settlements would be at a minimum. As I have earlier indicated, Tooke rendered this distinction as one between 'currency' and 'capital', forgetting that currency existed in both spheres, representing capital at one moment and revenue at another (1844, ch. 7). Later in the cycle, the position was reversed, when firms demanded notes to liquidate their debts (or even coin if the notes were not legal tender). This distinction between 'currency' and 'capital' occupied a large part of nineteenth-century discussion and was by no means just a scholastic exercise; it helped to categorise specific phases of the business cycle, though without venturing beyond the sphere of credit into the production process itself (Daugherty, 1942/43, p. 152).

Disentangling Tooke's 'false distinction' was a task which Marx set for himself in the third volume of *Capital*: 'The fact that the gentlemen of the currency theory confuse two different things is no reason to present them as two different concepts' (1867/94, III, p. 446).[43] Fullarton, too, accepted the distinction as outlined by Tooke, but added a further dimension. He wanted to show that it was a 'great error' to imagine 'that the demand for pecuniary accomodation (that is, for the loan of capital) is identical with a demand for additional means of circulation, or even that the two are frequently associated' (1848, p. 96).[44] What he meant was that the demand for money as a *means of purchase*, which could take the form of credit, was not the same as the demand for *means of payment* – the former predominating in the growth phase of the cycle and the latter at the point of crisis.

Counterposing specific functions of money in this way as a distinction between currency and capital suggested to Marx 'the narrow-minded banker's conception of circulation'; bank notes circulating as means of payment and immediately returning to the issuing bank were 'simply not circulation in the eyes of those economists' (1867/94, III, pp. 458–9). Yet he recognised that underlying Fullarton's misleading classification was a discovery of some significance for the validity of the reflux law. It was apparent to Fullarton that fluctuations in the securities held by the Bank of England and in the note issue were *mutually compensating*; this fact indicated to him both that the note circulation was governed by the demand of the non-bank public and that any additional advances by the Bank would constitute not just *money* (issued in exchange for securities) but *capital* (deducted from the Bank's own resources).

Once the Bank accommodated this demand with its notes, Fullarton argued, 'everything adjusts itself in conformity with the necessities of the market; the loan remains, and the currency, if not wanted, finds its way back to the issuer. . .'. The meaning was clear: '[N]o bank can enlarge its circulation, if that circulation be already adequate to the purposes to which a bank-note currency is commonly applied; but that every addition to its advances, after that limit is passed, must be made from its capital . . .' (1844, pp. 96–7). Fullarton was here developing a point first made by Adam Smith (see above, Chapter 5).

The demand for 'pecuniary accommodation' was thus a demand for capital – a sum of actual values – but it was a demand specifically for *money capital*. Furthermore, Marx explained, this capital, 'if not available in the actual form of money, . . . represents a *mere title* on capital' (ibid., p. 457, emphasis added). In other words, it was the banking capital, or what has been termed fictitious capital that was demanded. To recognise that capital took this form was important, according to Marx, 'since a scarcity of, and pressing demand for, *banking* capital is confounded with a decrease of *actual* capital, which conversely is in such cases rather abundant in the form of means of production and products, and swamps the markets' (ibid., pp. 457–8). The Banking School, in refusing to analyse production in the business cycle, could not account for *overproduction*.

The distinction between 'currency' and 'capital' therefore expressed a fundamental contradiction within the market economy itself, which was 'resolved' only by periodic crises. On the one hand, these crises were characterised by a shortage of capital just described, and on the other by its abundance, an 'over-supply of capital' (Fullarton, 1844, p. 162). The Banking School could have uncovered this contradiction had they been prepared, like Malthus, to challenge Ricardo's denial of the possibility of a 'general glut'; they would have seen that it was *money* capital which was in short supply, not capital in the form of *commodities*.[45]

Paradoxically, the failure of the Banking School to challenge Ricardo on this point may be taken as a further indication of the degree to which their discussion of money and credit was grounded in classical value theory. Only Marx, in the end, made the attempt to trace the connection between the overaccumulation of capital and its reflection in an overproduction of commodities, though, in the context of Say's law, as a temporary deviation from normal output (Eatwell, 1970, pp. 100–3; Milgate, 1982, p. 55). His contribution therefore, while it permitted a fuller comprehension of the 'credit cycle', still lacked a theory for the determination of output in the long-run. If this was a handicap for Marx, it was an even greater one for the Banking School.

Speculation

Fullarton's analysis in the *Regulation of Currencies* linked the 'over-supply of capital', which was apparent from observation, with a fall in the rate of profit during the progress of the business cycle. He repeated the Smithian view that, 'the amount of capital seeking productive investment accumulates in ordinary times with a rapidity greatly out of proportion to the increase of means of advantageously employing it' (ibid., p. 162).[46] The effect of this over-supply was to intensify competition in the money market and maintain a downward pressure on interest rates (ibid.). A climate was thus created for speculation both in existing commodities and in titles to future production – hence 'future surplus value' – although the causal weight to be attached to 'cheap money' was, as we saw in the preceding section, a matter of some dispute within the Banking School itself (Tooke, 1844, ch. 13; Fullarton, ibid., especially p. 163 fn.).[47] Speculation was acceptable provided that it was limited to ensuring a more efficient allocation of resources. There was a threshold, however, beyond which legitimate speculative activity gave way to 'excesses'. In Fullarton's words:

> It is true, indeed, that such excesses seem to be scarcely separable from the existence of the things themselves. . . . And when, with circumstances inviting to speculation, there concur any extraordinary facilities of credit, and those facilities are freely turned to use, the effect in general is anything but that of equalizing prices and supply, or moderating sudden transitions from plenty to scarcity and from scarcity to plenty. (Ibid., pp. 155–6)

Speculation was thought to lead to an overexpansion of credit at a specific point in the cycle, namely when the rate of profit on capital had declined to such an extent that quick gains were sought from the purchase and sale of commodities or of titles to commodities, whose existence in reality was a minor consideration:

> [T]he difficulty of procuring secure and productive investments for capital is at the root of nearly all those violent paroxysms of speculative excitement which occasionally convulse the money market. . . . [I]n every speculative undertaking, the amount of interest which the speculator has to pay if he acts with borrowed capital, or which he must forego if he acts with his own, constitutes an important item in his calculation of profit. . . . The real incentive of speculation, whether in the more hazardous class of securities or in merchandise, . . . operates like a contagion on the minds of capitalists themselves. (Ibid., pp. 161–2)

While an atmosphere of speculative activity might thus create an uncontrollable momentum, it was the *expectation of profit* which give rise to an excess demand and this demand in turn required the support of credit. In Tooke's words, '[t]he prospect of advantage supplies the motive, and the credit of the buyer constitutes the power of purchase . . .' (1844, p. 73; see also Mill, 1873, p. 318).[48] Once purchasing power in the shape of credit outstripped production, market prices were forced to rise. Tooke made it clear that, 'the greater part, if not the whole of the fluctuations of prices which are over and above those that are necessarily incidental to the nature of the commodities, are attributable to the expansion and contraction of credit, under the influence of the opinion of dealers or speculators, more or less exaggerated, of the prospect of markets' (ibid., pp. 86–7).[49] The overextension of credit and ensuing inflation might take place, as we have already indicated, without any measurable growth in the note circulation (Fullarton, 1844, p. 105; see Laidler, 1972).

Nevertheless, Tooke, contended, the banks would contribute to the inflation if they permitted the expansion of their demand liabilities on inadequate security (Rist, 1940, p. 200). Then they would no longer merely be providing more convenient circulating media, but actually advancing capital from their own resources; Tooke again presented his argument in terms of the distinction he made between currency and capital:

> The mischief of commercial revulsions from overtrading, whenever traceable to the banks, has been from over advances of capital, on insufficient or inconvertible securities, or both. . . . Advances so made are . . . likely to be recklessly employed, and prices may experience a temporary inflation from credit so unduly extended. . . . The recoil of speculation and overtrading would, in most cases, not be caused in the first instance by a want of bank notes, but by a want of demand from a view to the supply and consumption. (1844, pp. 157–9)[50]

The crisis, Tooke therefore maintained, was finally precipitated by an inability to sell at the prevailing prices both on the domestic and the world market (Rist, 1940, pp. 214–19).

The Banking School was so preoccupied, however, with the phenomenon of 'speculation and overtrading', that they made no attempt to account for the overproduction of commodities which reflected the overaccumulation of capital. It was left to Marx to draw the connection between 'overproduction promoted by credit and the general inflation of prices that goes with it' (1867/94, III, p. 492). As we have seen in Chapter 4, the overaccumulation of real capital was defined in relation to the available surplus value, and expressed the growth of social productivity through a rising organic composition of capital. Now, the development of credit superimposed upon this process an accumulation of fictitious capital which, by enlarging aggregate demand beyond the limits of real accumulation, was able both to conceal and sustain the extent of overproduction. In doing so, however, this fictitious capital claimed its share of surplus value in the form of interest, which, especially in the period leading up to the crisis, reduced the share for commercial and industrial profits (Schumpeter, 1954, pp. 745–6).

While interest rates were low, the scope for risky projects was considerable; but as soon as additional demand began to outstrip the production of real values, attempts to offset the declining profit rate by marking up commodity prices gave a further impetus to speculation and set in motion an inflationary spiral. An export of bullion on top of that tied up in foreign loans was the result, indicating a fall, as Fullarton put it, not in the 'nominal' but in the 'real' value of the currency on the foreign exchanges (1844, pp. 114–15 and see previous fn. 50). An import of bullion took place, according to Marx, in phases of the cycle when loan capital was relatively abundant; it was reversed 'as soon as returns no longer flow, markets are overstocked, and an illusory prosperity is maintained by means of credit; in other words, as soon as a greatly increased demand for loan capital exists and the interest rate, therefore, has reached at least its average level' (1867/94, III, p. 571). The financial panic which followed was characterised, as we saw in an earlier chapter, by the sudden conversion of the credit system into a monetary system; just at the point when external pressure on the metallic reserve of the Bank of England had reached a peak, credit no longer met with ready acceptance and means of payment (notes and coin) were demanded by the public to discharge their obligations.

Initially, however, as Marx pointed out, borrowing for speculation as well as for productive activity was superseded by 'distress' borrowing; indeed, 'the effect of continued withdrawal of . . . loanable money capital . . . must have a direct influence on the interest rate. But instead of restricting credit transactions, the rise in the interest rate extends them and leads to an over-straining of all their resources. This period, therefore, precedes the crash' (ibid.).[51] It was not the sheer *quantity* of bullion exported that made its influence felt but rather its capacity of 'acting like a feather which, when added to the weight on the scales, suffices to tip the oscillating balance definitely to one side' (ibid.). As we have seen, this conception underlay Thornton's distinction – adopted by the Banking School – between 'temporary' and 'permanent' factors affecting the balance of payments; the distinction was not merely a theoretical one, since it necessarily entered into the day-to-day judgement of the monetary authorities (Viner, 1937, p. 261 ff.).

'State of credit'

We have seen how speculation can both conceal and exacerbate the tendency toward crisis which Marx and the Banking School diagnosed in the market economy. The significance of commodity money in this context, according to Marx, was shown by the way in which the attempt to contract the unproductive gold reserve as far as possible continually came into conflict with the need to preserve it as 'the pivot of the entire credit system'. It was precisely the development of this system which created the 'over-sensitiveness of the whole organism', because it tended, on the one hand, 'to press all money capital into the service of production (or what amounts to the same thing, to transform all money income into capital), and, . . . on the other hand, [to] reduce the metal reserve to a minimum in a certain phase of the cycle, so that it can no longer perform the functions for which it intended' (ibid., p. 572).

The appropriate course of action for the Bank of England at the moment of crisis was indicated by Fullarton:

> What has chiefly, I suspect, given currency to the notion, that the issues of the Bank of England are in a high degree accessory to the extravagances of the speculative mania, has been the pressure on the Bank of England for discounts, after the malady has reached its concluding stage, when the excitement has come to a pause, when the market is irrecoverably sinking, discredit spreading rapidly, and payments can no longer be deferred. Then certainly, if the Bank complies with those applications, it must comply with them by an issue of notes, for notes constitute the only instrumentality through which the Bank is in the practice of lending its credit. (1844, p. 105)

Fullarton showed that notes lent for this purpose would not add to the money supply, but, on the contrary, 'the rapid decline of prices . . . would necessarily contract the demand for circulation'. This meant that the notes would either be 'returned to the Bank of England, as fast as they were issued, in the shape of deposits', or they would be 'locked up in the drawers' of the private London and country banks, or they might be 'intercepted by other capitalists' and held in reserve to meet outstanding claims. At no stage, according to Fullarton, could the notes contribute to inflation: 'The notes themselves never find their way into the produce markets; and if they at all contribute to retard the fall of prices, it is not by promoting in the slightest degree the effective demand for commodities, not by enabling consumers to buy more largely for consumption, and so giving briskness to commerce, but by a process precisely the reverse, by enabling the holders of commodities to hold on, by obstructing traffic and repressing consumption' (ibid., pp. 105–6).

Nevertheless, it was precisely at the moment when industry *needed* support from the banking system that the Currency School advocated a *withdrawal* of notes in step with the external drain, which would almost inevitably lead to a sharp rise in interest rates. No rule could have been more calculated to exacerbate the crisis (Andréadès, 1935, pp. 331–42). Although the Banking School opposed this course of action in the case of a temporary reverse in the balance of payments (e.g. Fullarton, 1844, p. 107 ff.), their practical recommendations when the drain had its source in the excessive growth of credit differed only in *degree* from those of the Currency School. It all depended upon the circumstances. The main recommendation was that the Bank of England should maintain an adequate reserve at all times, whose use was not impeded by the artificial division between a banking and an issue department (Fullarton, 1844, p. 215 and ch. 10; Tooke, 1844, pp. 114–17). The most important objection to that division was that it reduced the effective reserve available for sudden emergencies and thus contributed to unnecessarily severe fluctuations in the rate of interest. As Tooke pointed out, 'under a complete separation of the functions of issue and banking, the transition would be more abrupt and violent than under the existing system' (1844, p. 105; also pp. 108 and 165, and Fullarton, 1844, p. 190 and *passim*).[52]

That action on interest rates was desirable under certain conditions was not denied by the Banking School. Instead of attempting to contract the note issue, however, they argued that the Bank ought to operate upon what Tooke called the 'state of credit' (ibid., p. 124). How it would do so was a matter not for legislation but for skilfully applied discretion.[53] Fullarton, following the logic of Tooke's argument, maintained that it was 'obviously impossible to lay down any general rule'; but the timing and extent of the Bank's intervention 'must be determined by the circumstances of each particular case, by the nature and subjects of speculation, by the length of time which it has lasted, by the existing prospect as to its continuance or abatement, by the extent of mischief which it threatens, and by the state of the resources of the Bank itself' (1844, p. 157; Marx 1867/94, III, p. 447).[54]

Initially, at the onset of a drain, the Bank had no leverage in the money market and was obliged only to tighten its lending criteria, or, again in Fullarton's words, 'to hold itself aloof from all transactions of a speculative character, and refuse the aid of its credit in any shape to those who are avowedly or notoriously engaged in them' (ibid., p. 156). At a certain point, when the market became 'dependent' on the Bank for accommodations, interest rates could be raised with some effect. It followed that, 'a judicious exercise of the temporary power thus acquired by the Bank may be turned possibly to very beneficial account for the restoration of the exchanges, whatever be the nature of the speculation which has led to their derangement'; nevertheless, Fullarton emphasised, 'it would be a great mistake indeed to suppose, that it is in the will of the Bank of England . . . to regulate on the large scale, or for a length of time together, a thing so uncontrollable' (ibid., pp. 160–1).[55]

Tooke made a similar recommendation in his *Inquiry*, concluding that, 'it is only by a forcible action on their securities that they can influence the exchanges, so as to arrest a drain, or to resist an excessive reflux. By a forcible action on securities is meant a great advance in the *rate of interest* on the one hand, or a great reduction of it on the other' (1844, pp. 102–3).[56] This raising of the Bank rate through open market operations would not necessarily 'be attended with an immediate or direct effect on the prices of commodities. The effect, if any, can be only indirect, through the medium of credit, and dependent on the previous state of the market' (ibid., p. 103). The effect on prices, however, when it came, could be considerable. A devaluation of fictitious capital would be added to that of real capital in the form of commodities glutting the market, hence further contracting demand and ensuring generalised economic recession. The Banking School regarded the 'periodical destruction of capital' as inevitable and the 'errors and extravagances of credit' leading up to it as 'beyond the pale of legislation'; indeed, such interference 'would be more vexatious and intolerable than even the evil which it sought to correct' (Fullarton, 1844, p. 186).

The whole process was lucidly set out by Fullarton, who as we have seen, traced the origin of speculation to a combination of low interest rates and a diminishing return on productive investment. In short,

> The capitalist . . . becomes disposed to listen with avidity to any project which holds out the expectation of a better return for his money. . . . From the market for securities, the delusion spreads to the produce market. . . . Everything in the nature of value puts on an aspect of bloated magnitude; till at last the exchange becomes affected by the unnatural rise of prices, the bullion is sent abroad, a panic ensues, and the bubble bursts, with a destruction of capital which relieves the money market for a season of the load which had oppressed it, abates

competition, and restores the market rate of interest to the level from which it had declined. (Ibid., pp. 162–4)

Marx, too, recognised that, 'the whole crisis seems to be merely a credit and money crisis', since the central issue was the convertibility of bills of exchange into money (1867/94, III, p. 490). As we have seen, however, he went beyond this limited conception of the Banking School with an analysis of crisis which was grounded in the theory of value and distribution. It was his understanding, therefore, that, 'the majority of these bills represent *actual sales and purchases*, whose extension far beyond the needs of society is, after all, the basis of the whole crisis' (ibid., emphasis added).[57] Moreover, since commodity capital was simultaneously potential money capital, its consequent depreciation implied also a contraction of this money capital – irrespective of Bank action on interest rates. If this was the meaning of the conventional wisdom that money capital was reduced in times of stringency, it was 'identical with saying that the prices of commodities have fallen. Such a collapse in prices merely balances out their earlier inflation' (ibid., p. 491; see Hobson, 1913, p. 93).

Even supposing the Bank could operate to ease the crisis, it could do nothing to avert it. Marx's practical conclusion was well within the mainstream of monetary thought: 'The entire artificial system of forced expansion of the reproduction process cannot, of course, be remedied by having some bank, like the Bank of England, give to all the swindlers the deficient capital by means of its paper and having it buy up all the depreciated commodities at their old nominal values.' That the schemes of 'money cranks' might seem plausible was due to the fact that, 'everything here appears distorted, since in this paper world, the real price and its real basis appear nowhere' (ibid., p. 490; see Kuhne, 1979, p. 352).

Rules or discretion

In conclusion, it would seem that all that lay between the Currency and Banking Schools in policy terms was ultimately a matter of timing – when to act, in whatever way, on the state of credit (Fetter, 1965, p. 194). Yet this 'matter of timing' did reflect profound theoretical differences. Whereas the Currency School treated the business cycle as an outcome of monetary disturbances, the Banking School found the cause of periodic crises in the overaccumulation of capital. Although they identified 'capital' exclusively with money capital, the Banking School was able to establish the practical point of their analysis. This was fundamentally a rejection of preconceived rules in favour of discretion at the onset of a crisis. In other words, monetary contraction, even if it were necessary, should not be attempted according to the rigid Currency School criteria – notably fluctuations in the foreign exchanges – but it should be conducted by the monetary authorities in a pragmatic and discriminating way, taking account of the circumstances.[58]

The Banking School highlighted the futility of legislation such as that of 1844–45 in the fact of underlying movements in the business cycle; these movements, as Fullarton observed, 'proceed from too deep and too powerful causes to be effectually counteracted by any appliances within the reach of the law, and above all, by any appliances so mistaken and so entirely alien to their nature and origin as an artificial limitation of the currency' (1844, p. 165).[59] The form of discretion favoured by Fullarton, though other leading figures in the Banking School were not so explicit, emphasised the real bills doctrine as a practical expression of the law of reflux:

> [M]uch as I fear I am disgracing myself by the avowal, I have no hesitation in professing my own adhesion to the decried doctrine of the old Bank Directors of 1810, 'that so long as a bank issues its notes in the discount of *good* bills, at, not more than sixty days' date, it can never go far wrong.' In that maxim, simple as it is, I verily believe, there is a nearer approach to truth, and a more profound view of the principles which govern circulation, than in any rule on the subject which since that time has been promulgated'. (Ibid., p. 198)[60]

The new insights offered by the Banking School into the nature of a credit inflation were thus employed to sustain the earlier pragmatism of the anti-Bullionists; yet they were never fully developed into an alternative theoretical analysis to that of the Currency School. This was due partly to the continuing obstacle of Say's law and partly to limitations in their own theory of value and distribution. The Banking School accepted the long-run classical circulation law and related credit and fiduciary money to the value of money as a produced commodity. However, they also accepted that output was given by the level of accumulation and that only velocity was susceptible to exogenous monetary changes. The Currency School simply held velocity constant, which ensured that any adjustment would take place in prices. As against the real bills criteria proposed by the Banking School, they wanted a rule which would guarantee automatically the economic convertibility of bank notes into gold, and thus some degree of long-run price stability.

Neither side of the currency–banking debate was able to develop a theory of output, which would have countered the dominance of the quantity theory of money. Although long-run monetary circulation requirements were determinate in a system of commodity money, quantity theory was first allowed to dominate interpretations of the short-run in this system and then the long-run once commodity money was superseded by credit and fiduciary money. At a theoretical level, only the Banking School succeeded in retaining the link with commodity money in the credit system. In reality, however, as Marx pointed out, all that could be expected in a volatile market economy was the achievement of convertibility as an *average* over a period of time. This, after all, was the aim and justification of a monetary policy based upon the law of reflux:

> The point in dispute among the English who want to keep gold as the denomination of notes is not in fact the convertibility of the note into gold – which is only the practical equivalence of what the face of the note expresses theoretically – but rather the question how this convertibility is to be secured, whether through limits imposed by law on the bank or whether the bank is to be left to its own devices. The advocates of the latter course assert that this convertibility is achieved on the average by a bank of issue which lends against bills of exchange and whose notes thus have an assured reflux, and charge that their opponents despite everything never achieved better than this average of security. The latter is a fact. The average . . . is not to be despised. (Marx, 1973, p. 131)

Part IV

Conclusion

8 Theory and Policy

> Every addition to our generalised knowledge of society . . . is a contribution to our powers of social control.
>
> M. M. Postan, *Fact and Relevance: Essays on Historical Method* (1971)

It has been my intention in this work to trace the development of the classical (and Marxian) analysis of money and prices as an integral part of the 'surplus' approach to value and distribution in the market economy. Although the conventional interpretation suggests that this analysis implies a quantity theory of money, I have attempted to show that, in contrast with neoclassical analysis, the classical account of inflation treats the price level as an independent variable in the equation of exchange. It is only in the short run that quantity theory can have any relevance to classical economics; and this, I have argued, is due to its treatment not just of money and prices but also of output.

The universal assumption of Say's law may point up a superficial resemblance between the classical and neoclassical approaches to inflation. Yet the resemblance will remain purely superficial, for the versions of 'Say's law' adopted within these approaches are fundamentally different. Whereas in neoclassical economics, the dependence of the price level upon changes in the money supply is the outcome of a *theory* of output – Say's equality – in classical economics it is the result of the *absence of such a theory* – Say's identity – since output is given by the level of accumulation. The development of a theory of output as a counterpart to the classical analysis of value and distribution would remove the need for quantity theory and permit the emergence of a coherent alternative, in the short run as well as the long run. However, the neoclassical framework cannot do otherwise than encompass quantity theory, since prices and quantities are determined simultaneously by the forces of supply and demand, in turn reflecting utility maximisation subject to the constraints of endowment and technology. The differences *within* this framework concern varying notions of equilibrium rather than the theory of output, which is common to both 'monetarist' and 'anti-monetarist' positions (Eatwell, 1983).

I have considered the analysis of inflation in three key historical episodes, which were not only explained by classical economists but also influenced by them. The first episode was dominated by Hume's essays on money and interest, in which, we are told, '[t]he contemporary economist can . . . find few if any errors of commission' (Friedman, 1968, p. 36). The classical economists were at one with Hume in his rebuttal of mercantilism; the national interest no longer lay in the accumulation of precious metals but in the flourishing of enterprise. It was Adam Smith's view, therefore, that 'the attention of government never was so unnecessarily employed, as when directed to watch over the preservation or increase of the quantity of money in any country' (1776, p. 330). Yet, in his attempt to explain the 'price revolution', Hume found the source of inflation in monetary expansion. It thus became the task of classical economics to challenge the primitive supply and demand analysis which made the value of money dependent upon its quantity and replace it with an analysis which treated money as a *produced commodity*, whose value was determined prior to exchange. This analysis was the surplus approach to value and distribution; it necessitated the explicit repudiation of the 'erroneous view of Mr Hume' (Ricardo, 1951/58, V, p. 524).

According to the classical economists, the price level in the long-run was not determined by monetary circulation, but rather the reverse: the money supply (assuming a constant velocity) was dependent upon the sum of commodity prices (in turn a function of the conditions of production) and upon the level of output (given by past accumulation). It was only in the short-run that quantity theory acquired analytical significance, and, furthermore, that the unanimity within the classical school came to an end. The question now concerned not merely the effect of a change in the value of the money commodity, but the effect of monetary disturbances when the value of money remained *unchanged*. Acceptance of the fixed output assumption embodied in Say's law meant that the burden of adjustment to such disturbances had to fall upon either prices or velocity – alternatives thrown into bold relief by the equation of exchange. Since velocity was given by institutional factors, a short-run quantity theory associated mainly with Ricardo emerged to dominate economic thought for over a century. Opponents of this new monetary orthodoxy such as Tooke and Fullarton tried, as I have shown, to promote a different interpretation; however, without a coherent theory of output their efforts did not meet with practical success.

The concept of money was central to debate in each of the historical episodes I have examined. Although Hume, in opposing mercantilism, successfully identified the role of money as a medium of circulation, he ignored its role as a universal measure of value. Hence, its value as a commodity was established for him not by production but exclusively within the sphere of circulation. The consequent attention to its quantity, *pace* the view of Adam Smith, has an echo in modern monetarism: 'Acceptance of the quantity theory clearly means that the stock of money is a key variable in policies directed at the control of the level of prices' (Friedman, 1968, p. 62). However, since Hume shared the pre-classical supply and demand approach of the fading mercantilist orthodoxy, he was neither capable of explaining the 'price revolution' or, at a practical level, of advancing a consistent set of counter-proposals. He showed, in Marx's words, 'the same "backwardness" in still proclaiming the old-fashioned notion that the "merchant" is the chief mainspring of production – an idea which Petty had long passed beyond' (1894, p. 264).

During the 'bullion controversy', the classical theory of value and money was extended from a metallic to a fiduciary system. Here a principle of limitation was required, not because the value of money was determined by its quantity, but because the issue of paper currency could not exceed the amount of gold (or silver) that would otherwise circulate at a given level of output and velocity. Such overissue would proportionately reduce the capacity of the paper to represent gold (or silver) and would thus trigger their depreciation to a theoretically unlimited extent. All the classical economists understood that, with the suspension of legal convertibility, a new principle would have to be devised to maintain what I have called 'economic convertibility'. The bank notes of the Restriction period, however, could not be characterised as fiduciary money, that is to say inconvertible tokens given forced currency by the state; they were in fact a 'circulating token of credit' (Marx, 1867/94, III, p. 404). It was therefore quite wrong to superimpose a principle of limitation appropriate for a fiduciary system upon an economy in which credit had be come the main element of demand. Yet this was the rationale of 'Bullionism', whose short-run quantity theory implied strict monetary control in conformity with movements of gold across the foreign exchanges. It was given practical expression – after the reinstatement of cash payments – in the Bank Charter Acts of 1844–5, which set the pattern of the UK financial structure for the next 60 years. This legislation was at the heart of the third and final phase of debate, between the Currency and Banking Schools.

While the leading lights of what became known as the 'currency principle' did little except apply classical quantity theory to a regime of convertible notes, their Banking School opponents attempted to develop for the first time a theory specific to credit. Even if it is assumed that both sides of the debate were equally concerned to minimise the damaging fluctuations of the business cycle, the Banking School was alone in wanting to achieve this without needlessly sacrificing productive capacity to an inflexible monetary rule. Following Smith's real bills doctrine, they proposed a 'law of reflux', according to which debt creation would ultimately be self-liquidating under normal conditions, providing only that it had a counterpart in existing or future real value. It was the responsibility of banks themselves to design suitable lending criteria, which would be intended both to secure a proper rate of return and to avoid insolvency in the long-run.

The Currency School looked upon monetary policy almost as a panacea for the alternate bouts of inflation and economic recession; for them, gold was 'both the badge and the guarantee of bourgeois freedom' (Schumpeter, 1954, p. 406). The Banking School, on the other hand, was under no such illusions. They not only denounced the irrational banking legislation, as they perceived it, which required 'such enormous stores of coin . . . to be hoarded up at so vast an expense, [while] at all times inexorably withheld from the public' (Fullarton, 1844, p. 150); but they also recognised that repeal or replacement of the legislation would not subdue the inherently 'uncontrollable' movements of the business cycle (ibid., p. 161).

Likewise, Marx, in a scornful review of Darimon's *De la Réforme des Banques*, had declared that, 'the evil of bourgeois society is not to be remedied by "transforming" the banks or by founding a rational "money system" ' (1973, p. 134). Yet he supported the Banking School view that the law of reflux, even if it could not suppress crises entirely, could alleviate them by keeping the accumulation of 'fictitious' capital within manageable limits – at least up to a point. Beyond that, since the source of crises lay much deeper in the accumulation process of real capital, the monetary authorities could only operate upon what Tooke defined as the 'state of credit' through the Bank rate – and maintain an adequate bullion reserve. Each successive financial panic confirmed that, while the reserve of monetary metals could be reduced to a minimum in the modern credit system, it could not be dispensed with altogether. Gold drains from the Bank of England not only sounded a warning signal to the authorities, but also predetermined the scope of their response. Once crises were under way, the practical difference between the Currency and Banking School approaches became simply one of degree.

Marx's purpose, however, in recognising the limited role of monetary policy, was to set a course that was different in kind. For him, the only real solution to crises was a change in the organisation of production. The development of credit hastened this process in two ways. First, it turned the control of capital from a private into a social function: 'The banking system possesses indeed the form of universal book-keeping and distribution of means of production on a social scale . . .' (1867/94, III, p. 606). Second, banking and credit had become 'the most potent means of driving capitalist production beyond its own limits' (ibid., p. 607), that is to say beyond the limits established by private profit. Hence, Marx concluded, 'there is no doubt that the credit system will serve as a powerful lever during the transition from the capitalist mode of production to the mode of production of associated labour': but it would be 'only as one element in connection with other great organic revolutions in the mode of production itself' (ibid.).

To sum up, classical economics developed in part as a response to the quantity theory interpretation of the sixteenth and seventeenth century 'price revolution'. The distinguishing feature of the classical (and Marxian) approach which I have identified in this work was that the supply side of the equation of exchange determined long-run monetary requirements, whether metallic, fiduciary or credit. The role of quantity theory was limited to short-run price adjustment resulting from exogenous changes in the money supply. While this price adjustment was a necessary consequence of assuming a fixed level of output – Say's law – it was not accepted by all classical economists. Some counterposed a quantity adjustment associated with changes in velocity, although this was incompatible with the assumption of a stable demand for money. I have shown how Ricardo and the Currency School tried to seize upon this incompatibility to refute critics of quantity theory. Indeed, the inflation debate became a mirror image of the debate with Malthus on deflation. These critics, the Banking School among them, did much to develop the analysis of money and credit, but they were fatally compromised by their failure to overturn Say's law.

While monetarism is thus a necessary element of neoclassical economics, due to the nature of its theory of output, it simply reflects the 'incompleteness' of classical economics, since monetarism there follows from the lack of a theory of output comparable with the classical theory of value and distribution. I have depicted this difference between the classical and neoclassical variants of Say's law as a distinction between Say's identity and Say's equality respectively. The problem of 'incompleteness', however, has lent credibility to the claim that classical analysis implies a quantity theory of money and it has obstructed the further development of a theory of inflation and unemployment.

As a result, the neoclassical approach has dominated policy discussion on the future of market (and 'planned') economies almost by default (Eatwell and Green, 1984). This approach has been found wanting not only from the viewpoint of internal logic but also historically. A report on the 1970s' UK experience, for example, concludes that:

> Although over the long term the money supply and price level appear to have moved together, we have not been convinced by evidence of a direct causal relationship from growth in the money supply to inflation . . . [T]he Treasury's own evidence tends to refute the suggestion of any simple relationship in the short and medium term. (du Cann, 1981, p. lxxvii)

The development of a 'classical' theory of output encompassing a saving–investment analysis – a principle of effective demand – is an essential element of an alternative approach to money and price behaviour. Moreover, while a theory of output may be a 'separable' element of this approach, the corollary of my argument is that it cannot be treated as independent of its logical basis in classical value and distribution theory. A synthesis of the classical approach to value and distribution with the principle of effective demand offers a coherent alternative to monetarism and the neoclassical orthodoxy.

Appendix: Price Trends in History

Index (1451–75 = 100) of price of composite unit of consumables in Southern England, 1451–1858

Price revolution		*Bullion controversy*		*Currency–banking debate*	
1451–60	99	1792	883	1825	1400
1461–70	105	1793	908	1826	1323
1471–80	94	1794	978	1827	1237
1481–90	115	1795	1091	1828	1201
1491–1500	100	1796	1161	1829	1189
1501–10	105	1797	1045	1830	1146
1511–20	115	1798	1022	1831	1260
1521–30	151	1799	1148	1832	1167
1531–40	154	1800	1567	1833	1096
1541–50	203	1801	1751	1834	1011
1551–60	290	1802	1348	1835	1028
1561–70	282	1803	1268	1836	1141
1571–80	322	1804	1309	1837	1169
1581–90	362	1805	1521	1838	1177
1591–1600	478	1806	1454	1839	1263
1601–10	479	1807	1427	1840	1286
1611–20	527	1808	1476	1841	1256
1621–30	527	1809	1619	1842	1161
1631–40	611	1810	1670	1843	1030
1641–50	647	1811	1622	1844	1029
1651–60	621	1812	1836	1845	1079
1661–70	636	1813	1881	1846	1122
1671–80	614	1814	1642	1847	1257
1681–90	571	1815	1467	1848	1105
1691–1700	663	1816	1344	1849	1035
		1817	1526	1850	969
		1818	1530	1851	961
		1819	1492	1852	978
		1820	1353	1853	1135
		1821	1190	1854	1265
		1823	1099	1855	1274
		1824	1193	1856	1264
				1857	1287

Source: Phelps-Brown and Hopkins (1981).

References

1 The Aim of the Inquiry

1. This distinction is not the same as that made by Baumol and Becker (1960) who use it to denote two lines of approach *within* the framework of neoclassical analysis.
2. '[T]he theoretical foundations of monetarism . . . do not lie in the realm of monetary theory, but in theories of the determination of real output' (Eatwell, 1983, p. 203; see also Green, 1982a and 1987a).
3. Schumpeter has argued, rightly in my view, that, 'Nobody can hope to understand the economic phenomena of any, including the present, epoch who has not an adequate command of . . . what may be described as *historical experience* (1954, pp. 12–13); cf. Hegel's *Philosophy of Right*, where 'the concept develops itself out of itself. . . . Its development is a purely immanent progress . . .' (1821, p. 34).
4. Rubin has noted the 'two-sided nature' of this task: it would be necessary to impart 'at one and the same time an exposition of both the *historical* conditions out of which the different economic doctrines arose and developed, and their *theoretical meaning*, i.e., of the internal logical relationship of ideas' (1929, p. 10).
5. It should be borne in mind that the 'supply and demand framework' which occupies our attention in the following pages is quite distinct from supply and demand *theory*, i.e., the neoclassical theory of prices: see Eatwell (1982), p. 207.
6. As Postan has noted, 'Every historical fact is a product of abstraction . . .' (1971, p. 51).

2 The Classical Framework

1. Inevitably, as we shall see, such a procedure ran the risk of social detachment: '[T]he price of deduction is abstraction: the logical rigour and consistency of economic proportions is a direct consequence of the fact that the fundamental concepts, the original assumptions and the successive stages of economic argument are all treated in isolation from the rest of the social environment' (Postan, 1938, p. 27).
2. 'Different accidents may sometimes keep them suspended a good deal above it, and sometimes force them down even somewhat below it. But whatever may be the obstacles which hinder them from settling in this centre of repose and continuance, they are constantly tending towards it' (Smith, 1776, p. 44). It should be noted that the workings of competition which constitute the 'law' of supply and demand 'do not identify the phenomena which *determine* natural prices' (Eatwell, 1982, p. 207); that was to be the province of neoclassical theory one hundred years later.

3. Even earlier, Sir William Petty had broken with the natural law conception of a 'just price' and differentiated the value or 'natural price' of commodities from their 'political price', which was the price daily observable in the market (1899, I, p. 44 and *passim*). His achievement was recognised by Marx, who stated that, 'by classical Political Economy, I understand that economy which, since the time of W. Petty, has investigated the real relations of production in bourgeois society, in contra-distinction to vulgar economy, which deals with appearances only . . .' (1867/94, I, p. 85 fn.). For a more precise discussion of 'vulgar economy', see Garegnani (1984), pp. 303–4.
4. Ricardo also declared his opposition to those who would attempt to 'theorise' price formation from the standpoint of supply and demand, or, what I shall call the 'pure exchange' approach: 'It is the cost of production which must ultimately regulate the price of commodities, and not, as has often been said, the proportion between supply and demand: . . . this effect will be only of temporary duration . . .' (1951/58, I. p. 382).
5. 'The vulgar economist has not the faintest idea that the actual everyday exchange relations *cannot be directly identical* with the magnitudes of value. The essence of bourgeois society consists precisely in this, that *a priori* there is no conscious social regulation of production. The rational and naturally necessary asserts itself only as a blindly working average. And then the vulgar economist thinks he has made a great discovery when, in face of the disclosure of intrinsic interconnection, he proudly states that on the surface things look different. In fact, he boasts that he sticks to appearance, and takes it for the ultimate. Why, then, have any science at all?' (Marx to Kugelmann, 11 July 1868, in Marx and Engels, 1975, p. 197).
6. A striking illustration is Marx's treatment of the difference between labour and 'labour-power', where it is argued that, 'classical economy never arrived at a consciousness of the results of its own analysis . . .' (1867/94, I, pp. 503–4),
7. I have earlier examined the question of whether a 'realisation problem' exists for Marxist analysis in the context of the debate between Rosa Luxemburg and Nikolai Bukharin on imperialism and the accumulation of capital (Green, 1975).
8. Dobb is able to argue that Marx 'decisively rejected . . . "Say's Law"' only because he confines it to a denial of the possibility of hoarding (1973, p. 164).
9. On the problems of calculation, see Hawtrey (1934), ch. 3.
10. Most commentators recognise the importance of the 'transition from the discussion and analysis of general principles or long-run issues to . . . the analysis of particular events or short-run issues' (Niebyl, 1946, p. 146), but the role of money is not addressed from the viewpoint of Say's law and the classical theory of value and distribution.
11. The conventional wisdom was encapsulated in the following formula: 'price depends upon quantity of money, value depends upon quantity of labour. General or absolute prices depend upon the whole quantity of money in the market; relative prices, or the prices of commodities when compared with one another, depend on the values of commodities respectively' ('A Scotch Banker', 1868, p. 107).
12. Vilar takes a similar approach in his *History of Gold and Money*, though he describes it as 'the concept of the historical conjuncture', which 'involves

investigating the unevenness of the rhythm of development . . .' (Vilar, 1976, p. 39). See also Schumpeter (1954), pp. 4–24; Morgan (1965), p. 177; and Deane (1978), pp. ix–xv.

13. This is not to deny the widespread use of credit instruments even in medieval Europe: see Postan (1928).
14. The considerable problems of interpretation are described by Morgan (1950).
15. A formidable attempt to provide a quantity theory explanation of the Price Revolution is Hamilton (1934). See also Keynes's *Treatise on Money* on the 'extraordinary correspondence of periods of Profit Inflation and Profit Deflation respectively with those of national rise and decline (1933, pp. 151–2).
16. Deane further suggests that, 'the real forces pushing up the level of demand in the second half of the century were so evidently more substantial than those prevailing in the first half that what seems to need explanation is not that prices tended to rise but that the inflationary trend was so modest . . . However, wartime inflation was a different story . . .' (1979, p. 11).

3 Mercantilism and the Quantity Theory of Money

1. This terminology has no connection with the 'bullion controversy' of the early nineteenth century. Hence, to avoid confusion – and to fit in with popular usage – the scope and meaning of 'bullionism' will be subsumed under the general rubric of mercantilism.
2. This more sophisticated conception is found, for example, in Charles Davenant's *Essay upon the Probable Methods of Making a People Gainers in the Ballance of Trade*: 'Gold and Silver are indeed the Measure of Trade, but the Spring and Origins of it, in all Nations, is the Natural, or Artificial Product of the Country, that is to say, what their Land, or what their Labour and Industry produces . . .' (Davenant, 1699, p. 15; see also pp. 60–63).
3. It should be noted that the ethical content of 'just price' was subordinated to market considerations. As Schumpeter has pointed out, the Natural Law philosophers, following Aristotle, 'simply thought of the exchange values of market, as *expressed* in terms of money, rather than of some mysterious value substance *measured* by those exchange values' (Schumpeter, 1954, p. 61). Hence, the 'concept of the just value of a commodity is indeed "objective", but only in the sense that no individual can alter it by his own action' (ibid.). See also, pp. 93–4; and Milgate (1982), pp. 189–91.
4. 'It is the Exportation of our Product that must make England rich; to be Gainers in the Ballance of Trade, we must carry out of our own Product, what will purchase the Things of Foreign Growth that are needful for our own Consumption, with some Overplus either in Bullion or Goods to be sold in other Countries; which Overplus is the Profit a Nation makes by Trade, and it is more or less according to the natural Frugality of the People that Export, as from the low Price of Labour and Manufacture they can afford the Commodity cheap, and at a rate not to be undersold in Foreign Markets': Davenant (1699), pp. 45–6.
5. Wicksell regarded the emergence of quantity theory in this period as 'a reaction against the mercantile theory' (Wicksell, 1934/5, II, p. 144; also 1936, p. 38; Hollander, 1911, p. 438; and Rubin, 1929, p. 83 and *passim*).

6. The work of the early Spanish writers in the area of monetary theory was first unearthed by Grice-Hutchinson (1952); and it receives a lucid exposition in Gordon (1975), who also mentions the extraordinarily sophisticated development by the Belgian theologian, Leonard Lessins.
7. As Marx put it, Locke's view 'was the classical expression of bourgeois society's ideas of right as against feudal society'; and 'his philosophy served as the basis for all the ideas of the whole of subsequent English political economy' (1963/71, I, p. 367). See also Mill (1969), Part 3, ch. 4.
8. The debate was made to turn on whether the value of coin was really indicated by its metallic content or by the units in which it was denominated (see Andréadès, 1935, pp. 100–2). Disagreement persists over how Locke determined the value of of a given unit of weight. He advanced what has come to be called a 'consent hypothesis': 'The intrinsic value of silver, considered as money, is that estimate which common consent has placed on it, whereby it is made equivalent to all other things, and consequently is the universal barter, or exchange, which men give and receive for other things, they would purchase or part with, for a valuable consideration . . .' (1691, p. 318). Some interpret this statement to mean that, 'common consent simply established the fact that certain metals were to be used and universally accepted as money' (Vickers, 1960, p. 66). The context makes it clear, however, that it was the *magnitude* of value which was conventionally established. This approach, which divorced the 'intrinsic value' of money from its cost of production opened the way for Locke's quantity theory.
9. Locke here advanced to a standpoint which had some outward similarity to that of Petty and the classical economists. Value was no longer dependent upon the exchange process but appeared to be determined outside it. Hence a definite amount of money was required to support a given volume of commodity transactions: '[A] certain proportion of money [is] necessary for driving such a proportion of trade' (ibid., p. 226). This 'proportion of money' was also governed by its velocity: '[W]hat proportion that is, is hard to determine; because it depends [on] the quickness of its circulation.' That each unit of currency therefore represented a determinate weight of metal was illustrated in the debate with Lowndes by the case where the money supply was inadequate for the needs of trade: 'The necessity of trust and bartering is one of the many inconveniences springing from the want of money. This inconvenience, the multiplying arbitrary denominations will no more supply, nor any ways make our scarcity of coin commensurate to that need there is of it, by measuring it by a yard one-fifth shorter than the standard, or changing the standard of the yard, and so getting the full denomination of yards, necessary according to the present measure' (ibid., p. 340). Without a theory of value and distribution, let alone a theory of output, Locke was unable to take this aspect of his analysis any further. Indeed, he was mistaken in thinking that it justified his opposition to devaluation in the immediate circumstances. There was no suggestion of 'multiplying arbitrary denominations' to make up for a lack of metallic currency, but simply a recognition that debasement had already taken place through wear and tear. When Steuart later resurrected Lowndes' position, his repudiation of Locke's misconceived intervention in this policy debate allowed him to overlook the latter's vague but potentially fruitful attempt to locate the problem of value outside a supply

and demand framework. Locke himself failed to pursue the attempt not only because it was inconsistent with his quantity theory but also because he was reluctant to abandon mercantilist ideas. His persistent confusion of money with capital forced him to drop the constant output assumption and to make economic activity dependent upon the supply of available money. He claimed, for example, that, 'the over-balancing of trade, between us and our neighbours, must inevitably carry away our money; and quickly leave us poor, and exposed. Gold and silver, though they serve for few, yet they command all the conveniences of life, and therefore in a plenty of them consists riches' (ibid., p. 226).

10. In claiming to remedy 'the injustice to the creditors of reducing the bullion contents of the unit,' Locke, in Feavearyear's view, supported his argument against Lowndes 'with a great deal of purely deductive reasoning much of which is little more than truism' (1931, p. 124). In practical terms, the price which had to be paid for the victory of Locke's position was a severe and sustained deflation (ibid., p. 125 ff.). See Jay (1985) pp. 43–9; and, on the 'nominal standard of money', Marx (1859), pp. 76–86.
11. Rather curiously for an historian of thought, Roll, while prepared to admit the reliance by Hume upon his predecessors, nevertheless regards the connection as 'irrelevant' (1973, p. 118 fn.).
12. Tooke referred to Hume's essays as 'being written with all the charms of his popular style . . . But the opinions expressed in them are for the most part crude, and the conclusions are in many instances very loosely drawn' (1838/57, IV, p. 82).
13. Vickers questions the existence of any such contradiction (1960, p. 226 fn.); but see Rotwein's introduction to Hume (1955); Hegeland (1951) p. 34 ff.; and Rubin (1929) p. 84.
14. Hume made no reference to the important work of Jacob Vanderlint, *Money Answers All Things* (1784), though it must have been known to him: 'Money [i.e., gold and silver: R. G.] being, by the consent of all nations, become counters for adjusting the values of all things else . . . the prices of the produce or manufactures of every nation will be higher or lower according as the quantity of cash circulating in such nation is greater or less . . .' (Vanderlint 1734, pp. 2–3). The extent to which Hume simply took over Vanderlint's argument and presentation was originally pointed out by Dugald Stewar (Notes in Smith, 1812, V, p. 536 ff.). Compare, for example, the passages, i Hume (1752) pp. 195–8, and in Vanderlint, ibid., p. 55.
15. Here it was Montesquieu's formulation which had been employed, agai without acknowledgement: 'Gold and silver are either a fictitious or repres entative wealth. . . . But the more they are multiplied, the more they lose thei value, because the fewer are the things which they represent' (Montesquieu 1748, p. 172). Even earlier Isaac Gervaise had written: 'The value or propor tion of all things useful or necessary, is to gold and silver, in proportion to th quantity of gold and silver that is in the world; so that the more gold and silve is in the world, the greater the value of things will be' (Gervaise, 1720, p. 5)
16. 'If we compare the mass of gold and silver in the whole world with th quantity of merchandise therein contained, it is certain that every commodit or merchandise in particular may be compared to a certain portion of th entire mass of gold and silver. As the total of one is to the total of the othe

so the part of one will be to part of the other. Let us suppose that there is only one commodity or merchandise in the world, or only one to be purchased, and that this is divisible like money; a part of this merchandise will answer to a part of the mass of gold and silver; the half of the total of one to the half of the total of the other; [etc.] . . . [T]he establishment of the price of things fundamentally depends on the proportion of the total of things [cont.] to the total of signs': Montesquieu (1748), p. 176. Henry Thornton later remarked of this hypothesis that, 'though not altogether to be rejected', it was 'laid down in a manner which is very loose and fallacious' (1802, p. 247 and *passim*). See also Cantillon (1755), p. 161.

17. 'Thus as Labour draws the Denominator of the World, also the Denominator draws Labour from the World; so that if the particular Denominator of any Nation, be greater than its just proportion, it will draw from the other Nations a Portion of Labour, proportion'd to its Excess; and if its Denominator be less than its just Proportion, it will draw a Portion of Gold and Silver, proportion'd to what it wants of its just Proportion': Gervaise (1720), p. 7. 'But no Inconvenience can arise by an unrestrained Trade, but very great Advantage; since if the Cash of the Nation be decreased by it, which Prohibitions are designed to prevent, those Nations that get the Cash will certainly find every thing advance in Price, as the Cash increases amongst them. And . . . our Manufactures, and everything else, will soon become so moderate as to turn the Balance of Trade in our Favour, and thereby fetch the Money back again' (Vanderlint, 1734, pp. 44–5).
18. Marx noted Hume's 'correct discovery' that 'in the slow process of price equalisation, this depreciation [of the precious metals] only in the last instance "increases the price of labour" – *vulgo*, wages; . . . But he does not raise the problem which is of real interest to science, namely, whether and in what way an increase in the supply of the precious metals, if their value remains unchanged, affects the prices of commodities, and he confuses *every* 'increase of the precious metals' with their depreciation' (1894, p. 262). The evidence is adduced below.
19. Commenting on Hume, Price argued that, 'the increased commercial activity, which may follow on an augmented supply of the precious metals, may conceal, and neutralise the real influences exerted on prices (1909, p. 36).
20. Rist regarded Cantillon's *Essai* as 'one of the great works on money and credit' (1940, p. 74), and contrasted it, as we shall see below, with the writings of John Law.
21. Cantillon distinguished the 'intrinsic' price or value of a commodity, which was defined as 'the measure of the quantity of Land and of Labour entering into its production' (1755, p. 29).
22. Increased production of precious metals from mines in a closed economy gave rise, according to Cantillon, to a proportionately higher level of expenditure on the part of 'the Owner of these Mines, the Adventurers, the Smelters, Refiners, and all the other workers' (1755, p. 163). Their consumption 'will consequently give employment to several Mechanicks who had not so much to do before and who for the same reason will increase their expenses' (ibid.); but this stimulus to employment did not always imply an expansion of output. On the contrary, 'all this increase of expense in Meat, Wine, Wool, etc. diminishes of necessity the share of the other inhabitants of

the State who did not participate at first in the wealth of the Mines in question' (ibid.). At the same time, the growing pressure of demand would inevitably drive up the prices of these commodities. It was then the turn of farmers to benefit from the profits accruing from the sale of their produce at higher prices. The redistribution of resources set in train by this monetary inflation did, however, leave some classes and groups worse off: 'Those then who will suffer from this dearness and increased consumption who will be first of all the Landowners, during the term of their Leases, then their Domestic Servants and all the Workmen or fixed Wage-earners who support their families on their wages' (ibid., p. 165). Faced with the need to 'diminish their expenditure in proportion to the new consumption', many would be forced to emigrate, others would become unemployed, and the rest would seek to have their real wage restored to previous levels. The process only went into reverse once a re-evaluation had taken place of all incomes – of landowners, workmen, artisans, etc. – and hence of all commodities in conformity with the new monetary standard.

23. Cantillon also extended the analysis to other sources of money, such as subsidies from abroad, plunder and expenditure by travellers, ambassadors and immigrants (1755, pp. 171–5).

24. Elsewhere, Marx wrote: 'Steuart's great work . . . permanently enriched the domain of political economy' (1894, p. 276). The best treatment of Steuart is provided by Meek in his 'Rehabilitation of Sir James Steuart' (1967). Sen's account (1957) is uncritical.

25. Tooke was later to remark that while Steuart's treatise 'contained a great deal of miscellaneous information relating to the circulation of coin and paper, . . . it disclosed no general views of the principles upon which variation in their value depended' (1838/57, IV, p. 82).

26. Since Steuart only considered money as it appeared in circulation – as standard of price and money of account – he saw it as 'no more than an arbitrary scale of equal parts'; it 'might exist, although there was no such thing in the world as any substance which could become an adequate or proportional equivalent for every commodity'. Indeed, he answered the question as to what should be the 'standard value' of a given part of the scale 'by putting another question; what is the standard length of a degree, a minute, a second? It has none . . . But so soon as one part becomes determined, by the nature of a scale, all the rest must follow in proportion' (1967, II, pp. 408, 410, 411; see Marx, 1859, pp. 79–81). The fact that when the values of commodities are converted into prices they are measured in imaginary quantities of gold and silver, had led Steuart wrongly to suppose that the unit of account (pound, franc, etc.) must denote ideal or arbitrary fractions of value, rather than any fixed weight of metal. As we shall see below, this vision of an ideal monetary standard could only be fulfilled for Steuart by a paper currency.

27. Cameralism was an increasingly popular doctrine at this time, which Engels later described as 'an eclectic economic sauce covering a hotchpotch of sundry trivialities, of the sort a junior civil servant might find useful to remember during his final examination' (1859, p. 219).

28. It is noteworthy that Smith did not once refer to Steuart's work in the *Wealth of Nations*. In a letter to Pulteney in 1772, he had already confided: 'I have the

same opinion of Sir James Steuart's book that you have. Without once mentioning it, I flatter myself that any fallacious principle in it will meet with a clear and distinct confrontation in mine' (cited by Meek, 1967, p. 6). Earlier still Hume had written privately to Smith: 'I am positive you are wrong in many of your speculations, especially where you have the misfortune, to differ from me' (10 April 1767, in Hume, 1955, p. 216). Although there is considerable confusion in the literature over the theoretical status and relationship of these three leading figures of the 'Scottish Enlightenment', it has at least been recognised by Jacob Hollander that, in the context of monetary analysis, 'Adam Smith was neither convinced by Hume nor converted by Steuart' (1911, p. 439).

29. As Rubin put it, 'The "price revolution" . . . could not, therefore, be explained simply as the product of an increase in the quantity of money: the fact that the prices of commodities were rising reflected a fall in the value of the precious metals themselves' (1929, p. 84).
30. A similar conclusion was reached by Hammarström, who, in response to Hamilton's quantity theory interpretation of the 'price revolution', stated: 'It seems to me that, when price historians using the quantity theory take as their starting point figures of bullion imports or production, they leave out important elements in the dynamic process going on behind the facade of rising price trends' (1957, p. 57).

4 Classical Theory of the Metallic System

1. Roll's assessment of Petty was apt: 'His very method of analysis shows that . . . he was far removed from the primitive errors of the mercantilists' (1973, p. 110).
2. On the 'surplus' approach to value and distribution, see Garegnani (1984) and the collection in Eatwell and Milgate (1983).
3. Steuart distinguished 'relative profit', which 'implies no addition to the general stock', from 'positive profit', which 'results from an augmentation of labour, industry or ingenuity, and has the effect of swelling or augmenting the public good' (1767, I, pp. 179–80). His exposition was therefore described by Marx as the 'rational expression' of mercantilism, in the sense that he 'reproduced it in scientific form' (1963/71, I, pp. 41, 43). Although Steuart locates the origin of 'positive profit' in the physical 'superfluity' of total production for subsistence, he is unable to present this insight as a theory outside the supply and demand framework.
4. 'Gold and silver are indeed the Measure of Trade, but the Spring and Original of it, in all Nations, is the Natural, or Artificial Product of the Country, that is to say, what their land, or what their Labour and Industry produces' (Davenant, 1698, p. 15).
5. '[H]owever the standard of necessary labour may differ at various epochs and in various countries, or how much, in consequence of the demand and supply of labour, its amount and ratio may change, at any given epoch the standard is to be considered and acted upon as a fixed one by capital' (Marx 1973, p. 817; also p. 892).

6. The source of difficulty for many commentators lies in their treatment of classical quantity theory as a mere extension of Hume's (pre-classical) approach (e.g. O'Brien, 1975, ch. 6).
7. Later, in the *Political Arithmetic*, Petty presented the reasoning behind this assertion. Having resolved the social product into its constituent income shares – wages and rent – he estimated their magnitude and rate of turnover. The money supply of £6 million was one-ninth of annual output: 'If there be six Millions of Souls in England, and that each spendeth 7l. *per annum*, then the whole expence is forty two Millions, or about eight hundred thousands pounds *per* week; and consequently, if every Man did pay his expence weekly, and that the Money could circulate within the compass of a Week, then less than one Million would answer the ends proposed. But forasmuch as the Rents of the Lands in England (which are paid half yearly) are eight Millions *per annum*, there must be four Millions to pay them. And forasmuch as the Rent of Housing of England, paid quarterly, are worth about four Millions *per ann.* there needs but one Million to pay the said Rents; wherefore six Millions [are] enough to make good the three sorts of Circulations . . .' (1899, I, p. 310).
8. Petty argued that, 'the law . . . should allow the Labourer but just wherewithall to live; for if you allow double, then he works but half so much as he could have done, and otherwise would; which is a loss to the Publick of the fruit of so much labour' (1899, I, p. 87). This magnitude was further conditioned by natural factors, such as the fertility of the land, and the influence of climate upon physiological needs. Hence, Petty went on, 'natural dearness and cheapness depends upon the few or more hands requisite to necessaries of Nature: As Corn is cheaper where one man produces Corn for ten, then where he can do the like but for six; and withall, according as the Climate disposes men to a necessity of spending more or less' (ibid., p. 90).
9. Smith argued that whatever the 'advantage' possessed by the 'masters' in wage disputes, there was always a 'certain rate' which formed an irreducible minimum. This was the 'natural wage rate: 'A man must always live by his work, and his wages must at least be sufficient to maintain him. They must even upon most occasions be somewhat more; otherwise it would be impossible for him to bring up a family, and the race of such workman could not last beyond the first generation' (1776, pp. 51–2).
10. It could not be presumed, therefore, that this natural rate 'is absolutely fixed and constant. It varies at different times in the same country, and very materially differs in different countries' (Ricardo, 1951/58, I, p. 96).
11. For Marx, 'the general movements of wages are exclusively regulated by the expansion and contraction of the industrial reserve army, and these again correspond to the periodic changes of the industrial cycle. . . . [T]hat would indeed be a beautiful law, which pretends to make the action of capital dependent on the absolute variations of the population, instead of regulating the demand and supply of labour by the alternate expansion and contraction of capital . . .' (1963/71, II, pp. 597–7). The role of trade unions was 'to hinder the *sinking of the level* of wages beneath the various branches of business, the forcing of the *price* of the labour-capacity down below its value' (Marx, 1879/80, p. 184).
12. 'Suppose a man could with his own hands plant a certain scope of Land with

Corn, that is, could Digg, or Plough, Harrow, Weed, Reap, Carry home, Thresh, and Winnow so much as the Husbandry of this Land requires; and had withal Seed wherewith to sowe the same. I say, that when this man hath subducted his seed out of the proceed of his Harvest, and also, what himself hath both eaten and given to others in exchange for Clothes, and other Natural necessaries; that the remainder of Corn is the natural and true Rent of the Land for that year; and the *medium* of seven years, or rather of so many years as makes up the Cycle, within which Dearths and Plenties make their revolution, doth give the ordinary Rent of the Land in Corn' (Petty, 1899, I, p. 143).

13. 'Of all the values which shot up in the feverish atmosphere of [Law's] system, nothing remained except ruin, desolation and bankruptcy. Landed property alone did not go under in the storm . . . [but] arose for the first time from the condition of torpor in which the feudal system had kept it for so long. This was a real awakening for agriculture . . .'; Blanqui, *Histoire de l' Economie Politique en Europe* (1839) (cited in Marx, 1963/71, I, p. 64)

14. 'By this new arrangement the produce of the land is divided into two parts. The one includes the subsistence and the profits of the Husbandman, which are the reward of his labour and the condition upon which he undertakes to cultivate the field of the Proprietor. What remains is that independent and disposable part which the land gives as a pure gift to him who cultivates it, over and above his advances and the wages of his trouble; and this is the portion of the Proprietor, or the *revenue* with which the latter can live without labour and which he carries where he will' (Turgot, 1770, p. 14).

15. Turgot initially depicted the surplus, or 'produit net', both as a pure gift of nature and as a surplus labour, by which he meant labour performed in excess of that required to produce the means of subsistence (1770, p. 9). While he went beyond Petty in recognising that, with the development of landed property, the various categories of revenue accrued to specific social classes, he located the transition from feudal to capitalist relationships exclusively within agriculture. Hence the landowner became a capitalist, who paid the wages not only of his immediate employees, the 'classe productrice', but also of the manufacturing occupations, the 'classe stipendiée' (ibid., pp. 10–12). Ultimately, what appeared as a gift of nature was recognised as a function of the labour expended in agriculture, whose surplus product was appropriated by the landowning class, and partially redistributed as consumption spending to the 'sterile' manufacturing sector (ibid., p. 16).

16. 'The rational foundation of the principle of the determining role of the profits of agriculture, which is never explicitly stated by Ricardo, is that in agriculture the same commodity namely corn, forms both the capital (conceived as composed of the subsistence necessary for workers) and the product; so that the determination of profit by the difference between total product and capital advanced, and also determination of the ratio of this profit to the capital, is done directly between quantities of corn without any question of valuation' (Sraffa, in Ricardo, 1951/58, I, p. xxxi). Hollander, by contrast, argues that the corn model was of 'little significance' for Ricardo (1979, p. 183; also p. 259 and *passim*). See, however, the exchange of views between Hollander (1973, 1975) and Eatwell (1975b); also Groenewegen (1972).

17. 'And forasmuch as possibly there may be more Art and Hazzard in working about the Silver, then about the Corn, yet all comes to the same pass; for let

a hundred men work ten years upon Corn, and the same number of men, the same time upon Silver; I say, that the neat proceed of the Silver is the price of the whole neat proceed of the Corn, and like parts of the one, the price of like parts of the other . . .' (Petty, 1899, I, pp. 43–4).

18. It was only in his last writings, such as the *Quantulumcunque concerning Money* (1682), that Petty shed these final traces of mercantilist doctrine. He asked, for example, whether a country was necessarily the poorer for having less money, and answered in the negative: 'For as the most thriving Men keep little or no Money by them, but turn and wind it into various commodities to their great Profit, so may the whole Nation also' (1899, II, p. 446). Petty thus anticipated the predominance of industrial over merchant capital; he had no difficulty in reconciling rapid monetary velocity (or a low propensity to hoard) with his conception of the circulation law.

19. In his idiosyncratic terminology, Steuart called the natural or physical element in the commodity its 'intrinsic worth' and the labour-time its 'useful value' or, in other places, its 'real value'. Two problems arose immediately, one in connection with the definition of this real value, and the other as we have noted, with its transformation into price. First, real value was said to include not just the amount of labour 'upon an average only, a workman of the country in general may perform . . . in a day, a week, a month . . .', but also the wage and raw material costs (ibid., I, p. 160). Second, it excluded the 'manufacturer's profit' which is added in exchange to form the 'fundamental price' (ibid., I, pp. 160–1). Like the Physiocrats, Steuart recognised the creation of a material surplus in agriculture, but his attempt to develop the concept of surplus into a general category precipitated a reversion to mercantilist pure exchange analysis.

20. It was to make this point that Samuel Bailey correctly stated: 'The excellence of any thing as a measure of value is altogether independent of its own variableness in value' (1825, p. 10). Marx suggested that Smith 'confuses – as Ricardo also often does – labour, the *intrinsic* measure of value, with *money*, the *external measure*, which presupposes that value is already determined . . .' (1963/71, II, p. 403).

21. As Marx put it, Smith 'confuses the determination of value by means of the quantity of labour expended in the production of commodities, with the determination of the values of commodities by means of the value of labour' (1867/94, I, p. 53 fn.).

22. Thomas de Quincey commented on the economists before Ricardo: 'When it was asked what determined the value of all commodities: it was answered that this value was chiefly determined by wages. When again it was asked – what determined wages? – it was recollected that wages must . . . be adjusted to the value of the commodities upon which they were spent; and the answer was in effect that wages were determined by the value of commodities' (1824, p. 560). Similarly Marx: '[W]hen Adam Smith is examining the "natural rate" of wages or the "natural price" of wages . . . he falls into a vicious circle. By what is the natural price of the means of subsistence determined, which determine the natural price of wages? By the natural price of "wages", of "profit", or "rent", which constitute the natural price of those means of subsistence as of all commodities. And so *in infinitum*. The twaddle about the law of demand and supply of course does not help us out of this

vicious circle. . . . It is one of Ricardo's chief merits that he put an end to this confusion' (1963/71, I, pp. 96–7).

23. 'We have seen that with Adam Smith, the entire value of the social product resolves itself into revenue. . . . It follows necessarily that the money required for the circulation of the yearly revenue must also suffice for the circulation of the entire annual product. . . . [This opinion] is repeated by Th. Tooke' (Marx, 1867/94, II, p. 479; also III, pp. 841–42, and 1963/71, II, p. 479–80).
24. 'David Ricardo, unlike Adam Smith, neatly sets forth the determination of the value of commodities by labour-time, and demonstrates that this law governs even those bourgeois relations of production which apparently contradict it most decisively' (Marx, 1859, p. 60; also 1963/71, II, pp. 164–69).
25. Putting to one side Ricardo's limiting identification of surplus value with profit, Marx held up his correction of the Smithian price theory as a major breakthrough for political economy: 'Since the value of the commodities is determined by the quantity of labour contained in them, and since wages and surplus-value (profit) are only *shares*, proportions in which two classes of producers divide the value of the commodity between themselves, it is clear that a rise or fall in wages, although it determines the rate of surplus-value (profit), does not affect the value of the commodity or the price (as the monetary expression of the value of a commodity)' (1963/71, II, p. 418).
26. 'Instead of postulating this general rate of profit, Ricardo should rather have examined how far its *existence* is in fact consistent with the determination of value by labour-time, and he would have found that instead of being consistent with it, *prima facie*, it *contradicts* it, and that its existence would therefore have to be explained through a number of intermediary stages, a procedure which is very different from merely including it under the law of value. He would then have gained an altogether different insight into the nature of profit and would not have identified it directly with surplus-value' (Marx, 1963/71, II, p. 174).
27. Dobb has argued that Ricardo's 'refutation' of Smith's theory can, therefore, be seen to have 'turned on his bringing money itself within the circle of commodities, and in doing so postulating that the price of any commodity or group of commodities can only rise if more labour is required to produce it relatively to the amount of labour required to produce an ounce of gold' (1973, p. 77). As we have already seen, however, Smith had shown long before that money was a commodity; Ricardo's contribution was confined to the determination of its value – along with that of other commodities – by the quantity of labour embodied in it.
28. 'The liability to variation in value over intervals of time has led economic writers, both old and modern, to seek for a more stable measure . . .' (Price, 1909, p. 10 and *passim*).
29. 'Ricardo often gives the impression, and sometimes indeed writes, as if the quantity of labour is the solution to the false or falsely conceived problem of an 'invariable measure of value' in the same way as corn, money, wages, etc., were previously considered and advanced as panaceas of this kind' (Marx, 1963/71, III, p. 137).
30. On the passage in the text suggesting gold as such a commodity, Marx commented: 'This is far more applicable to those commodities into whose composition the various organic constituents enter in the average proportion,

and whose period of circulation and reproduction is also of average length. For these, cost-price and value coincide, because for them, and only for them, average profit coincides with their surplus-value' (1963/71, II, p. 199; also 1867/94, II, pp. 173–4). The 'inadequate' consideration in the *Principles* of the 'influence of the variations in the value of labour on "relative values" ', Marx went on, was 'theoretically a secondary matter compared with the transformation of values into cost-prices through the average rate of profits'; yet 'so important is the conclusion which Ricardo draws from this, thereby demolishing one of the major errors that had persisted since Adam Smith, namely that the raising of wages, instead of reducing profits, raises the prices of commodities' (ibid.).

31. In his notes on Wagner's *Textbook on Political Economy*, Marx insisted that he did not 'proceed on the basis of "concepts" hence also not from the "value-concept". . . . What I proceed from is the simplest social form in which the product of labour in contemporary society manifests itself, and this is as "commodity"' (1879/80, p. 214).

32. This procedure is all the more necessary in the light of the numerous conflicting accounts of Marx's theory of money. These range between the 'faithful', such as de Brunhoff (1976) and Rosdolsky (1977), and the 'creative', such as Mandel (1978) and Kuhne (1979). See also Green (1975), Rowthorn (1980, chs 5–6), Harris (1979) and Fine (1979).

33. 'It is one of the chief failings of classical economy that it has never succeeded, by means of its analysis of commodities, and, in particular, of their value, in discovering that form under which value becomes exchange value. Even Adam Smith and Ricardo, the best representatives of the school, treat the form of value as a thing of no importance, as having no connexion with the inherent nature of commodities. . . . We consequently find that economists, who are thoroughly agreed as to labour-time being the measure of magnitude of value, have the most strange and contradictory ideas of money . . .' (Marx, 1867/94, I, p. 85 fn).

34. To simplify the exposition, Marx assumed a reduction of the different degrees of skilled labour to a uniform expenditure of unskilled labour: 'Skilled labour counts only as simple labour intensified, or rather, as multiplied simple labour, a given quantity of skilled being considered equal to a greater quantity of simple labour. Experience shows that this reduction is constantly being made . . . For simplicity's sake we shall henceforth account every kind of labour to be unskilled, simple labour . . .' (1867/94, I, pp. 51–2). See Rowthorn (1980, ch. 8).

35. 'The necessity of money thus arises from the nature of commodity producing society, which derives its law from the exchange of commodities as products of socially necessary labour time' (Hilferding, 1910, p. 35. See Harris (1979), pp. 142–5.

36. The notion of an ideal standard was also pressed by the advocates of inconvertible paper-money, as we shall see in the next chapter. Some spoke of the pound as an 'ideal unit' (Wright and Harlow, 1844, p. 266–72). Similarly, it was inherent in the popular demand for a banking system which would issue 'labour money'. On this demand, Marx commented: 'The dogma that a commodity is immediately money or that the particular labour of a private individual contained in it is immediately social labour, does not of course

become true because a bank believes in it and conducts its operations in accordance with this dogma. On the contrary, bankruptcy would in such a case fulfil the function of practical criticism' (1859, p. 86).

37. 'Prices are thus high or low not because more or less money is in circulation, but there is more or less money in circulation because prices are high or low. This is one of the principal economic laws, and the detailed sustantiation of it based on the history of prices is perhaps the only achievement of the post-Ricardian English economists' (Marx, 1859, pp. 105–6). The debate among Ricardo's successors will be assessed when we come to look at credit.

38. Steedman claims 'with the benefit of hindsight' that Marx's criticism of Ricardo on this score was 'ill-judged' (1982, p. 124). Although it may be accepted that Marx himself 'was not able to construct a coherent theory of the rate of profit and of prices of production . . .' (ibid.), his analysis may be seen as a constructive development of Ricardo's theory (de Vivo, 1982; Harcourt, 1982). But see, for a contrary interpretation, Rowthorn (1980, ch. 1) and Shaikh (1977).

39. It was, after all, the purpose of Ricardo's 'invariable standard' to *reduce* prices to values in this way. Had he succeeded, Marx's criticism would have lost its force. See above and Eatwell (1975a).

40. Garegnani has illustrated the difficulty (1984, pp. 306–8) with a two-sector economy producing corn and steel. The rate of profit, according to Marx's equation, would be given by:

$$r = \frac{(s_s A_s + s_c A_c)}{(c_s A_s + c_c A_c) + (v_s A_s + v_c A_c)} \qquad (1)$$

where A_s and c_c denote the output of steel and corn respectively. The prices of production of the two commodities may then be calculated as follows:

$$p_s = c_s + v_s (1 + r)$$
$$p_c = c_c + v_c (1 + r) \qquad (2)$$
where $c_s + v_s + s = c_c + v_c + s_c = 1$

If we now modify the equations (2) by expressing constant capital (steel) and variable capital (corn) in terms of prices, we have:

$$p_s = c_s + v_s (1 + r)$$
$$p_c = c_c + v_c (1 + r) \qquad (3)$$

Since the equations (3) contain only one unknown, the *relative* price p_s/p_c, they will be contradictory if r is to be determined by equation (1).

41. Garegnani argues that there is 'a sense in which Marx's error was suggestive'. It can be seen as 'the result of treating as integral parts of a single method (for the determination of the rate of profit) what are in fact when consistently developed, two equivalent methods, each of which is sufficient to determine that rate' (1984, pp. 308–9). The first, which he calls the 'price-equation method', is exemplified by equations (3) in the previous footnote and determines the rate of profit – or more generally the relationship between the wage and the profit rate – *simultaneously* with relative prices. The second method, which he calls the 'surplus equation method', is exemplified by the profit equations of Ricardo and Marx, where commodities exchange according to the labour embodied. This method reveals more transparently the

nature of profit as a surplus product, which may be expressed, along with the capital, in terms proportionate to their values; and, since they do not contain the unknown prices, the profit rate is left as the only unknown in the equation. Garegnani's survey and development of the surplus approach attests to its continuing validity (see Kurz, 1985).

42. This is not the same as the proposition by Smith that a rise in corn prices, through its impact on wages, would increase the prices of commodities generally. We have seen earlier that Ricardo and Marx rightly rejected this proposition, demonstrating instead that, so long as the value of commodities (and of total output) remains unchanged, any rise in corn prices could only lower the rate of profit (or surplus value). Furthermore, in reality, the value of commodities was more likely to fall than to rise due to the growing productivity of labour (see Marx, 1867/94, III, p. 226 and *passim*).
43. Schumpeter, who could scarcely be accused of a favourable bias, has written: 'The leading "classics" solved the problem of this rather dubious value of money simply by extending to it their general theory of value. Accordingly, they distinguished a natural or long-run normal value of money and a short-run equilibrium value. The former or, as they also said – misleadingly – the "permanent" value was determined by the cost of producing (or obtaining) the precious metals, the latter by supply and demand' (1954, pp. 701–2). It is this 'short-run' value which will be the subject of the present section.
44. Schumpeter went on (see previous footnote) to identify this issue as 'the vexed and vexing questions [sic] how far the "classics" accepted the quantity theorem and whether or not it acquired illegitimate authority with them' (1954, p. 702). See also Hollander (1911, pp. 436 ff.).
45. In the first edition of the *Principles*, Ricardo cites Say with approval to the effect that any superfluous gold and silver 'will not be employed' (1951/58, I, p. 352). The contrast with Hume could not be drawn more sharply.
46. Elsewhere, commenting on Malthus's *Principles of Political Economy*, Ricardo referred to the departure of the 'market price' of gold from its 'natural price' (1951/58, II, p. 83).
47. This is the case even in otherwise sound discussions of Ricardian trade theory (Shaikh, 1979, p. 293).
48. It should be borne in mind that Ricardo's example was also premised on constant returns to scale in mining. The additional complications introduced by diminishing returns were discussed by Senior (1828).
49. A result parallel to the import and export of precious metals on an international scale would be achieved in a closed economy with its own mines by the opening and closing of those mines in response to monetary fluctuations: Marx (1859), pp. 170–7.
50. It is remarkable to find the suggestion made that, 'Adam Smith accepted Hume's Quantity Theory . . .' (Low, 1952, p. 320). It is repeated, however, in Hollander (1978) pp. 174, 205 and (1979), pp. 425–26. The opposite view is held by O'Brien, but he, like Viner, treats Smith's rejection of a Humean quantity theory as 'a puzzle' (1975, p. 146). Schumpeter was less restrained: 'Adam Smith did not advance beyond Hume but rather stayed below him . . . Hume's theory, including his overemphasis on price movement as the vehicle of adjustments, remained substantially unchallenged until the twenties of this century' (1954, p. 367).

51. Smith concluded the 'Digression on Silver' by emphasising the separation between the rise in European output and the increased volume of precious metals following the discovery of the American mines: 'The increase in the quantity of gold and silver in Europe, and the increase of its manufactures and agriculture, are two events which, though they have happened nearly about the same time, yet *have arisen from the very different causes, and have scarce any natural connection with each other*. The one has arisen from a mere accident . . . The other from the fall of the feudal system . . .' (1776, p. 192, emphasis added). Again, there was no question of accepting Hume or Steuart's output response to monetary movements – transitional or otherwise – since the level of output was treated as externally given. As Vickers points out, 'not only is the question avoided of a possible dependence of the shape of the long-run growth path on the shorter-run activity variations conceivably attributable to monetary phenomena, but money is very much a veil over the ultimately determinative forces in the system' (1975, p. 498).
52. Smith set out the process of adjustment as follows: 'For some time after the first discovery of America, silver would continue to sell at its former, or not much below its former price. The profits of mining would for some time be very great, and much above their natural rate. Those who imported that metal in Europe, however, would soon find that the whole annual importation could not be disposed of at this high price. Silver would gradually exchange for a smaller and smaller quantity of goods. Its price would sink gradually lower and lower till it fell to its natural price . . .' (1776, p. 160).
53. It will be recalled that Marx's abstraction from market phenomena was undertaken in order to observe 'the real inner laws of capitalist production . . . in their pure state' (1867/94, III, p. 189).
54. Marx was careful to distinguish the references by Hume's followers to rising prices in ancient Rome brought about by the conquest of Macedonia, Egypt and Asia Minor. This involved a sudden and forcible transfer of hoarded money from one country to another'; but, Marx insisted, 'the temporary lowering of the production costs of precious metals achieved in a particular country by the simple method of plunder does not affect the inherent laws of monetary circulation, any more than, for instance, the distribution of Egyptian and Sicilian corn free of charge in Rome affects the general law which regulates corn prices' (1859, p. 161). Arguably, however, Marx had side stepped the real issue, which is whether the sudden influx of metal leads to a drop in its *market value*, just as the surfeit of corn is necessarily reflected in a diminished market price. While it is true that the monetary circulation law will not be invalidated by such an influx, it does not *exclude* the possibility of temporary market fluctuations.
55. Commenting on this passage, Wicksell took issue with Marx's refusal 'to admit that the quantity of money may possibly exert an influence on prices'; there was 'no logical reason why a change in the conditions of production of gold (a rise or fall in the *average* cost of production) should not at first, and perhaps for a fairly long period of time, be consistent with a temporarily constant exchange value of gold' (1936, pp. 35–36).
56. Any departure of output from the level established by the accumulation process was treated by Marx as purely temporary, due to his acceptance of Say's law. This applied as much to increased output resulting from monetary

influences – especially the over-extension of credit – as to reduced output during periodic crises. Nevertheless, Marx conceded that a higher level of economic activity – whatever the cause – could operate through the market to offset a tendency for the monetary metals to depreciate: 'When, therefore, [the supply of gold and silver] suddenly increased, even if their costs of production of their value does not proportionately decrease, they find a rapidly expanding market which retards their depreciation' (Marx, 1973, p. 169).

57. Ricardo too, at least in his early monetary writing, referred to this additional aspect of the short-run inflationary process. In the notes on Bentham's unpublished 'Sur les Prix', he observed that an 'augmentation of money . . . would seldom cause any augmentation of goods, and if it did it would be before prices had found their new level. It would be effected by turning a part of that fund destined for the wages of labour for a short time into capital' (1951/58, III, p. 302). He elaborated this contention as follows: 'There is but one way in which an increase of money no matter how it be introduced into the society, can augment riches, viz. at the expence of the wages of labour; till the wages of labour have found their level with the increased prices which the commodities will have experienced, there will be so much additional revenue to the manufacturer and farmer they will obtain an increased price for commodities, and can whilst wages do not increase employ an additional number of hands, so that the real riches of the country will be somewhat augmented. A productive labourer will produce something more than before relatively to his consumption, but this can be only of momentary duration' (ibid., pp. 318–19). This idea of a 'profit inflation' was developed later by Keynes (1933).

58. Marx only touched upon the effect of changes in the value of the monetary metals on different social groups and classes: 'It is well-known that the fall in the value of precious metals in Europe gave rise to a great social revolution, just as the ancient Roman Republic at an early stage of its history experienced a reverse revolution caused by a rise in the value of copper, the metal in which the debts of the plebians were contracted. . . . [I]t is clear that a fall in the value of precious metals favours debtors at the expense of creditors, while a rise in their value favours creditors at the expense of debtors' (1859, p. 148). This was a phenomenon that disturbed Ricardo greatly, and it was a factor which initially motivated his search for an invariable measure of value.

59. 'Now and then, . . . as in his criticism of the earlier systems of Political Economy, [Smith] takes the right view' (Marx, 1867/94, I, p. 124 fn).

60. Marx also noted that the nature and content of hoards were a function of the prevailing social conditions: 'It may be regarded as a general law that the conversion of gold and silver coin into luxury goods predominates in times of peace, while their reconversion into bars and also into coin only predominates in turbulent periods' (1859, p. 135; see also Kuhne, 1979, p. 338 ff.).

61. Earlier Marx had given the example of gold during the Napoleonic war inflation, 'When, although the metal content of the circulating coins had not fallen below their normal measure, they circulated at the same time as depreciated paper money, while to melt them down and to export them was prohibited. In that case, the 1/4 ounce of gold circulating in the form of £

shared in the depreciation of the notes; a fate from which gold in bars was exempt' (1978, p. 800).

62. 'Reserve funds' were nevertheless counted as part of the money supply: 'Hoards must not be confused with reserve funds of coin, which form a constituent element of the total amount of money always in circulation, whereas the active relation of hoard and medium of circulation presupposes that the total amount of money decreases or increases' (Marx, 1859, p. 137).

63. In the *Critique*, Marx had remarked on James Mill's 'metaphysical equilibrium of purchases and sales' that, in a glut, 'this gives poor comfort to the possessors of commodities who cannot accordingly make a purchase either' (1859, p. 97).

64. Although John Stuart Mill, as we saw in an earlier chapter, at least recognised the possibility of crises, he did not attempt to pursue the mechanism through which this possibility became a reality: '[T]hose economists are no better, who (like John Stuart Mill) want to explain the crises by these simple *possibilities* of crisis contained in the metamorphosis of commodities – such as the separation between purchase and sale. These factors . . . by no means explain their actual occurrance' (Marx, 1963/71, II, p. 502). Here, as in the later discussion of paper currency, J. S. Mill 'understands how to hold at the same time the view of his father, James Mill, and the opposite view' (Marx, 1867/94, I, p. 125 fn.). Wicksell regarded this assessment as 'not entirely without justification', but he was quick to add that, 'Marx himself had in no way succeeded in overcoming the difficulties involved' (Wicksell, 1936, p. 43). Say's law was a continuing obstacle to a theory of 'normal' output, whose magnitude might not coincide with the level of accumulation.

65. 'This sudden transformation of the credit system into a monetary system adds theoretical dismay to the actually existing panic, and the agents of the circulation process are overawed by the impenetrable mystery surrounding their own relations' (Marx, 1859, p. 146).

66. Ricardo conceded the possibility of a general deflation, however, following the 'utter discredit' of paper money: '[C]ommodities would no doubt fall very considerably *but the fall would be temporary not permanent*, provided the circulation of paper before the annihilation of credit was exchangeable for the precious metals at par. We should very soon obtain such a supply of gold in exchange for commodities that prices would nearly regain their former level' (*Notes on Bentham*, in 1951/52, III, p. 324, emphasis added).

67. The connection with his treatment of circulation was summed up by Marx as follows: '[T]he conception . . . adopted by Ricardo . . . that overproduction is not possible or at least that no general glut of the market is possible, is based on the proposition that products are exchanged *against products*, . . . and this led to [the conclusion] that demand is determined only by production' (1968/71, II, p. 493).

68. In Ricardo's analysis, 'the tendency of the rate of profit to fall can only be explained by the same factors which make the rate of surplus value fall. But, with a given working day, the rate of surplus value can only fall if the rate of wages is rising permanently. This is only possible if the value of necessaries is rising permanently. . . . [Ricardo] makes the false presupposition that the whole of the capital advanced consists only of variable capital' (Marx, 1963/71, II, pp. 463–4; also 1867/94, III, p. 241).

69. This argument has a parallel in Ricardo's treatment of inflation in a credit system (see *Reply to Bosanquet*, 1951/58, III, p. 215 ff., and below).
70. For Marx, crises 'periodically re-establish equilibrium and, by means of radical destruction of capital values, recreate the conditions for profitability of business' (Schumpeter, 1954, p. 749).
71. Marx went on to show that, 'the rate of increase falls sharply, however much the profit may rise and this fall in the rate of interest then leads to the most risky speculative ventures . . .' (1963/71, II, p. 495). This aspect of the crisis, which relates to the operation of credit, will be discussed in ch. 7. The mechanism is described at length by Mandel in his *Late Capitalism* (1978, ch. 13). But see Rowthorn (1980, ch. 4).

5 Introduction of Paper Currency

1. 'Name and substance, nominal weight and real weight, begin their process of separation. Coins of the same denomination become different in value, because they are different in weight. The weight of gold fixed upon as the standard of prices, deviates from the weight that serves as the circulating medium, and the latter thereby ceases any longer to be a real equivalent of the commodities whose prices it realises. The history of coinage during the middle ages and down into the eighteenth century, records the ever renewed confusion arising from this cause' (Marx, 1867/94, I, p. 126). See also Feavearyear (1931, p. 157 ff.).
2. Ricardo was later to sharpen the distinction between an increase of money and an increase of capital. In his *Notes on Bentham* he commented: 'No sum of money carried into Switzerland would enable the possessor to drain a marsh and render it productive. The money must first be exchanged with some other country for those commodities which would increase the capital and revenue of the country. The same observation is applicable to Scotland. *It was not by money, but by capital that Scotland has been improved*' (1951/52, III, pp. 286–87 emphasis added).
3. Despite his hostility to the development of credit, Hume, at least in his later essays, recognised the benefits which could flow from its 'right use'. He saw the discounting of bills of exchange by Scottish banks as 'favourable' to industry and loans upon collateral as 'one of the most ingenious ideas that has been executed in commerce' (1752, pp. 190–1). The systematic issue of bank notes in Glasgow, for example, permitted 'a stock of £5 000 . . . to perform the same operations as if it were six or seven; and merchants were thereby enabled to trade to a greater extent, and to require less profit in all their transactions' (ibid., p. 191). Hume concluded, remarkably, that this acceleration in turnover, 'renders the commodity cheaper, causes a greater consumption, quickens the labour of the common people, and helps to spread arts and industry throughout the whole society' (ibid., p. 209). Financial conservatism was by no means a consistent virtue on Hume's part.
4. A less than successful aspect of Steuart's classification was his distinction between banks 'which issue notes payable in coin to bearer' and those 'which only transfer the credit written down in their books from one person to another' (1767, II, p. 476). The former he called 'banks of circulation', the

latter 'banks of deposit'. It was an artificial distinction, and one that contributed later to the confusion between money and credit in the 'currency–banking debate'. At the time Steuart was writing, however, it happened to be an accurate description of the practice of the Bank of Amsterdam on the one hand (a bank of deposit), and the Bank of England and Bank of Scotland on the other (banks of circulation).

5. In this context, Davenant, the seventeenth century mercantilist, became a counterfoil to Steuart's promotion of deficit financing: 'Men, at that time, had a terror upon them in contracting debts for the public: they considered the nation as they would a private man' (1767, II, p. 607). The real target, however, was the fiscal orthodoxy of Hume and Montesquieu: 'It is no objection to this representation of the matter, that the persons from whom the money is taken, would have spent it as well as the state' (ibid., pp. 725–6).
6. According to his biographer, William Ainsworth, this was how Law explained his system to Lord Godolphin: 'On reflecting profoundly on the matter, I am satisfied that precious metals are improperly employed as agents of circulation. By means of paper money, and a system of credit, such as I propose, the circulation would immediately be quadrupled, and since every branch of trade and industry must be immensely stimulated and encouraged, so the prosperity of the country will infallibly be increased in the same ratio' (Ainsworth, 1874, p. 45).
7. 'During the year and a half following its institution, Mr Law's Bank continued to rise in credit and importance, and was constantly extending its operations. Received as cash at all the public offices, its notes were eagerly sought after, and preferred to specie – thus realising Law's prognostications. Moreover, the large deposits of gold and silver continually made at the Bank, under the eye of the public, removed all doubts as to the solvency of the establishment. Distrust, in fact, had long since disappeared, and given way to the blindest confidence. In eighteen months, Mr Law had changed the whole aspect of affairs, had immensely increased the circulation, restored credit, revived trade, and given a new and strong impulse to every kind of industry' (ibid., p. 167).
8. 'During all this time Law's efforts to uphold the System had been incessant but ineffectual. Decree after decree was issued, but with no other result than to aggravate the difficulties of the position. Specie was almost entirely banished, but though the billets de banque maintained their nominal value, the price of provisions and of all other necessaries was trebled, so that in effect the notes were depreciated to that extent. The shares of the Compagnie des Indes, which was now united to the bank, had undergone a rapid and continuous fall, and were now not worth a twentieth part of price to which they had been raised by the manoeuvres of the Realisers. Moreover, there was every prospect that they would sink still lower, while it appeared equally certain that the billets des banque must be further depreciated' (ibid., p. 369). As soon as it became clear that a 'terrible financial crisis' was at hand, 'Law at once lost the wonderful popularity he enjoyed' (ibid.).
9. Schumpeter, who placed Law 'in the front rank of monetary theorists of all times', regarded his 'gigantic enterprise' as 'not simply a swindle and it may well be doubted whether France was the worse off for it . . .' (1954, p. 295). Less extravagantly, Clapham has argued that Law's central ideas were 'nei-

ther fantastic nor fraudulent; and this plan for a *banque de France* with its provincial *succursales* was obviously sensible' (1944, I, p. 106). Whereas Rist dismissed Law as an 'intelligent crank' (1940, p. 65), Schumpeter was surely closer to the mark when he described him as the 'ancestor of the idea of a managed currency' (1954, p. 322).

10. Once again, Hume was here simply repeating the view of Vanderlint and Montesquieu: 'I believe our paper-effects have contributed as much to this decay of trade as all the rest put together, by enhancing the price of everything among us, above the rates our real specie would have supported them at, in such proportion as the paper-effects amongst us are greater than the real specie we have circulating; for this is the natural and unavoidable effect of any thing operating as cash, which is not such' (Vanderlint, 1734, pp. 164–5).

11. Steuart was prepared to allow this 'money of society' to become 'legal tender in every payment of domestic debts', confining the metals to the discharge of the 'grand balance', or balance of payments. He advocated unrestricted convertibility, however, 'as long as some persons of the most acute understanding in many things, consider all money, except coin, to be false and fictitious' (1767, II, p. 485). Thus, unlike his predecessor Law, Steuart conceded the necessity of a proportional metallic reserve to meet both international obligations and domestic withdrawals (see p. 000).

12. 'It is this circumstance, above all others, which distresses banks of circulation. Were it not for this, the obligation to pay in coin might easily be discharged; but when in virtue of this pure obligation, a heavy national balance is demanded from the bank, which has only made provision for the current and ordinary demand at home, it requires a little combination to find out, at once an easy remedy. This combination . . . is by far the most intricate, and at the same time the most important in whole doctrine of banks of circulation' (Steuart, 1767, II, p. 488).

13. 'Credits of this kind are, I believe, commonly granted by banks and bankers in all different parts of the world. But the easy terms upon which the Scotch banking companies accept of repayment are, so far as I know, peculiar to them, and have, perhaps, been the principal cause, both of the great trade of those companies, and of the benefit which the country has received from it' (Smith, 1776, p. 226).

14. Many commentators, as we have seen, could not understand why Smith failed to adopt explicitly Hume's specie-flow mechanism. The reason, quite simply, lay in Smith's opposition to the pure exchange quantity theory and in his attempt, however, inadequate, to establish 'the forces determining the normal amount of a country's money supply' (Hollander, 1911, p. 436). It is perhaps not surprising therefore, to find the following assessment of the real bills element in maintaining a paper currency equivalent to the value of the commodity money it replaced: 'Beside Hume's performance, this was a pretty weak one and indeed a puzzling one . . . [Smith] may have preferred to evade the issue [of quantity theory] in the *Wealth of Nations* rather than enter into lengthy public controversy with his friend' (O'Brien, 1975, p. 147).

15. In this context, Smith unequivocally rejected Hume's account of the rise in prices in mid-eighteenth century Scotland; this was due 'to the badness of the season, and not to the multiplication of paper money' (1776, p. 249). It should be borne in mind that Smith was here writing about bank notes, a species of

credit, not fiduciary money. As Rist has pointed out, 'he does not confuse bank-notes with paper money, as Ricardo did later . . . He saw that *in the long-run* credit does not affect prices. Their level depends at bottom on the long-period relationship between the quantity of goods [Rist should have said 'value of output': R. G.] and that of the precious metals' (1940, p. 89).

16. Andréadès describes the fiasco of the South Sea Company and the many other 'projects' launched in Change Alley (1935, pp. 127–45). He cites an example of the contemporary verse:

    A wise man laughed to see an ass
    Eat thistles and neglect good grass,
    But had the sage beheld the folly
    of late transacted in Change Alley,
    He might have seen worse asses there
    Give solid gold for empty air. (Ibid., p. 135)

6 Theory of the Fiduciary System

1. This point was to be developed later by the Banking School: 'The authority issuing such paper money, can determine exactly the quantity that shall remain permanently in the hands of the public. The power of issue is unlimited, because there is no reflux . . .' (Tooke, 1838/57, IV, p. 186).
2. Fiduciary money was also discussed in these terms by Marx, who pointed out that, 'While the denomination of paper is based on gold and silver, the convertibility of the note, i.e., its exchangeability for gold and silver, remains an economic law regardless of what juridical law may say' (1859, p. 83).
3. Hayek goes further in his Introduction to a new edition of *Paper Credit*; he argues that 'in the field of money the main achievement of the classical period is due to Thornton' (1802, p. 36). See also Rist (1940) pp. 135–40; Deane, (1978) p. 46.
4. The Bullion dispute marked the beginning of the Ricardo–Malthus correspondence. Following the publication of Ricardo's *High Price of Bullion* in 1810, Mathus's critical response in the *Edinburgh Review* of February 1811 and the rejoinder by Ricardo in the form of an appendix to a new edition of his work in April of that year, Malthus wrote to Ricardo directly for the first time on 16 June. He suggested that, 'as we are *mainly* on the same side of the question, we might supersede the necessity of a long controversy in print respecting the points in which we differ, by an amicable discussion in private' (Ricardo, 1951/58, IV, p. 21). A month later, however, Malthus admitted that, '[w]ith regard to the points of difference, between us, though perhaps we have approximated a little in our late conversations, I think, it seems, that we are not likely entirely to agree'; he recommended that Ricardo read Steuart's *Principles of Political Oeconomy*, which would allow him to see 'what I mean by a comparative rise of prices not occasioned by a comparative redundancy of currency' (Malthus to Ricardo, 14 July 1811, ibid., pp. 33–4).
5. 'Bank notes, though they yield an interest to the issuer, afford none to the man who detains them in his possession; they are to him as unproductive as guineas. The possessor of a bank note, therefore, makes haste to part with it.

The possessor of a bill of exchange possesses, on the contrary, that which is always growing more valuable. The bill, when it is first drawn, is worth something less than a bank note, on account of its not being due until a distant day; and the first receiver of it may be supposed to obtain a compensation for the inferiority of its value in the price of the articles with which the bill is purchased. When he parts with it, he may be considered as granting to the next receiver a like compensation, which is proportionate to the time which the bill still has to run. Each holder of a bill has, therefore, an interest in detaining it' (Thornton, 1802, pp. 92–3).

6. In the first chapter of his book, Thornton pointed out that commercial capital, 'consists not in paper, and is not augmented by the multiplication of this medium of payment. In one sense, indeed, it may be encreased by paper. I mean, that the nominal value of the existing goods may be enlarged through a reduction which is caused by paper in the value of that standard by which all property is estimated. The paper itself forms no part of the estimate' (1802, p. 79; see also p. 255). We have already struck the concept of 'fictitious' capital in Smith's analysis and shall have occasion to return to it in the next chapter.
7. Thornton's analysis was ahead of its time: 'It must also be admitted, that, provided we assume an excessive issue of paper to lift up, as it may for a time, the cost of goods though not the price of labour, some augmentation of stock will be the consequence; for the labourer, according to this supposition, may be forced by his necessity to consume fewer articles, though he may exercise the same industry. But this saving, as well as any additional one which may arise from a similar defalcation of the revenue of the unproductive members of the society, will be attended with a proportionate hardship and injustice' (1802, p. 239; see Niebyl, 1946, pp. 76–7; Schumpeter, 1954, p. 724).
8. How dependent was Ricardo on Thornton's path breaking work was indicated not just by frequent quotation, but also by the use even of the same terminology: 'The circulation can never be over-full. If it be one of gold and silver, any increase in its quantity will be spread over the world. If it be one of paper, it will diffuse itself only in the country where it is issued. Its effects on prices will then be only local and nominal . . .' (1951/58, III, pp. 91–2).
9. Thornton continued: 'In general it may, perhaps, also be assumed, that an excessive issue of paper has not been the leading cause of a fall in the exchange, if it afterwards turns out that the exchange is able to recover itself without any material reduction of the quantity of paper' (1802, p. 221 fn.).
10. Ricardo replied in the *High Price of Bullion*: 'Mr Thornton has not explained to us, why any unwillingness should exist in the foreign country to receive our goods in exchange for their corn; and it would be necessary for him to show, that if such an unwillingness were to exist, we should agree to indulge it so far as to consent to part with our coin. . . . We should not import more goods than we export, unless we had a redundancy of currency' (Ricardo, 1951/58, III, p. 61). Thornton's case was taken up by Malthus, but, again, it was found wanting on the grounds of internal inconsistency: 'You maintain that money is rendered cheap by a bad harvest as compared with corn only, but with all other commodities it is dearer than before, – and then what appears to be very inconsistent you insist that this commodity thus rendered scarce and dear will be exported, though before it had increased in value, it

had no tendency to leave us, whilst too there are commodities which have undergone an opposite change, which from being dearer have become cheaper, and which will nevertheless be obstinately retained by us. This is a mode of reasoning which I cannot reconcile' (ibid., VI, pp. 38–9).

11. Thornton's *practical* judgement was borne out by the facts: 'That whenever there was a pause or cessation of the unusually large foreign expenditure by the government, or of unusually large foreign expenditure by the government, or of unusually large importations of corn, there was also a tendency to a restoration of the value of the paper, by a rise in the exchange, without any contemporaneous or immediately preceding reduction in the amount of Bank notes . . . (Tooke, 1838/57, IV, pp. 132–3). See also Horsefield (1941/44).

12. 'To limit the total amount of paper issued, and to resort for this purpose, whenever the temptation to borrow is strong, to some effectual principle of restriction; in no case, however, materially to diminish the sum in circulation, but to let it vibrate only within certain limits; to afford a slow and cautious extension of it, as the general trade of the kingdom enlarges itself; to allow of some special, though temporary, encrease in the event of any extraordinary alarm or difficulty, as the best means of preventing a great demand at home for guineas; and to lean to the side of diminution, in the case of gold going abroad, and of the general exchanges continuing long unfavourable; this seems to be the true policy of the directors of an institution circumstanced like that of the Bank of England' (Thornton 1802, p. 259). Fetter comments that, 'This was the analysis of a policy maker, not of a pure theorist or an interested partisan' (1965, p. 45). See also Horsefield (1941/44, pp. 27–9); Rist (1940, pp. 135–40).

13. It was Ricardo's attempt to account for the 'high price of gold' that motivated his first appearance in print in the three letters to the *Morning Chronicle* in 1809, 'The immense transactions which he had with the Bank of England, in the course of business, tallying with the train of studies on which he was then engaged, led Mr Ricardo to reflect upon the subject of currency, to endeavour to account for the difference which existed between the value of the coin and the Bank notes, and to ascertain from what cause the depreciation of the latter arose' (*Annual Biography and Obituary for the Year 1824*, pp. 371–72, cited in Ricardo, 1951/58, III, p. 3). Sayers regards Ricardo's adoption of the quantity theory of money as 'a major disaster' (1953, p. 79). Deane points out that Ricardo 'swept aside, as unimportant or irrelevant, all qualifications which Thornton had noted to the simple monetary explanation' (1978, p. 51). See also Viner (1937, pp. 139–40); Fetter (1965, p. 47).

14. In his *Reply to Bosanquet*, Ricardo followed Smith's formulation, suggesting that a country 'might substitute paper instead of bullion for the uses of money, but that the value of such paper must be regulated by the amount of coin of its bullion value which would have circulated had there been no paper' (1951/58, III, p. 224; also IV, pp. 62–3).

15. Tooke attempted to distinguish the role of gold as a standard of price from its role as measure of value: 'As a mere instrument or medium of exchange, at the same time and in the same place, invariableness of value, though desirable, is not of so much importance; the immediate purpose of money in this capacity being to serve as a point, or rather a scale, of comparison. . . . It is . . . on the subject of engagements or obligations for future payment, that in

every view of justice and policy, the specific thing promised, in quantity and quality, should be paid at the expiration of the term' (Tooke, 1838/57, IV, p. 146).

16. As we have already seen, Ricardo did not accept Thornton's view that an unfavourable trade balance could arise even temporarily from a bad harvest and thus from a need to import grain. If coin were to be exported for such a purpose, it would be due only to its 'cheapness' and would be 'not the effect, but the cause of an unfavourable balance' (1951/58, III, p. 61). Thornton's error, according to Ricardo, 'proceeds from not distinguishing between an increase in the value of gold, and an increase in its money price' (ibid., p. 60). It was also the error of Malthus, who, in his review of the *High Price of Bullion*, spoke of the possibility of an unfavourable balance 'originating in causes which may exist without any relation whatever to redundancy or deficiency of currency' (ibid., p. 101). In a lengthy reply in an appendix to the fourth edition of that work, Ricardo regarded it as 'satisfactorily proved, that a bad harvest operates on the exchange in no other way than by causing the currency, which was before at its just level, to become redundant, and thus is the principle that an unfavourable exchange may always be traced to a relatively redundant currency most fully exemplified' (ibid., pp. 106–7). The position of Malthus was 'contradictory', for, in earlier supposing a glut of commodities (which Ricardo interpreted as applying only to the 'foreign market'), the export of money was due to its being 'relatively redundant with commodities, as compared with other countries' (ibid., p. 105; see also Ricardo's letter to Malthus of July 17, 1811, VI, p. 38 and *passim*). The logic of Ricardo's position, on the other hand, became still clearer in the context of a closed economy, where production shortfalls could not be remedied by imports, or by increased output given the Say's law assumption of fully utilised capacity. In the early monetary debates, Ricardo was content to expose the failure of his critics to treat bullion as an ordinary commodity: '[A]fter having requested their reader to consider money and bullion merely as commodities subject to "the same general principle of supply and demand which are unquestionably the foundation on which the whole superstructure of political economy is built"; [they] forget this recommendation themselves, and . . . argue upon the subject of money, and the laws which regulate its export and import, as quite distinct and different from those which regulate the export and import of other commodities' (ibid., pp. 103–4). Malthus nevertheless persisted in his view that, 'many of the modern writers in political economy in their zeal to correct the absurd notions of the mercantile classes about the balance of trade have over-looked the real differences that exist between the precious metals and other commodities, from the circumstance of their having been adopted as a medium of exchange . . .' (Malthus to Ricardo, June 16, 1811, ibid., VI, p. 21). This dispute about the nature of money continued, and became enmeshed with, the subsequent discussion of the 'corn ratio' approach to distribution (see Ricardo to Malthus, March 27, 1815, ibid., p. 203). Tooke regarded Malthus's criticism of Ricardo as 'just, as far as it goes' (1838/57, IV, p. 101).

17. Ricardo reiterated this proposition in his *Reply to Bosanquet*: 'If an addition be made to a currency consisting partly of gold and partly of paper, by an increase of paper currency, the value of the whole currency would be dimin-

ished, or in other words, the prices of commodities would rise, estimated either in gold coin or in paper currency'. In a closed economy, once gold had been "wholly withdrawn" from circulating it would 'rise above the value of paper, and would soon obtain that relative value to other commodities which subsisted before any addition had been made to the circulation by the issues of paper'. It would then become the function of the mine to supply the quantity of gold required, and the paper currency would continue to be 'permanently depreciated', anticipating the case of a fiduciary system: 'During this interval, the gold mines of a country . . . could not be worked, because of the low value of gold, which would have reduced the profits on capital employed in the mines below the level of other mercantile concerns. As soon as this equality of profit were established, the supply of gold would be as regular as before.' In an open economy, on the other hand, 'any excess of . . . currency would be counteracted by an exportation of specie, and if that excess did not exceed the amount of coin in circulation, . . . no depreciation of the currency would take place' (1951/58, III, pp. 210–12). This interpretation was affirmed by Ricardo in his notes on Bentham's unpublished manuscript, 'Sur les Prix' (ibid., pp. 269–70).

18. To Bosanquet, who took the opposite view, Ricardo responded: 'The analogy seems to me to be complete, and not to admit of dispute. The issues of paper not convertible are guided by the same principle, and will be attended with the same effects as if the Bank were the proprietor of the mine, and issued nothing but gold. However much gold may be increased, borrowers will increase to the same amount, in consequence of its depreciation; and the same rule is equally true with respect to paper. If money be but depreciated sufficiently, there is no amount which may not be absorbed . . .' (1951/58, III, p. 217). Marx commented that, 'Ricardo confuses the circulation of banknotes or of credit money with the circulation of simple tokens of value. The fact which dominates his thought is the depreciation of paper money and the rise in commodity-prices that occurred simultaneously. The printing presses in Threadneedle Street which issue paper notes played the same role for Ricardo as the American mines played for Hume' (1859, pp. 169–70). Tooke showed that very different effects would follow from a gold issue by the Bank, depending upon the 'mode of issue' (1838/57, IV, p. 200).

19. In his private notes on the minutes of evidence to the Bullion Committee, Ricardo referred to the reliance upon the real bills doctrine by the Bank of England directors as 'the source of all the errors of these practical men' (1951/58, III, p. 362). However, the facts were clearly against Ricardo, for, taking the period as a whole, the real bills doctrine operated as an effective principle of limitation (Tooke, 1838/57, I, p. 159 and *passim*). In his *Reply to Bosanquet*, Ricardo conceded that, given the Bank of England's attachment to the real bills doctrine, 'it is a matter of surprise that our circulation has been continued within such moderate bounds' (ibid., p. 221). Clapham comments with some justice: 'If the Bank witnesses showed up badly as economists, their critics showed up no better as politicians' (1944, p. 28).

20. As Tooke pointed out in his *History of Prices*, it was 'the coincidence . . . between the market value and the Bank rate of interest, that prevented the tendency through this medium to progressive increase and irremediable excess of issues, which might have been apprehended if the Bank rate had

been for any length of time much below the market rate' (1838/57, I, p. 162). But see Chapter 7.

21. In reality, 'the excess of the advances by the Bank to the Government over and above the amount of Government deposits, from the period of the suspension of cash payments in 1797, to the year 1811, was actually smaller in amount than the same excess during the seven years preceding that event . . . This comparative smallness of the advances to Government completely negatives the supposition, so commonly entertained and reasoned upon as a point beyond doubt, that the Bank was rendered, by the restriction, a mere engine in the hands of Government, for facilitating its financial operations' (Tooke, 1838/57, IV, pp. 94, 96; see also Cannan, 1919, p. xxxvi; Andréadès, 1935, pp. 208–9; Deane, 1979, p. 17).

22. Ricardo accepted that monetary contraction could have a damaging effect on individual borrowers. He observed in the letters to the *Morning Chronicle* which followed publication of the Bullion Report: 'As the paper system, pushed to the extravagant length which it now is, affords great facilities to this description of persons, there can be no doubt that every measure which tends to correct that system, every material reduction in the quantity of paper, will greatly embarrass and cause much distress amongst those who depend upon its continuance; and though the misfortunes of every part of the community must be deplored, it is to the pernicious system which has lately prevailed, that it will be alone to be ascribed'. The contraction, however, would not affect the level of output, for capital was not destroyed but merely *redistributed* among the 'channels of trade'. Hence, Ricardo continued: '[W]hatever may be lost in consequence of the difficulties to which the persons of whom we have been speaking may be exposed, cannot be regarded an national loss, as the capital which they could command by the credit which the abundance of circulating medium afforded them will revert to those hands which have been heretofore dispossessed of it, and where it will at least be as profitably employed as in those where this ruinous system has placed it' (1951/58, III, pp. 135–36).

23. Ricardo's analysis in his drafts of the *Plan for the Establishment of a National Bank* (1824) anticipated the functions of central banking: Arnon (1987).

24. The dubious advantages of 'consistency' were alluded to by William Blake in his rejoinder (prior to publication) to Ricardo's marginal notes on his *Observations on the Effects Produced by the Expenditure of Government during the Restriction of Cash Payments* (1823). Blake denied any observable relationship between the amount of bank notes and the high price of gold: '[M]ay, so far from it, that for months together they are found to run in opposite directions. It was this want of connexion, between the amount of Bank notes and the price of bullion, that first led me to suspect the accuracy of the theory, that attributed the high price of gold to the overissues of the Bank. . . .' Ricardo commented: '"Overissues of the Bank" Is not every thing an overissue after the market price of gold rises above the mint price, whether caused by a real rise in the value of gold or a real fall in the value of paper?' Blake responded: '[Y]es overissue in the sense in which it is used by *consistent* political Oeconomists but not in the sense in which the public use it – viz. that notes have been issued in such excess as to alter the value of currency in

respect *to all* commodities: there is a material difference between "overissue" and "non-contraction"' (Ricardo, 1951/58, IV, p. 335).

25. The importance of Tooke's work lay in his discovery of "the positive evidence that these expansions of the circulation, and those operations of the Bank which are described as "occasioning" the fall of the exchange could not have had any such consequence, unless it can be shown, that the date of a cause may be subsequent to the date of its effect' (Tooke, 1838/57, IV, p. 138). He was determined to correct Ricardo's persistent 'misapprehension of the facts' (ibid., p. 104). More recent commentators, such as Viner, have since demonstrated in some detail that Ricardo and his group 'were clearly wrong in their denial that extraordinary remittances would operate to depress the value of the English currency on the exchanges . . .' (1937, p.142).
26. While some interpreted it as a concession, Ricardo was right to impress upon his readers that he had never held that *every* increase in prices was due to monetary depreciation: '[W]here has it been disputed that there are not other causes besides the depreciation of money which may account for a rise in the prices of commodities? The point for which I contend is, that when such rise is accompanied by a permanent rise in the price of that bullion which is the standard of currency, then to the amount of that rise is the currency depreciated' (*Reply to Bosanquet*, in 1951/58, III, p. 251). Since the price of bullion *had* risen, this apparent concession did not materially affect Ricardo's assessment of the contemporary inflation.
27. Ricardo had earlier presented these causes as follows: '[T]here may be a great increase in the capital of a country, which may so increase the quantity of commodities to be circulated, that there may be required more circulating medium at one time than at another; there may be a great diminution in the value of gold and silver, generally, in Europe, which may make it possible, with the same commerce, to maintain an increased amount of circulation; I consider, in all cases, that the quantity of circulation must depend upon its value, and the quantity of business which it has to perform' (1951/58, V, pp. 372–3). At the time, however, statistics were lacking on changes in the level of output and the production costs of gold and silver.
28. This assessment is confirmed by Deane, who deduces from the accumulated evidence that the real bills doctrine 'provided a reasonably acceptable criterion on which to base a prudent credit policy' (1979, p. 17).
29. Tooke drew upon the vast empirical detail of his *History of Prices* to argue that, '[t]he notes of the Bank of England, and of the private banks of this country, were, for two years after the restriction, of the same value as if they had been convertible, and never experienced any discredit' (1844, p. 70 fn.), and that, during the subsequent phases of inflation, causation ran from prices to the money supply, not the other way round. Also, Tooke observed, the paper money of the Russian government 'seems never to have suffered any discredit; and the variation of the exchanges beyond those produced by the mere excess of the paper, were such only as are incidental to variations in the state of trade'. By contrast, the American colonial currencies during the war of independence and the French assignats 'became ultimately valueless, when all prospect of redemption had ceased' (ibid.). In other words, *economic* convertibility had not only not been maintained but had actually slipped out of reach.

30. '[T]he Currency School were not on very strong ground when they argued that the equilibrium gold value of notes could depreciate significantly in the presence of gold convertibility' (Laidler, 1972, p. 179). See further below, ch. 7.

31. 'It is manifest that the quantity of such money depends on the necessities and caprice of the issuer, and its value must fall in proportion to its increase': 'A Scotch Banker' (1868), p. 100. See Laidler, (1972), p. 177; Fetter (1965), pp. 190–91.

32. Marx noted that, 'the opinion of Adam Smith . . . is repeated by Thomas Tooke. This erroneous conception of the ratio of the quantity of money required for the realisation of revenues to the quantity of money required to circulate the entire social product is the necessary result of the uncomprehended, thoughtlessly conceived manner in which the various elements of material and value of the total annual product are reproduced and annually replaced' (1867/94, II, p. 479).

33. Quite separately, George Poulett Scrope, like Attwood a 'brilliant rebel' (Fetter, 1965, p. 140), had already made the case for 'an inconvertible paper money to be preserved at par with bullion ordinarily, but to be left free to deviate from par for short periods during which temporary fluctuations of the price level would otherwise occur' (Viner, 1937, p. 288).

34. Fullarton was adamant about the retention of convertibility: 'Let my views, however, not be misunderstood. Let it not be supposed, for a moment, that I am indifferent to the expediency and importance of maintaining intact the metallic basis of our circulation, and providing by the most judicious means of security that can be devised, for the perfect and uninterrupted convertibility of our bank paper' (1844, p. 20). Yet he also maintained that the suspension of cash payments 'had nothing like the share which has been commonly supposed, in producing those violent alternations of price' (ibid., pp. 20–1; also p. 7 fn.). He argued that all the functions of gold and silver coins could be performed 'as effectually by a circulation of inconvertible notes, having no value but that factitious and conventional value which they derive from the law', and, echoing Steuart, that such notes could 'supersede even the necessity for a standard, provided only the quantity of the issues be kept under due limitation' (ibid., p. 21). For Marx, this aspect of Fullarton's presentation showed 'want of clearness'; just because 'the commodity that serves as money is capable of being replaced in circulation by mere symbols of value, . . . its functions as a measure of value and a standard of prices are decared [by Fullarton] to be superfluous!' (1867/94, I, p. 129 fn.). As a result, Fullarton managed to identify three disadvantages of fiduciary money, which, in his view, would rule it out as a feasible system of currency. The first was the lack of any 'regulating principle' by which the quantity could be 'kept in exact proportion to the transactions which the currency has to perform'; fluctuations in the market-price of bullion 'would not be sufficient'. Second, the 'power of creating money' would most likely be 'abused' by the government. Finally, '[a] conventional currency is the creature of the law, and it is only within the range, in which the law which creates it prevails, that it can serve the purposes of money'; a metallic standard was required not just to provide a medium of exchange for domestic circulation, but also to 'facilitate our commercial intercourse with all the other nations of the world' (1844,

pp. 22–6). Fullarton was thus 'another Law' only to the extent that he imagined that the adoption of a fiduciary system would mean the complete abandonment of a metallic standard.

35. 'In the same way as the exchange value of commodities is crystallised into gold money as a result of exchange, so gold money in circulation is sublimated into its own symbol, first in the shape of worn gold coin, then in the shape of subsidiary metal coin, and finally in the shape of worthless counters, scraps of paper, mere *tokens of value*' (Marx, 1859, p. 114).
36. A rise or fall in the price level which corresponded with a change in the supply of fiduciary money was thus, according to Marx, 'merely a forcible assertion by the process of circulation of a law which was mechanically infringed by extraneous action; i.e., the law that the quantity of gold in circulation is determined by the prices of commodities and the volume of tokens of value in circulation is determined by the amount of gold currency which they replace in circulation' (1859, p. 121).
37. 'The quantity theory being rightly regarded as refuted, there is a reluctance to give due recognition to the influence of quantity on the value of money even where it really is the determining factor, as in the case of paper money and depreciated currency' (Hilferding, 1910, p. 50). On the suggestion that money was 'imbued with a magic power which was supposed to be capable of adjusting and regulating the process of production', see Niebyl (1946), p. 98.
38. Kuhne suggests that Marx's 'opposition to the theory of the Currency School was but a continuation of the polemics directed at Proudhon and his school (Darimon and others), who saw in the manipulation of banking policy the lever whereby to control cyclical developments and even to overcome capitalism' (1979, p. 351). This interpretation has some validity.

7 Theory of the Credit System

1. Some clarification of terminology may be required at this point. In the eighteenth century, for writers like Hume, all paper money was 'fictitious', whereas Smith confined the term only to credit instruments which lacked an equivalent counterpart in commodities or real assets of any kind. In other words, 'fictitious' was a description used either indiscriminately to cover all money and credit which had escaped from its golden prison, or, much more narrowly, to distinguish in practice commercial paper which did not furnish adequate security for bank lending from that which did, that is, 'real bills' (see above, ch. 5). The classification of fictitious capital in the nineteenth century, by contrast, included every instrument in the spectrum of credit, irrespective of its capacity for conversion into real assets; as Marx pointed out, the various kinds of interest-bearing paper 'are not capital but merely debt claims. If mortgages, they are mere titles on future ground-rent. And if they are shares of stock, they are mere titles of ownership, which entitle the holder to a share in future surplus value. All of these are not real capital' (1867/94, III, p. 457). Nevertheless, Smith's distinction retained at least a practical validity in the operation of the Banking School's 'law of reflux', a direct descendant of the real bills doctrine.
2. '[T]he essence of the transaction is that the credit is based upon the actual or

anticipated existence of real concrete goods, and that it is measured and limited by the value of those goods' (Hobson, 1913, p. 76).

3. Thornton had already pointed out that real capital 'cannot be suddenly and materially encreased by an emission of paper . . . [T]he rate of mercantile profit depends on the quantity of this *bona fide* capital and not on the amount of the nominal value which an encreased emission of paper may give to it. . . .' An expansion of bank lending might, however, 'cause paper to be for a time overabundant, and the price paid for the use of it [that is, the money rate of interest: R. G.] consequently, to fall' (1802, p. 255). See Wicksell (1936), pp. 81 ff.
4. Although Tooke was ready to criticise almost every aspect of the Currency School theory, there is no evidence for Schumpeter's view that he 'attacked Ricardo's theory as theory' (1954, p. 709). This view rests upon a confusion of long-run analysis with its short-run application.
5. Interest-bearing capital, according to Marx, was derived originally from 'usurer's capital' and played a significant role in the dissolution of feudalism: 'Both the ruin of rich landowners through usury and the improvement of the small producers lead to the formation and concentration of large amounts of money capital. But to what extent this process does away with the old mode of production, as happened in modern Europe, and whether it puts the capitalist mode of production in its stead, depends entirely upon the stage of historical development and the attendant circumstances' (1867/94, II, p. 594). For usury to have this 'revolutionary effect', it was essential that it be subordinated to emergent industrial capital. In eighteenth century England, this took the form of a campaign – led by Sir Josiah Child, whom Marx called 'the father of ordinary English private banking' – against high interest rates and for their compulsory reduction by legislation: 'This violent battle against usury, this demand for the subordination of interest-bearing capital to industrial capital, is but the herald of the organic creations that establish these prerequisites of capitalist production in the modern banking system, which on the one hand robs usurer's capital of its monopoly of the precious metal itself by creating credit-money' (ibid., p. 603). See Postan (1928).
6. Indeed, as Marx demonstrated, Massie 'laid down more categorically than did Hume, that interest is merely a part of profit' (1963/71, I, p. 373). Marx also suggested that, 'Adam Smith's discussion of the rate of interest is closer to Massie than to Hume' (1972, p. 265). Even before Massie, Sir Dudley North, in his *Discourses upon Trade* (1691), determined interest by the supply and demand for 'stock' by which he meant not only money, but capital: 'If there be more Lenders than Borrowers, Interest will . . . fall; . . . it is not low Interest makes Trade, but Trade increasing, the Stock of the Nation makes Interest low' (1691, p. 4)
7. Massie noted the correspondence between the fall in the rate of interest in England and Holland over the preceding hundred years and the fall in the rate of profit, and inquired, 'how it happens that . . . Profits are less now than they were when [Merchants and Tradesmen] first set out in the world' (Massie, 1750, p. 49). This he attributed 'either to an Increase of Traders or a Decrease of Trade, or to People in Trade lowering the Prices of their Commodities upon each other . . . through Necessity to get some Trade, or through Avarice to get most . . .' (ibid.). While he was able to deduce, therefore, that, 'the

Profits of Trade in general, are governed by the Proportion which the Number of Traders bears to the Quantity of Trade' (ibid., pp. 51–2), he made no attempt to analyse the production of a social surplus in the same way as Petty and his successors had done. As Marx put it, 'Neither Massie nor Hume know or say anything at all regarding the nature of "profit", which plays a role in the theories of both' (1972, p. 263; also 1963/71, I, p. 377).

8. Earlier, Massie dismissed any attempt to derive the 'natural', or more accurately, average, rate of interest from the rate on government securities: 'All Reasoning about natural Interest from the Rate which the Government pays for Money, is, and unavoidably must be fallacious; Experience has shown us, they neither have agreed, nor preserved a Correspondance with each other; and Reason tells us they never can; *for the one has its Foundation in Profit, and the other in Necessity; the former of which has Bounds, but the latter none*' (Massie, 1750, p. 32–3, emphasis added).
9. Smith as usual, made no reference to Steuart, who had earlier shown how 'property becomes transferred to a new set of men, once the monied interest, who . . . consolidate this quantity of money which is become superfluous to circulation' (Steuart, 1767, II, p. 638).
10. Smith also showed how, just as a given amount of money could be used for a number of purchases – depending upon its velocity of circulation – so it could be employed in a number of different *loan* transaction. He concluded that, 'the same pieces of money can thus serve as the instrument of different loans to three, or for the same reason, to thirty times their value' (1776, p. 271). When Marx applied Smith's example to deposits in the banking system, he found that, 'everything in this credit system is doubled and trebled and transformed into a mere phantom of the imagination, [including] the 'reserve fund' where one would at last hope to grasp onto something solid' (1867/94, III, p. 472).
11. In the *Principles*, Ricardo commented on Say's argument, 'that the rate of interest depends on the rate of profits; but it does not therefore follow, that the rate of profits depends on the rate of interest. One is the cause, the other the effect, and it is impossible for any circumstances to make them change places' (1951/58, I, p. 300 fn.). This implied a sharp break with Hume's more agnostic approach to the direction of causality.
12. 'If . . . the quantity of money be greatly increased, its ultimate effect is to raise the prices of commodities in proportion to the increased quantity of money; but there is probably always an interval, during which some effect is produced on the rate of interest' (Ricardo, 1951/58, I, p. 298).
13. Tooke's antagonists in the Currency School were largely responsible for this confusion. Marx ridiculed Overstone's parliamentary evidence of 1857 on the record of the Bank Acts: 'Overstone . . . confuses continually "capital" and "money". "Value of money" also means interest to him, but insofar as it is determined by the mass of money, "value of capital" is supposed to be interest, insofar as it is determined by the demand for productive capital and the profit made by it' (1867/94, III, p. 509).
14. This view had been put most uncompromisingly by Thornton in a House of Commons speech on the Bullion Report in May 1811. He maintained that the 'danger of excess', and hence of a rise in the price level in accordance with the quantity theory of money, 'was aggravated in proportion to the lowness of

the rate of interest at which discounts were afforded' (Appendix to Thornton, 1802, p. 335). This would especially be the case if the current interest rate was 'lower than that which was the natural one . . .' (ibid., p. 339). Thornton's view was widely shared, but, as Tooke was to demonstrate, it was contradicted by evidence (Tooke, 1838/57, IV, pp. 124–9).

15. Tooke had already argued in his *History of Prices* that, 'If there exist grounds for speculation in goods, a coincident facility of credit *may*, but will not *necessarily*, extend the range of it' (1838/57, III, p. 166). The key factor was the extent of *demand* (Fetter, 1965, p. 193; Schumpeter, 1954, p. 709).

16. Tooke spoiled this aspect of his case, however, by over-reaching himself. He cited J. W. Bosanquet's observation in his *Metallic, Paper and Credit Currency* that: 'Were the rate of interest reduced as low as one per cent, capital borrowed at that, or even a lower rate, should be considered nearly on a par with capital *possessed*, is a proposition so strange as hardly to warrant serious notice were it not advanced by a writer so intelligent, and, on some points of the subject, so well informed. Has he overlooked the circumstance, or does he consider it of little consequence, that there must, by the supposition, be a condition of repayment?' (1844, p. 80). As Marx rightly pointed out, Tooke's criticism of Bosanquet on this score was misconceived: "The nearer the rate of interest approaches zero, falling, for instance to one per cent, the nearer borrowed capital is to being on a par with owner's capital (1867/94, III, p. 371).

17. In the *History of Prices*, Tooke found that even '*given the motives* for speculation' and an 'undue extension' of credit, 'the prices of commodities are little, if at all, affected by temporary alterations, in the rate of interest; whilst a *permanent* increase of the rate of interest would have effects on the prices of produce directly opposite to those which are commonly supposed' (Tooke, 1838/57, III, p. 166). Fullarton, on the other hand, although prepared to accept that, 'a depression of the market-rate of interest has no necessary or direct tendency to raise prices', drew back from the proposition that it had no role at all in promoting speculative activity. He distinguished 'sound or rational speculations', in which interest rate movements might have very little part, from 'speculation extravagant and monstrous' which would be conducted 'without the slightest regard to the state or prospects of supply' (1844, p. 163 fn.). See Niebyl (1946) pp. 69–70.

18. There is also a significant discussion as 'addenda' to the third part of *Theories of Surplus Value*. Here interest-bearing capital is examined from the perspective of 'revenue and its sources' (1963/71, III, pp. 453–540).

19. Similarly, Steuart demonstrated not only that the rate of interest was generally 'in proportion to the profits upon trade and industry', but also that it was regulated by competition: 'The borrowers desire to fix the interest as *low* as they can; the lenders seek, for a like principle of self-interest, to carry the rate of it as high as *they* can. From this combination of interests arises a double competition, which fluctuated between the two parties' (1767, II, pp. 449, 452).

20. Marx distinguished between that portion of gross profit accruing as interest and the portion left to the 'active capitalist', which could be categorised as 'profit of enterprise'. This derived 'solely from the operations, or functions, which he performs with the capital in the process of reproduction . . .' (1867/

94, III, p. 374 and *passim*). Long before most observers, therefore, he recognised the growing separation between ownership and control under capitalism: '[S]tock companies in general – developed with the credit system – have an increasing tendency to separate this work of management as a function from the ownership of capital, be it self-owned or borrowed' (ibid., pp. 387–8; also, pp. 436–40). See also Hilferding (1910, ch. 7).

21. 'The price of commodities is extremely fluctuating; they are every one calculated for particular uses; money serves every purpose. Commodities, though of the same kind, differ in goodness: money *is* all, or *ought to be* all of the same value, relatively to its denominations. Hence the *price of money* (which is what we express by the term *interest*) is susceptible of a far greater stability and uniformity, than the price of any other thing' (Steuart, 1767, II, p. 450).

22. According to Kuhne, 'That Marx set his face against the Currency School is curious, as the latter dates back to Ricardo . . .' (1979, p. 349). It has been my contention that the Currency School represents a distortion of Ricardo's theory of interest and prices and that the Banking School comes much closer to a 'Ricardian' position, on what might have been Ricardo's view in the mid-nineteenth century. It is therefore not at all remarkable that Marx should 'align himself' with the Banking School.

23. As far as Marx was concerned, the *money supply* could have a 'determining influence' on the rate of interest 'only in times of stringency'. Under normal circumstances, however, it would have no effect, 'since – assuming the economy and velocity of currency to be constant – it is determined in the first place by commodity prices and the quantity of transactions. . . , and finally by the state of credit, whereas it by no means exerts the reverse effect upon the latter; and, secondly, since commodity prices and interest do not necessarily stand in any direct correlation to each other' (1867/94, III, p. 530).

24. Panico (1980) also takes up Sraffa's suggestion (1960, p. 33) that the rate of interest may be treated as an independent variable in the formation of prices of production, thus 'closing' the system outlined by Garegnani (see above ch. IV). I have reservations about this argument, but its assessment is beyond our present scope.

25. Fullarton dismissed the idea that simply by 'operating on the interest-market', the Bank of England 'might succeed in arresting [a gold drain], without any material stock to credit or disturbance of mercantile affairs'. It might have been possible 'if the Bank held at all times the control of the market-rate of interest in its own hands', but 'that power only accrues to the Bank, when the public has already to some extent become dependent on the Bank for its discount accommodations' (1844, p. 160).

26. Although Fullarton and the Banking School recognised the dangers in the overaccumulation of money capital, they ignored its counterpart in the overaccumulation of *real* capital, expressed in an overproduction of commodities, and the role of credit, in promoting this overproduction. Marx, on the other hand, depicted the credit system as 'the main lever of over-production and over-speculation in commerce . . . because the reproduction process, which is elastic by nature, is here forced to its extreme limits'. The further development of the credit system would therefore 'constitute the form of transition to a new mode of production' (1867/94, III, p. 441).

27. The argument for a separation of Bank of England functions derived its authority from David Ricardo's posthumously published *Plan for the Establishment of a National Bank* (1824): 'The Bank of England performs two operations of banking, which are quite distinct, and have no necessary connection with each other: it issues a paper currency as a substitute for a metallic one; and it advances money in the way of loan, to merchants and others. That these two operations of banking have no necessary connection, will appear obvious from this, – that they might be carried on by two separate bodies, without the slightest loss of advantage, either to the country, or the merchants who receive accommodation from such loans' (1951/58, IV, p. 276). See Arnon (1987).
28. Andréadès, for example, found that, 'the discussion of the merits and demerits of these two systems is . . . somewhat futile and very dull . . . whatever may in reality be the advantages of the Banking Principle, . . . it was very soon rejected in England. Hence it is more important to examine the practical form given by the exponents of the currency principle to their theory . . .' (1935, p. 277). The Banking School has received more attention as successive inquiries upheld their main conclusions (Macmillan, 1931; Radcliffe, 1959; du Cann, 1981).
29. The little headway Tooke was able to make initially against the prevailing orthodoxy of the Currency School was partly explained by Fullarton as follows: 'Mr Tooke himself has been exceedingly slow in following out his original conclusions on the subject of price to all their consequences. . . . He adhered to [quantity theory] doctrines even after he had refuted them by his discoveries, and seems to have parted with them at last only by degrees and with reluctance, under the pressure of his growing convictions. . . . These slight appearances of wavering, which, rightly viewed, ought rather to be considered as proofs of the caution and deliberation with which he formed his judgements, *have been charged against him as inconsistencies*, and advantage has been taken of them to detract from the weight of his authority' (1844, pp. 18–19). The chief 'inconsistency' as we shall see, lay in Tooke's persistent failure to deal with Say's law; nevertheless, he was later to 'fully acquiesce' in Fullarton's 'sketch . . . of the progress of my opinions' (1838/57, IV, p. x).
30. 'The discussion between the two schools turned wholly . . . on short-run issues. On the question of what determined the quantity and value of a metallic currency in the long-run, both schools followed the "classical" or "Ricardian" doctrine' (Viner, 1937, p. 221). See also Laidler (1972).
31. Although this section is concerned largely with gold drains, the same principles apply to a gold *influx* of the kind discussed in chs 4 and 7; such an influx also took place later in the nineteenth century, following the new discoveries in California and Australia. Upon the constant velocity assumption, Hobson pointed out, 'hinges the whole of the theory that quantity of gold output is the sole ultimate regulator of prices, upon the money side of the equation of exchange' (1913, p. 145).
32. Fullarton also discussed the issue in some detail. In the first stage postulated by the specie-flow doctrine, he pointed out that an influx of bullion need have no effect on the domestic money supply: 'They never even allude to the existence of such a thing as a great *hoard* of the metals, though upon the

action of the hoards depends the whole economy of international payments between specie-circulating communities, while any operation of the money collected in hoards upon prices must, even according to the currency hypothesis, be wholly impossible' (1844, p. 140). In the second stage, a bullion outflow might be drawn entirely from available reserves: 'I would desire, indeed, no more convincing evidence of the competency of the machinery of the hoards in specie-paying countries to perform every necessary office of international adjustment, without any sensible aid from the general circulation, than the facility with which France, when but just recovering from the shock of a destructive foreign invasion, completed within the space of twenty-seven months the payment of her forced contribution of nearly twenty millions to the allied powers, and a considerable proportion of that sum in specie without any perceptible contraction or derangement of her domestic currency, or even any alarming fluctuation of her exchanges' (ibid., p. 141). Marx also maintained that, 'the movements of a hoard concentrated as a reserve fund for international payments have as such nothing to do with the movements of money as a medium of circulation' (1867/94, III, p. 453). See Viner (1937, pp. 222, 268).

33. Fullarton's commonsense produced a distant echo: 'We cannot regard as satisfactory a system under which so high a proportion of the gold stock is locked up in such a way as not to be available for export if the Central Bank should so desire' (Macmillan, 1931, p. 139). Fullarton distinguished drains of bullion for purchases of corn and war expenditure from those in which 'a foreign debt has been created by very extensive investments of capital in foreign securities' and where 'the mischief has originated in speculation and over-trading'. These latter categories 'have no claim to be treated with the same tenderness' (1844, p. 154). See also Tooke (1844), pp. 187–89 and below.
34. For Rist, the fact that, '[t]he beliefs of Peel and the Currency School were not weakened by Tooke's arguments . . . provides a further striking example of the weight carried by great names and by over-simplified thought in the tradition of political economy' (1940, p. 205).
35. It has been argued persuasively that, 'the currency principle and monetary base control are almost identical in intention' (Congdon, 1980, p. 2). See also du Cann (1981) ch. 9.
36. '[I]t cannot surely be pretended for an instant, that this question as to the action of a credit circulation on prices can, in one way or the other, or in the slightest degree, be affected by any variation in the form of credit through which the payments are made . . .': Fullarton (1844), p. 40. 'It appears, then, that there is neither authority nor reasoning in favour of the definition which invests Bank notes with the property of money, or paper currency, *to the exclusion of all other forms of paper credit*' (Tooke, 1838/57, IV, p. 163).
37. 'Though we do not regard the supply of money as an unimportant quantity, we view it as only part of the wider structure of liquidity in the economy' (Radcliffe, 1959, p. 132; see also Sayers 1960, pp. 516–17; Kaldor and Trevithick, 1981, pp. 11–13; du Cann, 1981, pp. lxxxvi–lxxxviii).
38. Rist subscribed to the law of reflux in the following terms: 'The banks' creation of credit, in all its forms, and particularly in the form of bank-notes, takes place only because the *public demand credit*. Banks cannot create notes

at will, anymore than they can create deposits' (1940, p. 213). Similarly Kaldor and Trevithick: 'Hence in a credit money economy . . . the outstanding "money stock" can never be in excess of the amount which individuals wish to hold; and this alone rules out the possibility of there being an "excess" supply of money which should be the *cause* (as distinct from the consequence) of a rise in spending' (1981, p. 7). Others have taken a different view: '[A]s long as a bank could find borrowers and had sufficient reserves it could increase its note issues indefinitely by granting more and more loans' (Daugherty, 1942/43, p. 151). The question which should have been asked is would the non-bank public have continued to demand credit, let alone 'indefinitely', if there were no further expectation of profit? This question is addressed below in the context of the business cycle.

39. Considerable confusion enters into the literature at this point, for which the Banking School itself is partly responsible. According to Fetter, 'it is never quite clear whether . . . the fundamental idea was that changes in note issues alone had no effect on prices, or that a change in the total means of payment created by banks that loaned only on real bills had no effect on prices' (1965, p. 191). My argument is that the reflux law contains *both* these aspects; however, some commentators, who find the first aspect congenial, recoil from the real bills dimension (e.g. Laidler, 1972, pp. 173–4).

40. The Banking School view has been cited in recent debate on credit control: 'The Currency School was incorrect . . . to claim that excessive increases in the note issue were responsible for price inflation or the subsequent commercial crises which threatened convertibility. Rather it was commercial crises which were responsible for excessive increases in the note issue' (Congdon, 1980, p. 4). Ironically, the opposite view is held by Kuhne, a Marxist economist. He claims that the Banking School must 'surely' have been wrong to assume 'the improbability of an inflation of bank notes' (1979, p. 350). He even suggests that, 'in the area of regulations the ideas of the Currency School had some success' (ibid.) It is now widely accepted that the banking legislation inspired by the Currency School only served to exacerbate subsequent crises (Clapham, 1944, II, pp. 211–16; Fetter, 1965, pp. 201–15).

41. 'The main constructive proposal made by the Banking School was that the Bank of England should maintain a larger average reserve' (Daugherty, 1942/43, p. 153). See also Gregory's introduction to Tooke (1838/57, p. 100); Viner (1937, pp. 264–70); Clapham (1944, II, p. 240).

42. Wilson's argument is reinforced by the possibility of converting the notes into gold: 'Their equilibrium price could never fall below their gold redemption value minus the cost of the redemption transaction . . . [I]t is hard to believe that [this cost] could have been a significant amount' (Laidler, 1972, p. 179). Fetter regards Wilson's articles compared with the writings of Tooke and Fullarton, as 'a better statement of the theoretical case against the Act of 1844' (1965, pp. 199–200).

43. Marx agreed, however, that 'the demand for currency between consumers and dealers predominates in periods of prosperity, and the demand for currency between capitalists predominates in periods of depression. During a depression the former decreases, and the latter increases' (1867/94, III, p. 450). See Kuhne (1979), p. 353; Harris (1979), p. 140.

44. 'Each demand originates in circumstances peculiarly affecting itself, and

very distinct from each other. It is when everything looks prosperous, when wages are high, prices on the rise, and factories busy, that an additional supply of currency is usually required to perform the additional functions inseparable from the necessity of making larger and more numerous payments; whereas, it is chiefly in a more advanced stage of the commercial cycle, when difficulties begin to present themselves, when markets are overstocked, and returns delayed, that interest rises, and a pressure comes on the Bank for advances of capital' (Fullarton, 1844, p. 96).

45. The issue was posed by Marx as follows: '[W]hich is it, capital or money in its specific function as a means of payment that is in short supply in periods of stringency? And this is a well-known controversy . . . It is not a contradiction here between a demand for money as a means of payment and a demand for capital. The contradiction is rather between capital in its money-form and capital in its commodity-form; and the form which is here demanded and in which alone it can function, is its money-form. Aside from this demand for gold (or silver) it cannot be said that there is any dearth whatever of capital in such periods of crisis. . . . On the contrary, the markets are overstocked, swamped with commodity capital. Hence, it is not in any case, a lack of *commodity* capital which causes the stringency' (1867/94, III, pp. 459–60).

46. It should be kept in mind that this over-supply of capital was seen as an oversupply of *money* capital. Marx noted that, 'this plethora of loanable money capital merely shows the limitations of *capitalist* production. The subsequent credit swindle proves that no real obstacle stands in the way of the employment of this surplus capital' (1867/94, III, p. 507).

47. Stocks and shares, for example, did not transfer control over real capital, but 'merely convey legal claims to a portion of the surplus value to be produced by it' (Marx, 1867/94, III, p. 477). They could be seen as 'duplicates' of the capital; but, 'as duplicates which are themselves objects of transaction as commodities, and thus able to circulate as capital-values, they are illusory, and their value may fall or rise quite independently of the movement of value of the real capital for which they are titles. Their value, that is, their quotation on the Stock Exchange, necessarily has a tendency to rise with a fall in the rate of interest – insofar as this fall, independent of the characteristic movements of money capital, is due merely to the tendency for the rate of profit to fall; therefore, this imaginary wealth expands, if for this reason alone, in the course of capitalist production . . .' (ibid., pp. 477–8).

48. Thornton had long before in his *Paper Credit* insisted that the scope for speculation turned 'principally on a comparison of the rate of interest taken at the bank with the current rate of mercantile profit'. His description of the nature of the demand brought by borrowers was perceptive: 'It will not be the privation of that quantity of circulating medium which is necessary for carrying on the accustomed payments, for these will be very immaterially encreased; the cause of the extraordinary applications to the bank will be the temporary advantage which may be gained, or the loss which may be avoided, by borrowing, during the three months in question, at the rate of five per cent' (1802, p. 257).

49. Hobson also attributed price fluctuations of this kind 'to an increase in the quantity of credit which each unit of negotiable capital supports during a rise of prices'; he called this 'a temporary and adventitious increase of supply of

money' and distinguished it from 'that increased credit which is the natural financial result of enabling larger masses of wealth to figure as securities' (1913, p. 93).

50. The mechanism of a credit inflation was explained by Fullarton: 'It is true, that the prices of an extensive class of commodities may occasionally be affected for a time by *speculation*, and that such speculation may be more or less supported by extraordinary facilities of credit. But albeit bank-notes are nothing more than credit embodied in a particular shape, this indirect action of credit on prices is quite a different thing from the action on prices ascribed to bank-notes by the partisans of the currency theory. . . . The object of the speculative purchaser is to withdraw from consumption a portion of the stock of the commodity in which he speculates, and to hold it back from the market until he can sell it at a profit; his action is on the value, not of the money, but of the commodity; and he causes a rise of price by thus disturbing the natural course of supply and demand. He first creates an artificial demand, by entering into competition with the consumer for the possession of the commodity, and then he contracts the supply, by refusing for a time to sell it to any-one else. When he succeeds in his object, however, the rise rise of price is not *nominal* but *real*; when he at last brings his commodity to market, he obtains for it not merely a larger numerical amount of coin or notes than he paid for it, but a larger money value' (1844, pp. 58–9).

51. As the crisis assumed an international dimension, it 'becomes evident that all these nations have simultaneously over-exported (thus over-produced) and over-imported (thus over-traded), that prices were inflated in all of them, and credit stretched too far. And the same break-down takes place in all of them . . . prov[ing] precisely by its general character . . . that gold drain is just a phenomenon of a crisis not its cause' (Marx, 1867/94, III, p. 492). Clapham has referred to the 'commercial crisis of the autumn of 1857, in which all the feverish and gold-dazzled activity of the mid-fifties ended', as 'the first really world-wide crisis in history . . .' (1944, II, p. 226).

52. It was not until 1931 that a firm recommendation was made to end the separation of departments and the associated fixed fiduciary issue: 'This peculiar provision arose out of long-dead controversies which we need not revive; for the reasons which originally led to the separation of the departments have no interest or relevance to-day' (Macmillan, 1931, p. 143).

53. Again, it was not until 1959 that the Banking School view was embodied in official policy: 'The authorities thus have to regard the structure of interest rates rather than the supply of money as the centre-piece of the monetary mechanism' (Radcliffe, 1959, p. 135). See also Sayers (1960).

54. The position was summarised by *The Economist*: 'Practically, then both Mr Tooke and Mr Loyd would meet an additional demand for gold . . . by an early . . . contraction of credit by raising the rate of interest, and restricting advances of capital. . . . But the principles of Mr Loyd lead to certain [legal] restrictions and regulations which produce the most serious inconvenience' (11 December 1847, p. 1418). Marx's comment was apt: 'That the greatest sacrifices of real wealth are necessary to maintain the metallic basis in a critical moment has been admitted by both Tooke and Loyd–Overstone. The controversy revolves merely round a plus or a minus, and round the more or less rational treatment of the inevitable' (1867/94, III, p. 573).

55. On the relationship between Bank rate and the market rate of interest, see Cramp (1962) ch. 1.
56. Four years earlier, the third volume of his *History of Prices*, Tooke argued that, in response to a gold drain, 'the Bank rate of discount should be kept so steadily above the market rate, as progressively to reduce the securities, through that channel, without increasing them by other investment'. The effect would be to replenish the Bank's reserve – up to a predetermined amount – and to allow it to 'preserve that amount *on an average*', depending upon the circumstances where the drain was due to temporary factors, such as the purchase of corn, 'the balance of payments would in all probability be satisfied by the export of that amount of bullion'. If the drain continued, however, the Bank would have 'reason to apprehend the existence of more extensive and deeper-seated causes of demand for the metals', namely a speculative boom. Under these circumstances, 'measures might be taken for its counteraction, without producing alarm and disturbance of the money market on the one hand, or endangering an extreme and unsafe degree of reduction of the Bank treasure on the other'. Tooke concluded that regulating the securities in this way would be 'more easily practicable than either that of maintaining the securities even, or of presenting the bullion in any given proportion to the liabilities'; and that, 'the principle of limitation would operated less rigidly' if the issue and deposit departments of the Bank were fused rather than separated (1838/57, III, pp. 187–9).
57. It is now possible to correct a widespread misinterpretation in the literature (Sweezy, 1970, p. 178 and *passim*) of Marx's contention that, 'The ultimate reason for all real crises always remains the poverty and restricted consumption of the masses as opposed to the drive of capitalist production to develop the productive forces as though only the absolute consuming power of society constituted their limit' (1867/94, III, p. 484). Although it has been alleged that Marx was here elaborating an 'underconsumptionist' theory of crisis, the context – a discussion of *credit* – makes it clear that he viewed the 'limits of consumption' as being set by 'the reproduction process itself' (ibid., p. 482). The point he wanted to make was simply that it was 'erroneous . . . to blame a scarcity of productive capital' for conditions of economic stagnation. On the contrary, it was "precisely at such times that there is a *super abundance of productive capital*, partly in relation to the normal, but temporarily reduced scale of reproduction, and partly *in relation to the paralysed consumption*' (ibid., p. 483, emphasis added). In other words, the 'consuming power of society' was a factor in the crisis only to the extent that it was restricted by the overriding need to maintain the rate of profit on capital. Nor was there any point in looking to a Malthusian 'third party' to 'realise' surplus value: 'The incomes of the unproductive classes and of those who live on fixed incomes remain in the main stationary during the inflation of prices which goes hand in hand with over-production and over-speculation. Hence their consuming capacity diminshed relatively, and with it their ability to replace that portion of the total reproduction which would normally enter into their consumption. Even when their demand remains nominally the same, it diminishes in reality' (ibid., p. 491).
58. Laidler concludes that, 'Tooke's emphasis on bank lending as a key variable in short-run business fluctuations surely put him closer to the truth than did the Currency School's emphasis on the size of the note issue' (1972, p. 183).

59. 'Ignorant and mistaken bank legislation, such as that of 1844/45, can intensify [a] money crisis. But no kind of bank legislation can eliminate a crisis' (Marx, 1867/94, III, p. 490).
60. Rist pointed out that this argument 'remains valid only so long as the banks really put the "law of reflux" into operation and confine themselves to making short-term loans and not advances which immobilise their funds for indefinite periods. Tooke makes this assumption throughout his argument' (1940, p. 200). Tooke himself later notes: 'It is certainly a striking fact, that for so long a period after the Restriction Act, so uniform a value of the currency and of the amount of the circulation should have been preserved ... [N]o attempt has ever been made to explain it by the vast majority of those who, under the influence of the currency theory, or of the Birmingham school, write or talk of the period of the Bank restriction as having been characterised in its whole course by abundant or excessive issues of paper money, and consequent depreciation' (1838/57, IV, pp. 92–3). See also Deane (1979, p. 17).

Bibliography

Ainsworth, W. (1874) *John Law: The Projector* (London: Chapman & Hall).

Andréadès, A. (1935) *History of the Bank of England 1640 to 1903* 3rd edn (London: Staples Press) (1st edn, 1909).

Arnon, A. (1987) 'Banking between the Invisible and Visible Hands: A Reinterpretation of Ricardo's Place within the Classical School', *Oxford Economic Papers*, vol. 39, June.

Ashton, T. S., and Sayers, R. S. (eds) (1953) *Papers in English Monetary History* (Oxford: Clarendon Press).

Aston, T. (ed.) (1965) *Crisis in Europe, 1560–1660: Essays from 'Past and Present''* (London: Routledge & Kegan Paul).

Bailey, S. (1825) *A Critical Dissertation on the Nature, Measures, and Causes of Value* (London: London School of Economics and Political Science, reprinted, 1931).

Baumol, W. J., and Becker, G. S., (1952) 'The Classical Monetary Theory: The Outcome of the Discussion', *Economica*, vol. 19, November.

Berkeley, G. (1750) *The Querist, Containing Several Queries, Proposed to the Consideration of the Public* (London: W. Innys).

Beveridge, W. (1957) 'Wages and Inflation in the Past', *The Incorporated Statistician*, vol. 7.

Bodin, J. (1568) *The Response of Jean Bodin to the Paradoxes of Malestroict, and the Paradoxes* (Washington, 1946).

Bradley, I., and Howard, M. (1982) *Classical and Marxian Political Economy: Essays in Honour of Ronald L. Meek* (London: Macmillan).

Brown, M., Sato, K. and Zarembka, P. (eds) (1976) *Essays in Modern Capital Theory* (Amsterdam: North Holland).

Cannan, E. (1918) *Money: Its Connexion with Rising and Falling Prices* (London: Staples Press).

Cannan, E. (1919) *The Paper Pound of 1797–1821: A Reprint of the Bullion Report* (London: P. S. King).

Cantillon, R. (1755) *Essai sur la nature du commerce en général* H. Higgs, ed. (London: Macmillan, 1931).

Carus-Wilson, E. M. (ed.) (1954) *Essays in Economic History* (London: Edward Arnold).

Cassel, G. (1903) *The Nature of Necessity of Interest* (New York: Kelley & Millman, reprinted 1957).

Cesarano, F. (1976) 'Monetary Theory in Ferdinando Galiani's *Della Moneta*', *History of Political Economy*, vol. 8.

Chamley, P. (1962) 'Sir James Steuart, inspirateur de la theorie générale de Lord Keynes?' *Revue d'Economie Politique*, no. 3.

Clapham, J. (1944) *The Bank of England: A History* (Cambridge: Cambridge University Press).

Congdon, T. (1980) 'The Monetary Base Debate: Another Instalment in the Currency School vs Banking School Controversy?' *National Westminster Bank Quaterly Review*, August.

Cramp, A. B. (1962) *Opinion on Bank Rate, 1822–60* (London: London School of Economics and Political Science).

Daugherty, M. R. (1942/43) 'The Currency–Banking Controversy', *Southern Economic Journal*, vol. 9, October 1942 and January 1943.

Davenant, C. (1699) *An Essay upon the Probable Methods of Making a People Gainers in the Ballance of Trade* (London: James Knapton).

Deane, P. (1978) *The Evolution of Economic Ideas* (Cambridge: Cambridge University Press).

Deane, P. (1979) 'Inflation in History', in D. Heathfield (ed.) *Perspectives on Inflation: Models and Policies* (London: Longman, 1979).

De Brunhoff, S. (1976) *Marx on Money* (New York: Urizen).

De Quincey, T. (1824) 'Dialogues of Three Templars on Political Economy, chiefly in relation to the Principles of Mr Ricardo', *The London Magazine*, vol. 9, April/May.

De Vivo, G. (1982) 'Notes on Marx's Critique of Ricardo', *Contributions to Political Economy*, vol. 1, March.

Dobb, M. (1973) *Theories of Value and Distribution since Adam Smith: Ideology and Economic Theory* (Cambridge: Cambridge University Press).

Du Cann, E. (1981) *Report of the Treasury and Civil Service Committee on Monetary Policy* (London: Her Majesty's Stationery Office).

Eatwell, J. (1975a) 'Mr Sraffa's Standard Commodity and the Rate of Exploitation', *Quarterly Journal of Economics*, vol. 89.

Eatwell, J. (1975b) 'The Interpretation of Ricardo's *Essay on Profits*'. *Economica*, vol. 42, May.

Eatwell, J. (1979) 'Theories of Value, Output and Employment', in J. Eatwell and M. Milgate (eds) *Keynes's Economics and the Theory of Value and Distribution* (London: Duckworth, 1983).

Eatwell, J. (1982) 'Competition', in I. Bradley and M. Howard (eds) *Classical and Marxian Political Economy* (London: Macmillan, 1982).

Eatwell, J. (1983) 'The Analytical Foundations of Monetarism', in J. Eatwell and M. Milgate (eds) *Keynes's Economics and the Theory of Value and Distribution* (London: Duckworth, 1983).

Eatwell, J., and Green, R. (1984) 'Economic Theory and Political Power', in B. Pimlott (ed.) *Fabian Essays in Socialist Thought* (London: Heinemann, 1984).

Eatwell, J., and Milgate, M. (eds) (1983) *Keynes's Economics and the Theory of Value and Distribution* (London: Duckworth).

Eatwell, J., Milgate, M., and Newman, P. (eds) (1987) *The New Palgrave: A Dictionary of Economics* (London: Macmillan).

Engels, F. (1859) 'Review of Karl Marx, *A Contribution to the Critique of Political Economy*', in K. Marx *A Contribution to the Critique of Political Economy* (Moscow: Progress, 1970).

Engels, F. (1894) *Anti-Dühring* (New York: International, 1972).

Feavearyear, A. E. (1931) *The Pound Sterling: A History of English Money* (Oxford: Clarendon Press).

Fetter, F. W. (1965) *Development of British Monetary Orthodoxy, 1797–1875* (Cambridge, Mass.: Harvard University Press).

Fine, B. (1979) 'World Economic Crisis and Inflation: what bourgeois economics says and why it is wrong', in F. Green and P. Nore (eds) *Issues in Political Economy: A Critical Approach* (London: Macmillan, 1979).

Franklin, B. (1836) *Works*. (ed.) J. Sparks, (Boston).

Friedman, M. (1968) 'The Quantity Theory of Money', in A. A. Walters (ed.) *Money and Banking* (Harmondsworth: Penguin, 1973).

Friedman, M. (1974) 'A Theoretical Framework for Monetary Analysis', in R. Gordon (ed.) *Milton Friedman's Monetary Framework: A Debate with his Critics* (Chicago: University of Chicago Press, 1974).

Fullarton, J. (1844) *On the Regulation of the Currency* (London: John Murray).

Garegnani, P. (1976) 'On a Change in the Notion of Equilibrium in Recent Work on Value and Distribution', in M. Brown, K. Sato and Zarembka (eds) *Essays in Modern Capital Theory* (Amsterdam: North Holland, 1976).

Garegnani, P. (1978/79) 'Notes on Consumption, Investment and Effective Demand', in J. Eatwell and M. Milgate (eds) *Keynes's Economics and the Theory of Value and Distribution* (London: Duckworth, 1983).

Garegnani, P. (1984) 'Value and Distribution in the Classical Economists and Marx' *Oxford Economic Papers*, vol. 36, June.

Gervaise, I. (1720) *The System or Theory of the Trade of the World* (London).

Gordon, B. (1975) *Economic Analysis before Adam Smith* (London: Macmillan).

Gordon, R. (ed.) (1974) *Milton Friedman's Monetary Framework: A Debate with his Critics* (Chicago: University of Chicago Press).

Green, F., and Nore, P. (eds) (1979) *Issues in Political Economy: A Critical Approach* (London: Macmillan).

Green, R. (1975) *Imperialism and the Accumulation of Capital: The Debate between Rosa Luxemburg and Nikolai Bukharin*, unpublished honours dissertation.

Green, R. (1982a) 'Money, Output and Inflation in Classical Economics', *Contributions to Political Economy*, vol. 1.

Green, R. (1982b) Review of R. Hilferding, *Finance Capital*, *Contributions to Political Economy*, vol. 1, March.

Green, R. (1983) Review of N. Kaldor, *The Scourge of Monetarism. Contributions to Political Economy*, vol. 2, March.

Green, R. (1987) Various entries, in J. Eatwell, M. Milgate and P. Newman (eds) *The New Palgrave: A Dictionary of Economics* (London: Macmillan, 1987).

Grice-Hutchinson, M. (1952) *The School of Salamanca* (Oxford: Clarendon).

Groenewegen, P. D. (1972) 'Three Notes on Ricardo's Theory of Value and Distribution', *Australian Economic Papers*, vol. 11, June.

Hahn, F. (1982) *Money and Inflation* (Oxford: Blackwell).

Hamilton, E. J. (1934) *American Treasure and the Price Revolution in Spain, 1501–1650* (Cambridge: Harvard University Press).

Hammarström, I. (1957) 'The Price Revolution of the Sixteenth Century: Some Swedish Evidence', in P. Ramsey (ed.) *The Price Revolution in Sixteenth Century England* (London: Methuen, 1971).

Haney, L. H. (1949) *History of Economic Thought* (London: Macmillan).

Harcourt, G. C. (1982) 'The Sraffian Contribution: An Evaluation', in I. Bradley and M. Howard (eds) *Classical and Marxian Political Economy* (London: Macmillan, 1982).

Harris, L. (1979) 'The Role of Money in the Economy', in F. Green and P. Nore (eds) *Issues in Political Economy: A Critical Approach* (London: Macmillan, 1979).

Hawtrey, R. G. (1934) *Currency and Credit*, 3rd edn (London: Longmans, 1st edn, 1919).

Heathfield, D. (ed.) (1979) *Perspectives on Inflation: Models and Policies* (London: Longman).

Horsefield, J. K. (1941/44) 'The Duties of a Banker', in T. S. Ashton and R. S. Sayers (eds) *Papers in English Monetary History* (Oxford: Clarendon Press, 1953).

Hegel, G. W. F. (1821) *Philosophy of Right* (Oxford: Clarendon Press, 1952).

Hegeland, H. (1951) *The Quantity Theory of Money* (Göteborg: Elanders).

Helfferich, K. (1903) *Money* (New York: Kelley, reprinted, 1969).

Hilferding, R. (1910) *Finance Capital: A Study of the Latest Phase of Capitalist Development* (London: Routledge & Kegan Paul, 1981).

Hill, C. (1969) *Reformation to Industrial Revolution* (Harmondsworth: Penguin).

Hobsbawm, E. J. (1954) 'The Crisis of the Seventeenth Century', in T. Aston (ed.) *Crisis in Europe, 1560–1660: Essays from Past and Present* (London: Routledge & Kegan Paul, 1965).

Hobson, J. A. (1913) *Gold, Prices and Wages, with an Examination of the Quantity Theory* (Clifton: Kelley, reprinted, 1973).

Hollander, J. (1911) 'The Development of the Theory of Money from Adam Smith to David Ricardo', *Quarterly Journal of Economics*, vol. 25, May.

Hollander, S. (1973) 'Ricardo's Analysis of the Profit Rate, 1813–15', *Economica*, vol. 40, August.

Hollander, S. (1975) 'Ricardo and the Corn Profit Model: Reply to Eatwell', *Economica*, vol. 42, May.

Hollander, S. (1979) *The Economics of David Ricardo* (London: Heinemann).

Horner, F. (1957) *Economic Writings* (F. W. Fetter, ed.) (London: London School of Economics and Political Science).

Hume D. (1752) *Essays, Literary, Moral and Political* (London: Ward, Lock & Co, n.d.).

Hume, D. (1955) *Writings on Economics* (E. Rotwein, ed.) (Edinburgh: Nelson).

Jay, D. (1985) *Sterling* (London: Sidgwick & Jackson).

Jevons, W. (1881) 'Richard Cantillon and the Nationality of Political Economy', in R. Cantillon (1755) *Essai sur la nature du commerce en général*, ed. H. Higgs (London: Macmillan, 1931).

Johnson, H. G. (ed.) (1972) *Readings in British Monetary Economics* (Oxford: Clarendon Press).

Kaldor, N. (1982) *The Scourge of Monetarism* (Oxford: Oxford University Press).

Kaldor, N., and Trevithick, J. (1981) 'A Keynesian Perspective on Money', *Lloyds Bank Review*, no. 139, January.

Kenway, P. (1980) 'Marx, Keynes and the Possibility of Crisis', in J. Eatwell and M. Milgate (eds) *Keynes's Economics and the Theory of Value and Distribution* (London: Duckworth, 1983).

Keynes, J. M. (1933) *Treatise on Money* (London: Macmillan).

Keynes, J. M. (1936) *General Theory of Employment, Interest and Money* (London: Macmillan, 1970).

Kuhne, K. (1979) *Economics and Marxism* (London: Macmillan).

Kurz, H. D. (1985) 'Sraffa's Contribution to the Debate in Capital Theory', *Contributions to Political Economy*, vol. 4, March.

Laidler, D. (1972) 'Thomas Tooke on Monetary Reform', in M. Peston and B. Corry (eds) *Essays in Honour of Lord Robbins* (London: Weiderfeld, 1972).

Landes, D. (1969) *The Unbound Prometheus: Technological Change and Industrial Development in Western Europe from 1750 to the Present* (Cambridge: Cambridge University Press).

Law, J. (1705) *Money and Trade Considered* (New York: Kelley, reprinted, 1966).

Locke, J. (1691) 'Consequences of the Lowering of Interest and Raising the Value of Money', in J. McCulloch (1825), *Principles of Political Economy* (London: Ward, Lock & Co.).

Low, J. M. (1952) 'An Eighteenth Century Controversy in the Theory of Economic Progress', *Manchester School.*

Macmillan, H. (1931) *Report of the Committee on Finance and Industry* (London: Her Majesty's Stationery Office).

Malynes, G. (1601) *A Treatise of the Canker of England's Commonwealth* (London).

Mandel, E. (1978) *Late Capitalism* (London: Verso).

Marcuzzo, M. and Roselli, A. (1987) 'Profitability in the International Gold Market in the Early History of the Gold Standard', *Economica*, vol. 54, August.

Marshall, A. (1923) *Money, Credit and Commerce* (London: Macmillan).

Marx, K. (1859) *A Contribution to the Critique of Political Economy* (Moscow: Progress, 1970).

Marx, K. (1867/94) *Capital* (Moscow: Progress, 1971).

Marx, K. (1879/80) 'Marginal Notes to A. Wagner's "Textbook on Political Economy"', in A. Dragstedt (ed.), *Value: Studies by Karl Marx* (London: New Park, 1976).

Marx, K. (1894) 'From the *Critical History*', in Engels (1894) *Anti-Dühring* (New York: International, 1972).

Marx, K. (1963/71) *Theories of Surplus Value* (Moscow: Progress).

Marx, K. (1973) *Grundrisse* (Harmondsworth: Penguin).

Marx, K., and Engels, F. (1975) *Selected Correspondence* (S. W. Ryazanskaya, ed.) (Moscow: Progress Publishers).

Massie, J. (1750) *An Essay on the Governing Causes of the Natural Rate of Interest* (Baltimore: Johns Hopkins, reprinted, 1912).

McCulloch, J. R. (1825) *Principles of Political Economy* (London: Ward, Lock & Co.).

Meek, R. L. (1967) *Economics and Ideology and Other Essays* (London: Chapman & Hall).

Milgate, M. (1982) *Capital and Employment: A Study of Keynes's Economics* (London: Academic Press).

Mill, J. (1844) *Elements of Political Economy*, 3rd edn (New York: Kelley, reprinted, 1965).

Mill, J. S. (1873) *Principles of Political Economy*, 6th edn (London: Longmans).

Mill, J. S. (1874) *Essays on some Unsettled Questions of Political Economy*, 2nd edn. (1st edn., 1844) (London: Longmans).

Mints, L. (1945) *A History of Banking Theory in Great Britain and the United States* (Chicago: University of Chicago Press).

Mitchell, B. R., and Deane, P. (1962) *Abstract of British Historical Statistics* (Cambridge: Cambridge University Press).

Monroe, A. (1923) *Monetary Theory before Adam Smith* (Cambridge: Harvard University Press).

Montesquieu, C. (1748) *The Spirit of Laws* (Chicago: Encyclopaedia Britannica, 1952).

Morgan, E. V. (1950) *The Study of Prices and the Value of Money* (London: George Philip).

Morgan, E. V. (1965a) *The Theory and Practice of Central Banking, 1797–1913* (Cambridge: Cambridge University Press).

Morgan, E. V. (1965b) *A History of Money* (Harmondsworth: Penguin).

Mun, T. (1664) *England's Treasure by Forraign Trade* (Oxford: Blackwell, reprinted, 1982).

Nef, J. V. (1941) 'Silver Production in Central Europe, 1450–1618', *Journal of Political Economy*, vol. 49.

Niebyl, K. (1946) *Studies in the Classical Theories of Money* (New York: Columbia University Press).

Nobay, A. R., and Johnson, H. G. (1977) 'Monetarism: A Historic-Theoretic Perspective', *Journal of Economic Literature*, vol. 15, June.

North, D. (1691) *Discourses upon Trade* (Baltimore: Johns Hopkins, reprinted, 1907).

O'Brien, D. P. (1975) *The Classical Economists* (Oxford: Clarendon Press).

Outhwaite, R. B. (1969) *Inflation in Tudor and Early Stuart England* (London: Macmillan).

Panico, C. (1980) 'Marx's Analysis of the Relationship between the Rate of Interest and the Rate of Profits', in J. Eatwell and M. Milgate (eds) *Economics and the Theory of Value and Distribution* (London: Duckworth, 1983).

Peake, C. F. (1978) 'Henry Thornton and the Development of Ricardo's Economic Thought', *History of Political Economy*, vol. 10, no. 2.

Peston, M., and Corry, B. (eds) (1972) *Essays in Honour of Lord Robbins* (London: Weidenfeld & Nicholson).

Petty, W. (1899) *The Economic Writings of Sir William Petty* (C. H. Hull, ed.) (New York: Kelley, reprinted, 1963).

Phelps-Brown, E. H., and Hopkins, S. V. (1955a) 'Seven Centuries of the Prices of Consumables', *Economica*, vol. 23.

Phelps-Brown, E. H., and Hopkins, S. V. (1955b) 'Seven Centuries of the Prices of Consumables compared with Builders' Wage Rates', *Economica*, vol. 23.

Phelps-Brown, E. H., and Hopkins, S. V. (1957) 'Wage Rates and Prices: Evidence for Population Pressure in the Sixteenth Century', *Economica*, XXIV.

Phelps-Brown, E. H. and Hopkins, S. V. (1981) *A Perspective of Wages and Prices* (London: Methuen).

Pimlott, B. (ed.) (1984) *Fabian Essays in Socialist Thought* (London: Heinemann).

Postan, M. M. (1928) 'Credit in Medieval Trade', *Economic History Review*, vol. I, no. 2.

Postan, M. M. (1944) 'The Rise of a Money Economy', in Carus-Wilson (ed.) *Essays in Economic History* (London: Edward Arnold, 1954).

Postan, M. M. (1971) *Fact and Relevance: Essays on Historical Method* (Cambridge: Cambridge University Press).

Postan, M. M. (1975) *The Medieval Economy and Society* (Harmondsworth: Penguin).

Price, L. L. (1909) *Money and its Relation to Prices* (London: Swan Sonnenschein).

Radcliffe, Lord (1959) *Report of the Committee on the Working of the Monetary System* (London: Her Majesty's Stationery Office).

Ramsey, P. (ed.) (1971) *The Price Revolution in Sixteenth Century England.* (London: Methuen).

Ricardo, D. (1923) *Economic Essays* E. C. K. Gonner, ed. (London: Frank Cass & Co).

Ricardo, D. (1951/73) *The Works and Correspondence of David Ricardo* P. Sraffa, ed. (Cambridge: Cambridge University Press).

Rist, C. (1940) *History of Monetary and Credit Theory from John Law to the Present Day* (London: Allen & Unwin).

Robinson, J. (1970) 'Quantity Theories Old and New: A Comment', *Journal of Money, Credit and Banking*, vol. 2, November.

Rogers, J. E. T. (1866/1902) *A History of Agriculture and Prices in England* (Oxford).

Roll, E. (1973) *A History of Economic Thought*, 3rd edn (London: Faber and Faber 1st edn, 1938).

Rosdolsky, R. (1977) *The Making of Marx's 'Capital'* (London: Pluto).

Rowthorn, R. (1980) *Capitalism, Conflict and Inflation*, London: Lawrence & Wishart).

Rubin, I. I. (1929) *A History of Economic Thought* (London: Ink Links, 1979).

Sayers, R. S. (1953) 'Ricardo's Views on Monetary Questions', in T. S. Ashton and R. S. Sayers (eds) *Papers in English Monetary History* (Oxford: Clarendon Press, 1953).

Sayers, R. S. (1960) 'Monetary Thought and Monetary Policy in England', in H. G. Johnson (ed.) *Readings in British Monetary Economics* (Oxford: Clarendon Press, 1972)

Schumpeter, J. A. (1954) *History of Economic Analysis* (London: Allen & Unwin).

Schwartz, J. (ed.) (1977) *The Subtle Anatomy of Capitalism* (Santa Monica: Goodyear).

'A Scotch Banker', (1868) *The Theory of Money, in connection with some of the prominent doctrines of Political Economy* (Edinburgh: William P. Nimmo).

Sen, S. R. (1947) 'Sir James Steuart's General Theory of Employment, Interest and Money', *Economica*, vol. 14.

Sen, S. R. (1957) *The Economics of Sir James Steuart* (London: G. Bell).

Senior, N. (1828) *The Transmission of the Precious Metals from Country to Country* (London: London School of Economics and Political Science, reprinted, n.d.).

Shaikh, A. (1977) 'Marx's Theory of Value and the "Transformation Problem" ', in J. Schwartz (ed.) The Subtle Anatomy of Capitalism (Santa Monica: Goodyear, 1977).

Shaikh, A. (1979) 'Foreign Trade and the Law of Value', *Science and Society*, vol. XLII, Fall.

Skinner, A. (1967) 'Money and Prices: A Critique of the Quantity Theory', *Scottish Journal of Political Economy*, vol. XIV.

Skinner, A. and Wilson, T. (eds) (1975) *Essays on Adam Smith* (Oxford: Clarendon Press).

Smith, A. (1776) *An Inquiry into the Nature and Causes of the Wealth of Nations* (D. Stuart, ed.) (London: George Routledge 1890).

Smith, A. (1812) *Works*, D. Stewart, ed. (London: T. Cadell & W. Davies).

Sraffa, P. (1960) *Production of Commodities by Means of Commodities* (Cambridge: Cambridge University Press).

Stark, W. (1944) *The History of Economics in its Relation to Social Development* (London: Kegan Paul, Trench & Co.).

Steedman, I. (1982) 'Marx on Ricardo', in I. Bradley and M. Howard (eds) *Classical and Marxian Political Economy* (London: Macmillan, 1982).

Steuart, J. (1767) *An Inquiry into the Principles of Political Oeconomy*, A. Skinner, ed. (Edinburgh: Oliver & Boyd).

Sweezy, P. (1970) *The Theory of Capitalist Development: Principles of Marxian Political Economy* (New York: Modern Reader, 1st edn., 1942).

Thornton, H. (1802) *An Enquiry into the Nature and Effects of the Paper Credit of Great Britain* F. A. van Hayek, ed. (New York: Farrar & Rinehart, 1939).

Tobin, J. (1974) 'Friedman's Theoretical Framework', in R. Gordon (ed.) *Milton Friedman's Monetary Framework* (Chicago: University of Chicago Press, 1974).

Tooke, T. (1838/57) *A History of Prices and of the State of the Circulation from 1792 to 1856* (London: P. S. King, reprinted, 1928).

Tooke, T. (1844) *An Inquiry into the Current Principle* (London: London School of Economics and Political Science, reprinted, 1959).

Torrens, R. (1837) *A Letter to the Right Honourable Lord Viscount Melbourne* (London).

Turgot, A. R. J. (1770) *Reflections on the Formation and Distribution of Riches* (London: Macmillan, 1898).

Vaggi, G. (1983) 'The Physiocratic Theory of Prices', *Contributions to Political Economy*, vol. 2, March.

Vanderlint, J. (1734) *Money Answers All Things* (New York: Johnson, reprinted, n.d.).

Vickers, D. (1960) *Studies in the Theory of Money, 1690–1776* (London: Peter Owen).

Vickers, D. (1975) 'Adam Smith and the Status of the Theory of Money', in A. Skinner and T. Wilson (eds) *Essays on Adam Smith* (Oxford: Clarendon Press, 1975).

Vilar, P. (1976) *A History of Gold and Money, 1450–1920* (London: New Left Books).

Viner, J. (1937) *Studies in the Theory of International Trade* (New York: Harper).

Walters, A. A. (ed.) (1973) *Money and Banking* (Harmondsworth: Penguin).

Wicksell, K. (1934/35) *Lectures on Political Economy* (Fairfield: Kelley, reprinted, 1977).

Wicksell, K. (1936) *Interest and Prices: A Study of the Causes Regulating the Value of Money* (New York: Kelley, reprinted, 1965).

Wilson, J. (1859) *Capital, Currency and Banking* (London: The Economist).

Wood, E. (1939) *English Theories of Central Banking Control, 1819–1858* (Cambridge: Harvard University Press).

Wright, B.,and Harlow, J. (eds) (1844) *The Currency Question: The Gemini Letters* (London and Birmingham, published anonymously).

Young, A. (1774) *Political Arithmetic* (London).

Name Index

Subject Index

332.4 G825c
Green, Roy, 1951-
Classical theories of money, output and inflation